D0948816

INTERNATIONAL DIPLOMACY, STATE ADMINISTRATORS AND NARCOTICS CONTROL

For Valerie, Amitai, Daniel, Ilana-Marie and Natalia
with much love

International Diplomacy, State Administrators and Narcotics Control

The Origins of a Social Problem

S. D. STEIN
Senior Lecturer,
Department of Economics and Social Sciences
Bristol Polytechnic

Published for the London School of Economics
and Political Science by
Gower

Published by

Gower Publishing Company Limited,
Gower House, Croft Road, Aldershot, Hampshire, England.

Gower Publishing Company Limited,
Old Post Road, Brookfield, Vermont 05036, USA.

British Library Cataloguing in Publication Data

Stein, S.D.
   International diplomacy, state administrators
   and narcotics control : the origins of a social
   problem.
   1. Drug abuse——Government policy——History
   I. Title
   363.4'5   HV5801

ISBN 0-566-00980-3

Printed in Great Britain by
Paradigm Print, Gateshead
Tyne and Wear

Contents

Preface

This book is about narcotics control. I first became interested in the subject when an undergraduate student at the London School of Economics. At the same time, criminology in social science courses was being translated into the sociology of deviant behaviour as the writings of American theorists gradually supplanted the more arid empirical preoccupations of their European counterparts. Central to their concerns was the conviction that our understanding of deviant patterns of behaviour would be enhanced if attention were deflected from the detailed examination of deviants toward an analysis of the processes associated with the control of deviance. They argued that the origins of deviant subcultures, and the perpetuation of deviant lifestyles, were explicable in terms of policies employed to regulate such patterns of behaviour. They illustrated the analytic potential of their model by applying it in relation to a rather limited range of deviant behavioural configurations. Included amongst these was the non-medical consumption of dangerous drugs, especially of narcotic substances. Of particular relevance in this connection were differences in the control policies being implemented in the United States and Great Britain.

Students of drug addiction, particlarly Alfred Lindesmith, Edwin Schur and Troy Duster, drew attention to the radically different approaches prevailing in the two countries. They contended that these had important implications relating to the extent of narcotic addiction, and the characteristics of drug consumers and drug subcultures. Whilst they drew attention to the existence of different approaches to control, no detailed attempt was made to account for why they arose in the first place. Implicit in their analyses were explanations which placed emphasis on certain cultural dichotomies, such as American moralism versus British pragmatism. Others, such as Howard Becker, drew attention to the role played in the evolution of American narcotics policies by forceful and charismatic personalities, particularly Harry J. Anslinger, who for many years was in charge of the Federal Bureau of

Narcotics. Whatever the merits of these accounts they did not amount to a detailed comparative analysis of the origins of these policies.

During the same period, the middle to late sixties, sociologists of law were approaching questions of this sort from a different vantage point. Concerned more with the origins of legislative instruments than with their impact on criminals or deviants, they eschewed micro socio-psychological perspectives in preference for macro-sociological ones. Conflict models, often Marxist in origin were regularly invoked to account for the enactment of various laws. Although the resulting arguments were quite sophisticated, considerable stress was placed upon the role of ruling elites in introducing legislation designed to secure their interests at the expense of the less powerful. These models were necessarily intra-state orientated. Laws succeeded the emergence of domestic social conflicts, resolving them in favour of elite groups at the expense of those lower down the socio-economic hierarchy.

In the context of both of these perspectives I expected to find that American and British narcotics laws emerged in response to domestic problems, and that their dissimilarities were traceable to differences in the organisation of social control agencies. It did not take an inordinate amount of preliminary archival research to establish that the origins of domestic narcotics laws introduced at the beginning of this century could not be accounted for in terms of these models. First, they were enacted, not in response to domestic considerations, but to comply with international agreements, in particular the International Opium Convention 1912, the Treaty of Versailles 1919, and the Covenant of the League of Nations. The International Opium Convention of 1912 originated with attempts to control the consumption of raw and prepared opium in China. American foreign policy personnel were responsible for setting in motion the circumstances which led to the convening of the conference which drafted the convention. They were motivated, not by a concern for the consequences of extensive opiate consumption in China and other parts of the Far East, as has been suggested by some historians, but by the need to advance American foreign policy interests in a situation in which they had few means of exerting the required leverage. Secondly, the purpose of narcotics control policies introduced in Britain was not to control the consumption of narcotic substances. There was no significant addiction problem in this country during the first two decades of the century, although, as I endeavour to establish, a considerable quantity of narcotics was being consumed. Narcotics control policies introduced in Britain and other Western European countries during the early part of this century were directed at regulating the distribution of narcotics, · not their consumption. Generally speaking, that continues to be the case. The distinction is important because the types of policies appropriate to the control of distribution are not necessarily suited to the control of consumption. Thirdly, there was no important difference in the thrust of British and American drug control policies during the early part of the twentieth century. In both countries the overwhelming proportion of national resources devoted to narcotics control were aimed at eradicating consumption, albeit, through the control of distribution. Home Office and Ministry of Health officials were strongly of the view that "the mere satisfying of the craving of a drug addict without further object, whether this is attained by the provision of the drugs by the addict himself or through an intermediary, comes under the heading of illicit dealing". This viewpoint is wholly congruent with opinions delivered by the United States Supreme Court during the early decades of this century.

To the extent that there were differences in the types of control policy being implemented in the two countries, they evolved along separate paths because of differences in the ways in which decision-making organisations interacted. Elsewhere I have argued that "the distinctive attributes of the law-making process in particular social systems can only be grasped analytically by focusing attention on the ways in which separate rule-creating institutions interlock. Each has a feedback effect on the norm-creating activities of the others". (1980) In the present study I attempt to demonstrate the utility and necessity of adopting this approach in order to explain the distinctive characteristics of narcotics legislation. Only by focusing on the interplay of officials representing the interests of the Foreign, India and Colonial Office, is it possible to account for the content of the Hague International Opium Convention. Similarly, differences between narcotics control policies enforced in Great Britain and the United States are best understood in the context of the relations which obtained between administrative entities and pressure groups representing the interests of those involved in medical and ancillary medical activities.

An author has numerous debts. My greatest is to my wife Valerie who, through no choice of her own, has had to live with the problems of international narcotics control for more than a decade. During this time she provided much needed support as well as practical assistance with the typing of several drafts. My children have put up with my frequent trips to archives in London, weekends cloistered in my study, and so forth. Paul Rock was the first to arouse my interest in the subject of deviant behaviour. He also had the unenviable task of supervising my Ph.D. thesis. Had some administrator in the registry at the London School of Economics not decided to burden him with tutoring me during my undergraduate years it is certain that I would never have undertaken this research, or embarked upon an academic career. To Mr P.D.C. Davis and members of the Publications Committee at the London School of Economics I am indebted for their assistance in connection with the publication of the manuscript. My friend and colleague Charles Harvey rescued me from various errors grammatical and syntactical and occasioned me to remove some of my worst horrors of expression. To Mr W. Tozer and the secretarial staff at Bristol Polytechnic, Ena Briers, Christine Hunt, Elizabeth Davidson, I am thankful for the valuable support and encouragement given freely over the years it took to complete this research.

1 Introduction

Over the last two and a half decades various issues relating to the non-medical consumption of drugs periodically have been the subject of political and scholarly exchanges. The journalist, broadcaster and television commentator have all played an important part in keeping some of these issues before a wider public. Although interest in these matters has waxed and waned, and the drugs causing intense concern have varied - heroin in the late fifties, pot in the early sixties, heroin in the mid-sixties, LSD in the late sixties, glue sniffing in the late seventies, and currently a mixture of the latter and heroin and cocaine - it has never been an easy matter to assess the merits of the contending arguments being advanced by the interested parties. There are tens of scholarly treatises which proclaim that no ill-effects attend the regular consumption of such drugs as opium, morphine, heroin and cannabis, provided, of course, that they are consumed under optimally favourable conditions. On the other side is ranged an equally imposing army of experts. They point to the deleterious physical and mental consequences that accompany regular consumption of these substances. Many of the arguments on both sides are of respectable vintage. Those relating to the opiate-narcotics were detailed at length in the report of the Royal Commission on Opium, 1894-95. The Indian Hemp Drugs Commission 1893-94, reviewed many of those aired in connection with marihuana consumption.

A major change since that time, however, is the increased regulation of the markets for drugs used for approved medical purposes on the one hand, and for disapproved of hedonistic and ameliorative purposes on the other. In the nineteenth century few controls were imposed on the consumption of opiates. Those that were, were organised on an intra-state basis. Frequently, their primary object was to augment administrative revenues. High ranking state officials were thereby led to extoll the benefits of consumption and the benign systems of control

1

they oversaw. They had little incentive to dwell on potential hazards associated with regular consumption of these substances. It was left to those outside the political and administrative establishments, missionaries, participants in moral and social reform movements, and some members of the medical profession, to point to the latter. Today, the situation is very different. Vast resources are allocated to controlling the availability of opiate-narcotics and other substances whose uses for non-medical purposes is disapproved of. The movement of these substances from points of cultivation to places of approved of uses is carefully monitored, first within particular states, and then within an international framework of police, health and medical supervisory organisations.

Whereas in the nineteenth century much of the controversy surrounding the availability of opiate-narcotic substances centred on the risks to health associated with consumption, today considerable emphasis is placed on the risks presumed to be associated with controlling supplies to potential customers. Prominent British and American experts have argued that a causal relationship exists between the types of policies designed to regulate non-medical drug consumption, and consumption patterns. The mechanism that relates the two is conflict. The relevant conflicts originate from differences in class, age, culture and ethnically-based orientations towards non-medical drug consumption. It is also generally assumed that the origins of regulatory policies can be traced to the desire of dominant groups to control an internal social problem which is associated with the activities of subordinate socio-economic, racial and ethnic categories. Control policies, therefore, are perceived as having originated in efforts to control consumption, rather than production and distribution. As the focus of critical assessment is upon consumption, it has been relatively easy to argue from this vantage point that drug control policies are ineffective and self-defeating. Instead of reducing the size of the problem they have an opposite effect. The more repressive the drug laws, the more intractable the `drug problem` is presumed to be.

The plausibility of many of these assumptions rests on the viability of a specific model of the law creating process. Variously characterised as a `conflict' or `Marxist' model, perspective or paradigm, its proponents suggest that legal instruments are simply the outcomes of legislative decision-making processes which are structured in such a way as to ensure that the interests of dominant segments of the population prevail over others. Accordingly, legal norms are percieved as originating in domestic conflicts of interest between superordinate and subordinate strata.

Probably the most important consequence of this approach has been the eclipse of attempts to account for legislative policies in terms of organisational variables. It is assumed implicitly that institutions which process divergent interests fail to impinge upon or shape them significantly. Unique and culturally specific configurations of pressure groups, administrative agencies, legislative bodies and political parties are considered irrelevant to an explication of the reasons underlying the adoption of particular legislative programmes. The same applies in respect of their internal structural characteristics and their complex power and organisational interdependencies. What should in fact be a central component of any analysis of legislative policy is omitted because of conceptual allegiances which as yet have not proved to be particularly fruitful.

Equally serious is the difficulty of employing such models in accounting for the genesis of international legislation. Since they have been evolved for the purpose of explaining the origins of legislation in terms of variables which are causally efficacious within circumscribed geographical areas, they cannot be adapted to account for policies which are by-products of inter-state rivalries, or used to explore the interrelationship of international and domestic legislation. They are, therefore, singularly unsuitable for analysing the genesis of international and domestic narcotics legislation, and assumptions deriving from their application in this context must be presumed to be of questionable validity.

Both the British Dangerous Drugs Act 1920, and the equivalent American statute, the Harrison Act 1914, were introduced to comply with the terms of the International Opium Convention 1912. Neither was primarily a response to an internal opiate-addiction problem. The circumstances that led to the convening of the conference which drafted the convention were Far Eastern and international in scope. Its most important provisions required the signatory countries to introduce: (a) restrictions on the production and distribution of raw opium, particularly on its importation and exportation; (b) equivalent restrictions on prepared opium, that is opium which had by a process of distillation been made suitable for smoking; (c) legislation designed to 'limit the manufacture, the sale and use of morphine, cocaine and their respective salts to medical and legitimate uses only', and the extension of such restrictions to 'every new derivative of morphine, cocaine or their respective salts or to any other alkaloid of opium which might ... give rise to similar abuse and result in the same injurious effects', and (d) the implementation of certain policies designed to reduce the extent of consumption of all the aforementioned drugs in China by those powers having treaty relations with that country.

In the light of the subsequent evolution of Anglo-American narcotics control, the most important articles of the convention were those relating to (c). These were also the most restrictive, inasmuch as the consumption of these substances was to be confined to 'medical and legitimate uses'. No such restrictions were agreed in relation to prepared opium, it being left to each signatory to determine whether its 'peculiar conditions' made such a policy desirable or feasible. The differences in approach were not, as might perhaps be expected, a product of the delegates' varying evaluation of their physiological, psychological or social effects. Most were of the opinion that all substances dealt with by the convention were productive of equally pernicious consequences. The content of the convention was not shaped by considerations of this order, but by the divergent interests of the participating powers in the cultivation, manufacture, distribution and consumption of the drugs brought within its framework of control. Of these Great Britain was the most important. Her delegates were largely responsible for incorporating relatively lax provisions concerning various aspects of the traffic in raw and prepared opium, as well as for including stringent controls on the traffic in manufactured narcotics and cocaine. British economic interests in the former were extensive, whereas those in the latter were not particularly significant. In order to defend the former, foreign office officials, in response to pressure exerted by British colonial administrators in the Far East, insisted

3

that the main thrust of any international narcotics control programme be directed against the traffic in manufactured narcotics and cocaine.

Although in the short-run this policy achieved its objective of deflecting attention away from the extensive consumption of raw and prepared opium in the Far East, which was in fact the issue initially used to justify the quest for an international approach to problems of non-medical drug consumption, it had important consequences. It meant that elaborate policies for controlling the manufacture, distribution and consumption of narcotics and cocaine were introduced in many countries at a time when most government officials were not aware that there was any domestic drug problem that necessitated such intervention. This, at least, was the situation in Britain. It was reflected in the fact that different government departments vied with each other in an endeavour to ensure that some other department would assume responsibility for implementing such measures.

Domestic British concerns featured more prominently in subsequent stages of the evolution of national and international drug controls. Here to, however, domestic preoccupation with an internal narcotics problem accounts for only certain aspects of these policies. It was the complex interaction of domestic and international issues which eventually led to the 'bringing into force' of the International Opium Convention, and the passage of the Dangerous Drugs Act. Although it is reasonably certain that had the League of Nations not assumed responsibility for monitoring the implementation of the regulatory system specified in the convention, some form of domestic legislation to control the internal traffic in and consumption of narcotics and cocaine would have been introduced, its contents would probably have been substantially different.

The predominantly international focus of domestic drug policies accounts partly for the fact that, when first introduced, the Dangerous Drugs and Harrison acts encountered little opposition in the legislature. Officials responsible for implementing domestic narcotics programmes could legitimately claim that they were merely complying with the terms of international agreements which had already been ratified. Opposition, when it arose, usually came too late to substantially modify domestic policies. Interested pressure groups were usually only equipped for negotiating with government departments responsible for internal programmes. By the time the implications of international conventions were fully understood and translated into domestic policies, it was usually too late to modify their general thrust, or contest the assumptions upon which they were based. The only scope left to domestic pressure groups lay in challenging the interpretations placed upon the relevant clauses in domestic and international legislation that directly affected them.

One of the most important justifications for exploring the interrelationship of domestic and international legislation is that it offers a rare opportunity for conducting a controlled comparative analysis. Since a significant number of domestic drug statutes are enacted and implemented in order to comply with the provisions of international conventions, it is possible to examine in detail the diverse ways in which dissimilar social structures refract an identical legislative policy. In substance the Dangerous Drugs and Harrison acts are virtually identical. They were, however, interpreted very differently by the administrative agencies which assumed responsibility for their implementation. Whereas British addicts were permitted under certain conditions to continue consuming heroin and morphine, American users were prevented from doing so. These differences are best explained, not in terms of British pragmatism and American puritanism, as has hitherto frequently been the case, but in terms of different configurations of domestic pressure groups, administrative agencies and legislative bodies. The historical records relating to early British and American narcotics policies indicate that such an analysis is crucial to an understanding of their origins and differences. Control strategies can only be accounted for in terms of internal conflicts within and between different government agencies, and between them and pressure groups representing the interests of pharmacists, medical practitioners and commercial organisations directly involved in the manufacturing and distribution of narcotics and cocaine. In this context, conflicts between politicians, administrators and enforcement agencies on the one side, and addicts on the other, are largely irrelevant. In fact, it is only because the addict played so unimportant a role in the evolution of national and international drug policies, that these programmes take the forms that they do. The main thrust of international narcotics control has been, and remains, the control of production, manufacture and distribution. Control of consumption is only important insofar as it assists in controlling these other components of the drug traffic. If the control of addicts, or addiction, had been the objective, most of the resources that have been directed at controlling the traffic, would have been channelled into domestic and international treatment and rehabilitation programmes. That they were not attests to the continuing influence of international considerations. The drug traffic is an inter-state phenomenon, addiction an internal social problem. International agencies such as the League's Advisory Committee on Traffic in Opium, and its successor, the United Nations' Commission on Narcotic Drugs, are precluded from directly effecting the latter. Consequently, their main concern is with cultivators, manufacturers and distributors, and not with addicts. Paradoxical though it may seem, much of the history of national and international narcotics control can be written without reference to addicts or addiction.

International considerations still impinge directly on domestic drug control programmes. In fact, the increasing influence of international bodies like the United Nations, the World Health Organisation and INTERPOL, has institutionalised the processes whereby the drug control policies of one country are dictated by considerations that do not emanate from, or have a direct bearing upon, its own domestic situation at the time they are introduced.

2 India, China and the Far Eastern opium traffic 1820-1906

The early history of the Indo-China opium trade, and that of the Anglo-Sino conflicts it provoked, has been related in many books, monographs and articles. Here, it is only necessary briefly to outline those issues which had a direct bearing on the subsequent development of an international system of narcotics control.

In 1773, Warren Hastings, Governor of Bengal, assumed control on behalf of the East India Company of poppy cultivation and the manufacture and sale of raw and prepared opium in those parts of India under the company's suzerainty. The reasons were strictly financial. At the time the company, as an Indian government, was virtually bankrupt. (Harlow 1964, Vol.2, p.485) Revenues were obtained from the sale of the raw product of the poppy plant to the indigenous population, who ingested it in liquid or pill form. The marketed product was referred to as excise opium. In addition, prepared opium was regularly auctioned off at Calcutta, the product being purchased by merchants who were licensed to ply the trade between India and other parts of the Far East. Known collectively as 'country traders', it was they who arranged for its distribution to various points along the China coast. The East India Company was not the only exporter of opium from India to China. The poppy was also cultivated in the Native States, the parts of India not under company control. The product they prepared for smoking, known as malwa opium, was also distributed in China by those engaged in the country trade.

During the second decade of the nineteenth century exports of Malwa increased substantially. Company officials feared that if a new policy was not embarked upon, revenues from this source would dry up as their share of the market dwindled. It was decided to increase the land area under poppy cultivation, and reduce the price at which prepared opium was sold to country traders. Henceforth, the company sought 'to secure command of the market by furnishing a supply on so enlarged a scale on such reasonable terms as shall prevent competition, and as shall make up for such depreciation of the Article by the Aggregate profit on an extended scale'. (Owen 1934, p.87) The new policy paid handsome dividends.   Until the eighteen-twenties the annual number of chests shipped from India to China rarely rose above 5,000.   By the 1930-31 season this had increased to 18,956, and in 1938-39 China imported approximately 40,000 chests.

Opium exported from India had to be smuggled into China since the Imperial authorities had repeatedly issued edicts prohibiting its importation and consumption.   The rapid rise in imports during the eighteen-thirties had a significant effect on the Chinese economy.   An Imperial edict published in 1838 noted that: 'the quantity of silver exported has yearly been on the increase, till its price has become enhanced, the copper coin depressed, the land and capitation tax ... all alike hampered.   If steps are not taken for our defence ... the useful wealth of China will be poured into the fathomless abyss of transmarine regions'.   (Canton Register, 1839) After consultations between leading officials of the Manchu bureaucracy, it was decided to embark upon a policy directed at the extinction of the smuggling trade and the practise of opium smoking.   (Phipps 1835, p.168)   The campaign was largely successful, and by January 1839 Sino-Foreign trade was at a virtual standstill: 'opium exports from Bombay dropped ... Foreign smuggling boats disappeared ... and Canton was virtually cleared of all opium traffic'. (Hsu 1976, p.225)

The British government considered that the actions taken by Chinese officials provided it with a suitable casus belli.   An expeditionary force was despatched to China to seek redress.   It encountered little opposition, and at the conclusion of the First Opium War a number of treaties were negotiated between British and Chinese officials.   Under their terms the number of Treaty Ports at which Sino-Foreign trade could be conducted was increased to five, and British consular officials were granted   extraterritorial rights of jurisdiction over their   own nationals.   This meant that violations of Chinese laws, including those relating to opium, would be dealt with by tribunals manned by British diplomatic officials.   Similar treaties were conclude with France and the United States. The single most important defect of the first treaty settlement was 'the failure to bring fully within its scheme of things that expanding drug trade which had so largely contributed to the collapse of the old order at Canton'.   (Fairbank 1953, Vol.1, p.57) Despite the efforts of British negotiators, the Chinese authorities steadfastly refused to legalise the trade.   Consequently, since the demand for the drug increased, and the smuggling trade was as profitable as ever, the East India Company's volume of exports continued to rise.

It took another Sino-Foreign war to convince the Chinese authorities of the futility of attempting to prohibit the importation of foreign opium in the face of support lent to the traffic by the British government and navy.   Subsequent to the signing of the Treaty of Tientsin of 1858, at the conclusion of the second Sino-Western conflict, negotiations took place at Shanghai on tariff and trade regulations. Chinese officials chose not to counter a British proposal that the importation of opium should be legalised.   Henceforth, subject to the payment of an import tax, there were to be no impediments to the

Government of India's policy of maximising its opium revenues:

> The organised smuggling, or delivery outside the treaty ports,
> ceased at once; henceforth all opium in foreign hands was taken to
> the authorised places of trade. For fifty years there was no
> renewal of the edicts against the distributing trade in opium, and
> for more than that term the treasury derived a revenue from the
> trade. (Morse and MacNair 1931, p.207)

As the quantity of opium exported from British India to China
increased steadily so did the financial and economic dependence of the
authorities along with their ideological and bureaucratic commitment to
sustaining the trade. In 1858, when the East India Company's political
control of India was transferred to the Crown, 68,004 chests were
exported. Thenceforth the trade continued to grow, peaking at 94,835 in
1879. From then onwards the quantity declined gradually, reaching
50,590 in the 1904-1905 season. The decline in exports was not due to a
decrease in the popularity of opium smoking in China, but to an increase
in the quantity of domestic opium produced there, the price of which was
considerably lower than that of the Indian variety. Revenues from opium
sales increased in parallel with the rise in exports. In 1800, revenues
from the sale of opium, for both internal and external consumption,
accounted for 3.35% of total revenue; in 1850 for 13.73%; and in 1876
for 15.55%.

India was not the only Far Eastern administration to derive
substantial revenues from the sale of opium in the nineteenth and early
twentieth centuries. The colonial authorities of some territories were
by 1906 more dependent financially upon opium revenues than the Indian
administration had ever been. The proportion of total revenue derived
from this source for various territories in 1906 was as follows: French
Indo-China: 16.25%; Hong Kong: 29.02%; India: 6.3%; Straits Settlements:
53.3%; Federated Malay States: 10.08%; Netherlands Indies: 14.91%;
Formosa: 14.3%; Macao (1908-1909): 25.7%; Siam: 15.5%. (Report of the
International Opium Commission 1909, Vol.2, pp.355-365) Most of the
opium sold and consumed in these territories was of Indian origin, and
it was used primarily for smoking purposes.

It has frequently been suggested, both by those who actively
campaigned against this traffic, and historians, that the principal
reason for the Government of India's total opposition to any
interference with its 'right' to cultivate the poppy, and export its
product to other countries, can be traced to its fiscal dependence upon
revenues obtained from this source. Although there is some truth in
this, it does not alone constitute an adequate explanation. It obscures
the fact that a large number of individuals secured their livelihoods
from this traffic. In India these included a veritable army of
officials working for the opium monopolies, cultivators, manufacturers,
distributors, wholesalers, retailers, merchants, seamen, financial
brokers and bank employees. A relatively small adjustment in the Land
or other Indian taxes could easily have made up for any decline in
revenues attending the abolition of the opium monopoly, the prohibition
of poppy cultivation, and the abolition of opium consumption. Fiscal
policies could not, however, ensure the redeployment of land and labour
that such steps would necessitate. A comparison of the available
statistical information relating to opium revenues, total government
revenue, and the quantity of land under poppy cultivation, suggests that

the latter problems were the main obstacles to change. Whereas the percentage of total revenue derived from the sale of opium declined steadily between 1876 and 1907, the number of acres under poppy cultivation remained about the same. In 1876-77 opium revenues accounted for 15.5% of total revenue, when the number of acres under poppy cultivation, deducting crop failures, was 556,013; in 1907 the figures were 6.4% and 564,585 acres. (Stein 1978, pp.385-388) Since poppy cultivation was concentrated in two states, any abrupt change in the quantity of opium produced would have caused serious economic dislocations. Given the large numbers of persons occupied directly and indirectly in the internal and external trade in opium, it is obvious that government revenues represented only a very small proportion of the gross national income directly linked to the opium trade. This applies equally to other Far Eastern territories, both those which were major transit ports for distribution to the Chinese interior, such as Hong Kong, and those which included a substantial number of opium-smokers.

Throughout the period 1840-1917, government of India and India Office officials were forced to embrace an essentially defensive rhetoric on all issues relating to the opium trade. Opposition to their policies, and the supportive role lent by the British government, first surfaced in the parliamentary debates that preceded and followed the government's decision to send an expeditionary force to China in 1840. Gladstone declared that 'a war more unjust in its origin, a war more calculated in its progress to cover this country with permanent disgrace, I do not know, and I have not read of'. (Hansard 1840, Vol.53, c.818) The idea of a war to uphold the opium trade was 'repugnant' to reform and humanitarian circles, the High Church party and the 'Saints'. (Blake 1960, p.41). Although a number of tracts criticising British and Indian policy were circulated at the time of the First and Second Opium Wars (Alexander 1856, 1857; Fry 1840), organised opposition to the traffic only emerged in 1874 with the founding of the Anglo-Oriental Society for the Suppression of the Opium Trade (AOS)

The society was the inspiration of Edward Pease, a Birmingham Quaker. Its main primary objective was to secure the release of China from her treaty obligations to import foreign opium. Suggestions that it should aim at the prohibition of all poppy cultivation in India, except for that necessary to provide for legitimate medical needs, were rejected. The leadership adopted a strictly pragmatic approach to the agitation: 'It is one thing ... to desire a moral reformation of society, another to propose demands for immediate legislation. Less than the abolition of the monopoly and the withdrawal of unfair pressure upon the Chinese government to admit our opium, we would not ask: more than this, it would be useless to ask at present'. (Friend of China March 1875, p.5) During the seventies and eighties the mainstay of their support was among non-conformists. As in the fight against slavery, members of the Society of Friends played a central role in the agitation conducted by this anti-opium society.

In June 1888 the first International Missionary Conference was held in London. Following an appeal made by James Maxwell and Benjamin Broomhall, its General Committee agreed that arrangements should be made for a debate on the subject of the opium trade. In a packed Exeter Hall, resolutions condemning the complicity of the British government in this traffic were passed without substantial opposition. Six days later the Christian Union for the Severence of the Connection of the British

Empire with the Opium Trade (CU) was formed. (National Righteousness 1911, p.2) Although there was a certain amount of cross-membership of the Executive Committees of the AOS and the CU, their tactics, and the social and occupational characteristics of their more active members differed. Whereas the CU adopted a populist approach to the conduct of the agitation, the AOS was more elitist in orientation.

The first issue of the organ of the new movement spelt out its campaign strategy: 'It is intended ... to form local committees in the principal towns of the Kingdom for the purpose of local organisation, and by all available means to prepare the public mind for speedy and decisive action'. The society was, the editorial continued, 'a union of those who believe that nations rise or fall in proportion as they have regard to the principles of moral rectitude', an association of Christian men and women who believe in the power of 'prayer and prayerful effort'. (National Righteousness December 1883, p.3) Missionaries and members of the clergy played a far more prominent role in the CU than they did in the AOS. Many had served in China. Close links between the CU and the numerous missionary societies gave it a wide platform for disseminating its members' views. Missionary magazines carried frequent articles inveighing against the traffic. Between 1882 and 1906, support for the agitation was lent increasingly by members of the clergy.

Missionary hostility to the traffic can only be understood in the context of the difficulties those who served in China encountered in the course of their attempts to convert the local population. Throughout the nineteenth century they met with fierce resistance and intense hostility from virtually all sections of Chinese society. Chinese of diverse social strata, including officials attached to the central government in Peking, and those in the provincial capitals, as well as the literati and the peasantry, directly or indirectly encouraged outbreaks of anti-missionary violence and lent assistance to those who attempted to render their proselytising efforts nugatory. The attitude of the literati towards Christianity throughout the nineteenth century was one of unswerving hostility:

> the vast majority of the educated classes of China either passively
> or actively rejected Christianity. Passively, they did so by
> remaining coldly indifferent to Christianity's message ... Actively
> they expressed their hostility by writing and disseminating
> inflammatory anti-Christian literature; creating countless stumbling
> blocks for the Christian missionary; issuing threats of retaliation
> against any who dared enter the religion or have any dealings with
> its foreign transmitters; and by the direct instigation of and
> participation in all anti-Christian riots. (Cohen, P.A. 1963, p.3)

With the dispersal of the missionaries from their previous points of concentration at the Treaty Ports to the interior of the empire, the potential sources of conflict multiplied. Missionary privileges contributed to an undermining of the authority of the local gentry. They responded by fermenting hostility and outbursts of violence against the foreign invaders and their converts. With the rapid rise in the number of missionaries that went to China in the last decade of the nineteenth century, outbursts of anti-missionary violence became more widespread and the Peking authorities found it more difficult to contain the situation.

The Sino-Japanese War was succeeded by a violent internal reaction to the defeat of Chinese troops by those of a neighbouring Asiatic state:

> The missionaries, hated for themselves and now more than ever regarded as just another species of the foreign foe, suffered a reign of death and destruction which equalled or surpassed the violence of 1891. (Wehrle 1966, p.59)

Serious though this anti-missionary outburst was in comparison with previous riots, it was mild in relation to the devastation that accompanied the Boxer uprising in 1900. That missionaries and their converts bore the brunt of the hostility that was generated, can partly be attributed to the fact that they were the foreigners who impinged most directly upon the way of life of the Chinese in the interior of the empire. (Steiger 1927, p.140; Purcell 1963, p.184)

It is not necessary to explore here the varied circumstances that contributed to the 'passive and active' resistance of the Chinese to the missionary enterprise. The consequences are more relevant to the current discussion. Missionaries and missionary societies were placed on the defensive. They found it necessary to account to their constituents, and often governments, for their apparent lack of success and the recurrent outbreaks of violence and abuse to which they were repeatedly subjected. Despite the fact that the number of Protestant missionaries had risen from 80 in 1858, to 3,500 in 1907, and the numbers of Catholic priests had increased proportionately, the number of converts to Christianity was probably considerably less than a million. It is, however, impossible accurately to estimate how many Chinese converted to Christianity because missionaries were frequently accused of employing some highly dubious practices to counter the impression that they were ineffective. Pseudo-conversion was one such technique. Low, in the course of discussing the circumstances which culminated in the massacre of French missionaries at Tietsin in 1870, reported that 'the priests or sisters, or both, have been in the habit of holding out inducements to have children brought to them in the last stages of illness, for the purpose of being baptised in articulo mortis'. (Morse 1918, Vol.2, p.241). Similarly, medical missionaries were often less concerned with the health of their patients, than with providing an environment conducive to pragmatic conversions. (Forsythe 1971, pp.17-18). Such practices suggest that regardless of whether their endeavours were adequately rewarded relative to the resources expended, many felt that there was some substance to the contention that their efforts were counter productive. When, in 1888, missionary delegates from all over the world converged on London to attend the Centenary Conference of Protestant Missions of the World, The Times could not resist the opportunity of writing a scathing editorial on the subject:

> An army of learned and diligent labourers is occupied in Missionary work. Two millions sterling are annually subscribed for their maintenance. An appeal is made for more men and more money ... But before the promoters of missionary work can expect to have greater resources confided to them, they will have to render a satisfactory account of their trust in the past. Their progress, it is to be hoped, is sure; indisputably it is slow ... It enjoys a sufficiency, which according to ordinary estimates might seem in abundance, of good will and funds. Still it marches at a pace which, unless it registered by the enthusiasm of Exeter Hall,

appears little more than funereal ... If some people profess to believe, as one speaker deplored, that they hear too little of Foreign Missions, the explanation is that they see too little of their results. (Quoted in <u>National Righteousness</u> December 1888, p.6)

In the course of parrying such attacks and explaining to their supporters the underlying reasons for the resistance they encountered, missionaries transferred the onus of responsibility onto the peoples they were attempting to convert. There being little love lost between China missionaries and their potential flock, it is hardly surprising that the descriptions they provided of their customs, institutions and behaviour, were far from flattering. Uncertain as to whether blame should be laid at the door of Chinese institutions or the perverse character of the people, they played safe by denigrating both. An <u>American Board of Missions</u> pamphlet warned missionaries that:

Underneath a calm and courteous exterior, foreigners have found them cunning and corrupt, treacherous and vindictive. Gambling and drunkeness, though abundantly prevalent, are far outstripped by their licentiousness, which taints the language with its leprosy ... and lurks beneath a thin layer as deep dead rot in society. (S C Miller 1969, p.76)

When some did find a few complimentary things to relate, they were quick to point out that these desirable traits were merely manifestations of an 'outward morality' which was only surface deep:

Side by side with their best traits of character are found habits which are gross and sensual, and practices which reveal a sorry lack of cultured moral sense ... To lie is with them a sort of Spartan virtue. Parents feel somewhat pleased at the dexterity with which a child of theirs can lie. They regard it as a touch of genius, a hopeful sign that their son will make his way in the world ... But the saddest point of view from which to study the manners of the Celestial is the question of his sexual morality ... below all the veneer of good manners there is often a state of corruption that is too terrible to think of. (Dukes 1887)

The Boxer crisis ushered in a brief period of mutual recriminations, during which politicians and diplomats blamed missionaries, missionaries blamed the imperialist powers for encroaching on Chinese territory and sovereignty, Catholics blamed Protestant missionaries, and the latter reciprocated in due course. (Wright, J.W. 1901; <u>Missionary Review of the World</u>, February 1901, p.740) It was a time during which the missionary Sinologist was given full scope for expounding on the real reasons for the direction that events had taken. Many old curios were resurrected. The <u>North American Review</u> carried an article on ancestor worship, a missionary bogey of long-standing. (Clark September 1900) The influential organ of Protestant missionary work, the <u>Missionary Review of the World</u>, traced the devastation to devil worship. (April 1901, pp.315-316). Confucianism, a corrupt political and administrative bureaucracy, the gentry, the Chinaman's 'perverse character', and the opium policy pursued by the British government, all alternated as scapegoats for missionary failure.

From the eighteen seventies onwards, British missionaries repeatedly drew attention to the connection between missionary failure and the responsibility of the British government for the spread of opium smoking in China. The Society of Friends linked the two in an appeal addressed to their 'fellow-countrymen' in 1881:

> It is not to be wondered at when such is the history of England's dealings with China, that Christian missionaries find it extremely difficult to overcome the prejudices of the Chinese people against the religion professed by those who force upon them opium. It is the universal testimony of the missionaries of every Society that this is the greatest obstacle to the progress of the Gospel in China. (Friend of China April 1881, pp.259-261)

This was a theme to which missionaries of all denominations, and of many different coutries, constantly. The views of Theodore Christlieb, Professor of Theology at the University of Bonn, were echoed widely in missionary journals, speeches and petitions:

> The opium traffic has, ... by the scandalous greed in which it originated, by the violence with which it was forced upon the country, contrary to the wishes of its inhabitants, by the physical and moral desolation which it has wrought: in a word, by the odious light in which it has placed Christianity ... it has been the means of closing millions of Chinese hearts to the influence of Christian preaching ... As long then as the opium traffic, that glaring proof of British avarice, continues, so long will the dark stain it has brought upon the honour of England incalculably retard the progress of the Gospel. (1879, p.68)

It was not only British policy which impeded such progress, but also the effects of the drug on its consumers. Bishop J.M. Thoburn of the American Methodist Episcopal Church of India and Malaysia, with 34 years experience in the East behind him, testified before the Royal Commission on Opium that smokers were less susceptible to moral and religious influence: 'It takes the moral stamina right out of a man'. (British Parliamentary Papers 1894, Vol.LXI, p.17) The strong links between China missionaries and the British anti-opium societies ensured that these views were disseminated widely in clerical and political circles, and that they became focal points of the agitation.

Whilst the Christian Union directed its efforts at rallying clerical support, the AOS concentrated its energies on attempting to secure the passage of resolutions in the Commons which would lead to the termination of the Indo-China trade. Between 1880 and 1907 the House debated the matter on nine occasions. The substance of the motions varied little from one debate to the next; nor did the arguments on either side. Anti-opium spokesmen directed their attacks against four aspects of the traffic. First, that the importation of Indian opium led to the physical, social and moral degradation of the consumer. The Rev. Silvester Whitehead painted a vivid description of the ravages wrought by the drug to one of the meetings of the 1888 missionary conference:

> Hollow eyes, sunken chests, protruding shoulder bones, emaciated frame, discoloured teeth, sallow complexion; are the signs which announce the opium smoker everywhere. And the evils thus set forth have their correspondence in the mental and moral degradation of the people ... It is obvious that the wife of such a man must be

reduced to prostitution ... daughters must be sold into slavery or
into shame, in order to procure the money requisite to stave off
hunger.   (Report of the Centenary Conference of the Protestant
Missions of the World 1888, Vol.1., p.128)

Since these views on the eventual consequences of repeated indulgence
were widely held by supporters of the agitation, they naturally drew
attention to the 'immorality' involved in deriving government revenues
from a trade which produced such human misery.   The editorial writer of
the Pall Mall Gazette noted in 1891 that:

> It does seem remarkable, to put it no stronger, that England at the
> close of the nineteenth century should be nursing and making huge
> profits from a trade, the direct outcome of which can only be
> demoralisation, disease and death ... Six millions per annum would
> be a serious loss to the public funds of India.   But even six
> millions may be earned at too great a cost ... The destruction of
> an injustice has always called forth from those upholding it the cry
> of 'the letting loose of hell to ravage the earth'.   It was so with
> slavery; it will be so in the case of the poppy.   But England dared
> to do right to the African, and the heavens did not fall.   They will
> not fall either when all that remains of the opium traffic is a
> black and blurred page of our national history. (April 11)

The arguments linking the traffic with the slow progress of missionary
work have already been mentioned.

All component parts of this critique had been fashioned by the end of
the eighteen seventies.   Some arguments were of longer standing, having
been employed by opponents of the Anglo-Sino wars of the late thirties
and fifties.   From the early eighties until 1917 these themes were
simply reiterated in stereotypical form.   The hundreds of pamphlets
published on the subject, the substance of every parliamentary debate,
and the contents of every memorial and petition, were virtual carbon
copies of each other.

The same was true of arguments advanced by those who sprang to the
defense of the traffic.   With few exceptions they were, or had been, in
the employ of the Government of India, or were responsible for defending
its policies in the Commons.   They strongly denied that opium smoking
had the effects attributed to it by their critics.   W.J. Moore, Deputy
Surgeon-General H.M. Forces, Presidency Division Bombay, maintained that
the Chinese were so generally depraved that opium smoking was unlikely
to do them any further harm:

> that a people distinguished by such characteristics as the Chinese,
> viz. avarice, poverty, cruelty, excessive venery, liability to all
> kinds of disease, drunkeness, Budhism, should become addicted to
> opium, certainly does not appear very wonderful; for opium in its
> effects is exactly the agent to minister to minds so diseased ...
> The only wonder indeed is, that opium was not sooner extensively
> adopted by the Chinese. (1882, p.20)

It was, however, the pragmatic and fiscal considerations which featured
most prominently in the attitudes of defenders of the traffic.   Their
appeal to successive British governments and parliamentarians, partly
accounts for the fact that during the nineteenth century no serious

attempt was ever made to compel the government of India to change its
policy. To discontinue the export of opium, it was contended, would
merely result in transferring the trade to other opium producing
countries, would increase the revenues of these countries at the expense
of India, and would do nothing to reduce the extent of opium smoking in
China. Some went so far as to argue that abolition of the monopoly
would exacerbate those evils which opponents of the traffic were
repeatedly inveighing against. The author of an early pamphlet on the
subject noted that the consequence of abolition would be that:

> The trade, instead of being prosecuted by merchants of credit, with
> capital sufficient to purchase a high-priced article prepared
> specially for the market, will fall into the hands of adventurers,
> ready, reckless, and desperate ... there would, undoubtedly, be more
> opium grown, and much more consumed in India. (The Opium Revenue of
> India 1857, p.8)

Another favourite line of defense was taken by Sir Richard Temple, a
former Finance Member of the Government of India. In the 1886 debate on
the subject, he stressed that since the Chinese insisted on smoking
opium, it was better that they should obtain 'first-class opium highly
taxed from India' than consume 'inferior opium from their own country or
elsewhere untaxed'. He felt sure that the House would perceive that
'this doctrine is as consistent with true morality as it is with sound
finance'. (Hansard 1886, Vol.CCCV, c.294) The views offered by the
Marquess of Hartington in defense of the policy of the Government of
India, in an earlier debate, typified those held by his predecessors and
successors in the office of Secretary of State for India:

> This is not a time at which we can afford to tamper with any branch
> of the Indian Revenue ... Among all the eloquent declamations on
> this subject I have not yet heard any suggestion that any but the
> Indian Government and the Indian people should bear any loss the
> Indian Revenue may sustain from the cessation of this trade ...
> Morality of this kind is extremely cheap; and we should, perhaps,
> here less of the immorality of this traffic and of the expediency of
> putting an end to it, immediately or prospectively, if these
> speeches had to be accompanied with a demand made on the English
> taxpayer for the 6,000,000 or 7,000,000 or some part of it which
> it is proposed so lightly that India should surrender. (Hansard
> 1880, Vol.CCLII, cc.1259-1260)

Anti-opium agitation reached its peak in 1891-92. The number of
petitions against continuation of the traffic submitted to parliament
rose from 10 with 190 signatories in 1883, to 36 with 690 in 1889, and
then to 3,353 with 192,108 in 1891. In terms of signatories,
petitioners against this traffic were more numerous in 1891 than those
against the Contagious Diseases Acts, Vivisection, or in favour of a
Local Option Bill, in any one year during the period 1877-91. (Report
of the Select Committee on Public Petitions Annual: 1877-91) In
response, the government agreed in 1893 to set up a commission to
investigate certain aspects of this question. Political astuteness in
drawing up its terms of reference ensured that its enquiries would focus
on the effects of opium consumption in India, where the drug was
ingested. It did not investigate in depth the problem of opium smoking,
which was the main issue which preoccupied supporters of the anti-opium
agitation. In their report, the commissioners concluded that they found

'a marked preponderance on the side of the view that the common use of opium in India is a moderate use leading to no evident ill efffects'. (British Parliamentary Papers 1895, Vol.XLII, p.69)

Support for the agitation had started to decline prior to the publication of the voluminous reports of the Royal Commisssion on Opium in 1895. This prompted the various wings of the movement to establish the Representative Board of British Anti-Opium Societies in 1894. Its Executive Committee included representatives of the AOS, CU, the Anti-Opium League and the Edinburgh Anti-Opium Committee. Its task was to co-ordinate their activities and endeavour to arouse new interest in and support for the agitation. Despite its efforts, and those of its constituent bodies, anti-opium agitation never again mobilised support on the scale that it had in 1891. Between 1895 and 1906, no further parliamentary debates on the subject were held. The financial position of the societies deteriorated considerably. By 1909 the annual income of the Church of England's Anti-Opium Committee had fallen to 28, and it could no longer afford to publish an annual report. The Archbishop of Canterbury was no longer convinced that there was any need for a separate Church of England anti-opium organisation. (Davidson Papers, Special Box: Opium) Decline of financial support was accompanied by a falling off in the number of public meetings held, failure to reemploy travelling lecturers, and a substantial reduction in the number of petitions submitted to parliament and the relevant departments of state.

It would be easy to conclude that the agitation had had little impact, particularly as this had failed to lead to the realisation of its primary objectives, despite thirty-three years of concerted effort. Although justified in substantive terms, such an evaluation oversimplifies the dynamics of the relationship between aims, agitation, and criteria of success. It is based on the premise that the achievements of this type of social movement can be measured solely in terms of policy changes that give effect to the objectives of their supporters. When, however, the aims are of a highly specific nature and do not entail a quest for power or fundamental dissent from governmental or administrative policies in other spheres, these can usually only be realised after the ideological and/or pragmatic conversion of those with the power to implement them. Since changed circumstaces may independently necessitate or facilitate shifts in policy, it becomes virtually impossible to establish the relative causal impact of ideological and substantive considerations. As Isaac noted in her study of the Israeli Peace and Land of Israel movements:

> The key function of an ideological movement is to provide sets of justifications and courses of action for decision-makers, who may be brought to adopt the alternative thus defined under pressure of constraints which limit their power to continue in the course they have defined as desirable. (1976, p.15)

In these terms the anti-opium agitation was at least partially successful, for in 1906 three separate events occurred which made it extremely unlikely that officials of the British and Indian governments would be able to pursue their Far Eastern opium policy for very much longer. In order of relative importance these were: an anti-opium campaign initiated by the Chinese authorities; an American diplomatic initiative directed at seeking an international solution to the Far Eastern opium problem; and the return of the Liberal Party to power in

Britain.

On 2 September 1906, an Imperial Decree was published in the Peking Gazette which heralded an early ending to the Indo-China opium trade. After a preamble which took note of some of the evils which were presumed to be associated with consumption of the drug, it commanded that:

> within a period of ten years the evils arising from foreign and native opium be equally and completely eradicated. Let the Government Council frame such measures as may be suitable and necessary for strictly forbidding the consumption of the drug and the cultivation of the poppy, and let them submit their proposals for our approval. (FO371/215/249)

Detailed regulations were set forth in an edict published in November. Henceforth, no new ground was to be placed under poppy cultivation; land currently used for this purpose was to be reduced by one-tenth annually. Opium smokers would have to be registered, and those under the age of sixty would be expected to reduce their consumption by twenty per cent per annum. Opium shops, and everything connected with the trade, would be officially registered and gradually closed down. No new opium shops were to be allowed to open. Arrangements would be made to distribute among people addicted to the use of opium, either prescriptions for, or medicines counteracting, withdrawal effects, at cost price or gratuitously, as long as these did not contain opium, morphia or its ashes. Anti-opium societies would receive governmental financial support.

The immediate reasons why the Chinese government took this line of action at this time are still not fully apparent. The general political and social climate at any time from the suppression of the Boxer rebellion in 1900-01, until the eventual overthrow of the dynasty in September 1911, was conducive to the initiation of a government sponsored anti-opium campaign. In other words, any analysis of the introduction of this legislation would identify the same causal factors regardless of the precise timing of the initiation of the campaign during these years. These factors would include dynastic decline, the rise of Chinese nationalism, and the belated attempts of Chinese officials to channel domestic opposition to their authority into programmes directed at fundamental social change.

By the late eighteen-seventies it had become apparent to some scholar-officials, that fundamental changes were needed in China's ancient political, economic and social institutions, if she was successfully to meet the challenges posed by Western imperialism. Some changes were made during the period of the T'ung Chih Restoration, 1861-74. The military was reorganised, a Board of Foreign Affairs was created with the specific purpose of conducting China's international relations with the Western powers, and minor reforms were made in the examination system to ensure the recruitment of men of talent to the bureaucracy. Most of these reforms were 'restorative rather than innovative in character'. (Cohen, P.A. 1970, p.39). Fundamental issues, the source of both internal and external difficulties, were not tackled. The problems of the peasantry were left unheeded, little was done to encourage the growth of industry, and there continued to be considerable opposition to the introduction of modern communication and transport systems. Until 1900 reform programmes were generally:

> additions to an unchanging core of administration ... New institutions ... were tacked onto the existing administrative structure ... Most programs of industrialization were segregated from the continuing traditional responsibilities of government ... There was, so to speak, a small modernizing enclave, walled off from the rest of government activities like the carrier of some dread disease'. (Young, E.P. 1970, p.157)

Administrative disintegration had progressed considerably by the late Ching period. This was most clearly revealed in times of severe social and economic dislocation. The Great Famine of 1876-79, regarded by historians as one of the worst catastrophies of the nineteenth century, is a case in point. It claimed between nine and thirteen million lives, ravaged all five of China's northern provinces, and resulted in the death of between 60 and 90 per cent of the population in the most severely effected regions. The severity of its effects were partly a consequence of the fact that the economic infrastructure had been allowed to fall into a state of decay. The road system, inadequate at the best of times, had deteriorated into a miserable condition: 'Carts moving over the loess-covered roads, which were scarred by ruts ten to fifteen feet deep, were often delayed for days or even weeks'. (Bohr 1972, p.67) Port facilities were equally imperfect. Water conservancy had been neglected and the Grand Canal had silted to such an extent that the movement of grain barges was seriously impeded. In the past the elaborate granary system had to some extent cushioned the impact of natural disasters on the peasantry. It had, however, been allowed to fall into decay:'Social upheaval and the suppression of rebellion had forced general government retrenchment' in its upkeep. (ibid., p.76)

Increased foreign penetration during the 1880s, the outcome of the Sino-Japanese War, and subsequent rivalries between the powers to exact industrial, commercial and territorial concessions from the imperial government, contributed to a further decline in the authority of the central and provincial administrations. Japanese success in her war with China was attributed by many of the traditional elite to her adoption of Western technological, educational and military programmes. They concluded that if China adopted certain facets of Western culture, the incursions of foreign powers on her sovereignty could be warded off more effectively. The Boxer uprising and its brutal suppression by the foreign powers, further undermined dynastic authority, whilst facilitating the dissemination of reform ideas amongst a wider cross-section of the population. The legacy of the incident 'was the achievement of consensus among politicized Chinese that the main task was to develop sophisticated responses to the imperialist danger. Anti-imperialism as a broad modern movement was born, and it was common property'. (E.P. Young 1970, pp.153-154)

The imperial government responded by initiating a number of important reforms. Significantly, the reforms of the last decade of the dynasty differed from those attempted in the past. This time they made important inroads upon the traditional political order. Major changes were introduced in the educational system. Strenuous efforts were made to reorganise the military. Preparatory steps were taken to a reform of the legal structure. An embryonic system of elected representative bodies, based on a limited franchise, emerged at the town, district, provincial and national level. (ibid., p.167) The reform associations that had been created in many of the provincial capitals since 1898 met new demands from the foreign powers for mining, commercial, industrial and territorial concessions with increasing hostility, and endeavoured to fortify the imperial government's resolve to resist further incursions on Chinese sovereignty. In those instances when the government had no alternative but to submit, nationalists frequently attempted to take matters into their own hands.

The spread of the opium habit symbolised the destructive impact of the Western powers more than any other manifestation of imperialism. Railway, mining, commercial and industrial concessions, the ceding of territory, extraterritoriality, and the like, directly effected only a minority of the population. The vastness of China's territorial expanse, the size of her population, and the concentration of foreigners in the coastal region, meant that these facets of imperialism impinged on only a minority of the populace. Foreign opium, on the other hand, spread deep into the interior, winding its way along the trade routes into virtually every corner of the empire. Consequently, the twin problems of opium consumption and poppy cultivation could more easily symbolise imperialism in its varied guises, than could the exaction by any particular foreign power of specific territorial, commercial or industrial concessions. Both were particularly potent symbols during a period which saw the rise of a nationalist movement because their repercussions were familiar to virtually every inhabitant of the empire. Moreover, it was relatively easy to relate the presumed effects of opium to diverse facets of China's contemporary predicament.

The impact of opium on the physical body was perceived as being equivalent to its effects on the body politic. The gradual tightening of the hold of opium on both was equated with the continued encroachments of the foreign powers on Chinese sovereignty. Just as habitual opium smoking was presumed to sap individual drive and initiative, the spread of consumption amongst large sections of the population was perceived as weakening the foundations of the social order. Poverty, lack of economic progress, and military incompetence and weakness were frequently ascribed to the pernicious effects of the drug. The widespread belief that opium consumption distorted the 'moral senses', was parallelled by the assumption that the internal and external trade in this substance contributed to bureaucratic inefficiency, dishonesty and incompetence. The soporific effects of the drug were assumed to exacerbate problems of individual and social control. Analagously, on the political and administrative level, the large revenues obtained from taxing the internal trade in opium by officials of the provincial governments were perceived as enhancing their autonomy at the expense of that of the central government.

An effective campaign against the domestic opium problem could be expected to contribute to the attainment of a number of distinct goals. A major social problem which was presumed to contribute to individual immorality and economic, political and social inefficiency, would be eliminated. Standards of living would be improved by shifting land from poppy cultivation to grain production. The central government would be able to reassert to some degree its control over provincial authorities by removing an important source of their revenues. Finally, the prestige of the dynasty could only be enhanced by its taking action which would adversely effect the economic interests of the pre-eminent imperialist power in the Far East.

The campaign was highly successful. In January 1907 Sir John Jordan, British Ambassador to China, notified the foreign office that the authorities were adopting the 'most active measures' for distributing anti-opium propaganda in the capital city and elsewhere: 'Proclamations are now posted all over Peking ... In Tien-tsin the anti-opium crusade is going on with unabated vigour'. (FO371/216, p.7676) The Chinese measures were so effective, some officials so energetic in implementing anti-opium directives, that poppy cultivation was eradicated in some provinces after only two years. Acting Consul Rose reported in May 1909 that a considerable degree of unrest had been generated in South Yunan, due to the Governor-General's policy of attempting to eradicate the opium crop in two years instead of ten. (FO371/615/408) By March 1911 Rose was able to report that most of the area that had been under poppy cultivation in Yunan was being used for other purposes. (FO371/1071, p.13304) Max Muller, charge d'affaires at the British Mission in Peking, reported in March 1910 that in Szechuan the area under poppy cultivation had been reduced by 80 per cent:

> It is quite remarkable that so great a change should have been effected with so little violent opposition in the economic conditions of a populous province formerly almost wholly dependent on the cultivation of opium. (FO371/846/295-6)

As early as April 1908 Jordan had expressed the opinion that it was unlikely that it would take ten years to eradicate poppy cultivation completely. The achievement was indeed remarkable, for in the course of four years poppy cultivation had been largely extinguished in the two main opium producing provinces. The success elsewhere was no less spectacular.

Reducing consumption was a more intractable problem, primarily because treaty obligations compelled the authorities to permit the continued import of opium and manufactured narcotics. Regulation 10 of the November edict was aimed at finding a solution to the former problem. It directed the Ministry of Foreign Affairs 'to approach the British Minister with reference to the annual reduction of opium imported, so that the importation may be ended within ten years'. (The Times 23 November 1906). The timing of the campaign may conceivably have been influenced by the return of a Liberal government in Britain in 1906, and a passing of a resolution in the Commons in May of that year which called for an early end to the Indo-China trade.

The victory of the Liberal Party at the polls encouraged expectations that 'radicals' amongst those elected to parliamentary, and government office, would oversee the implementation of wide ranging reforms in domestic and external affairs. One consequence of the victory was that the socio-demographic composition of the Commons changed significantly. No less than 220 Liberals and 39 Labour members had been elected for the first time. Non-conformists, 157 in all, now constituted nearly a quarter of the total membership. They were, as noted earlier, fervently opposed to the traffic and had been the mainstay of anti-opium agitation for over thirty years. On 30 May 1906, Theodore Taylor moved from the Liberal benches a motion condemning the association of the British government with this trade. The House, the motion read:

20

reaffirms its conviction that the Indo-Chinese opium trade is morally indefensible, and requests His Majesty's Government to take such steps as may be necessary for bringing it to a speedy close. (Hansard, Vol.158, p.516)

In speaking to the resolution, he and those who followed him advanced those arguments traditionally favoured by the anti-opiumists, all of which I have discussed earlier. It was expected, however, that the newly appointed Secretary for State for India would depart from defending the traffic as had done his predeccessors. The editor of the Illustrated Missionary News had in March expressed the view that now that a new government had been elected, the whole question of opium in China and India would be dealt with expeditiously. This conclusion was based on the belief that the new secretary, John Morley, and his under-secretary, John E. Ellis, were both anti-opium men. Moreover, it was a widely held belief that Morley was a radical. His reputation in this connection was largely based on the stand he had taken on the Irish question during Gladstone's ministry of 1892-95. It was not, however, particlarly deserved in the context of the expectations of members of the radical wing of the party in 1906. His general political philosophy, and his views on concrete issues, both domestic and foreign, were decidedly conservative. Presiding in the autumn of 1906 over a dinner party at the Athenaeum, he scorned the notion of old-age pensions and proposals to nationalise the railways, `decried the constitutional implications of proposed legislation to rectify abuses in the sweated industries, and fortified his arguments with quotations from the 1834 Poor Law Report'. (Koss 1969, p.71) In this respect, Morley was by no means unique amongst Liberal leaders: `they were conservative in their outlook in that they desired to preserve the good old nineteenth-century pattern of Liberalism without making any concessions to the demands of the twentieth ... (their) immediate programme was both reactionary and negative'. (Rowlands 1968, p.30) Morley, in particular, had learned from Burke the `profound lesson' that in politics one had to draw a distinction between abstract truth and practical morality; he also had a deeply ingrained reverence for law and order. (Wolpert 1967, p.16) Consequently, caution and gradualism became the foundation-stones of his India policies, including his approach to the opium question.

In his reply to the motion, he proceeded to advance all those arguments that for nearly seventy years had been put forward by defenders of the trade: that the monopoly system was `one of the best means of restriction that could be provided', that the cultivation and manufacture of Malwa opium was outside the control of the Government of India, something which was not in fact true; and that when proposing to whittle away Indian revenues, the House should proceed cautiously, so that righteous sentiments, `if righteous they were', would not inflict harm on the peoples of India. (Hansard 1906, Vol.158, cc.506-511) He did, however, make one concession, intimating that under certain conditions a significant change in policy might be contemplated:

It is, he said, no secret that the Chinese have been considering for two years or more whether some plan could be devised of dealing with the importation of opium into their country, other than that which now prevails ... if China wanted seriously and in good faith to restrict the consumption of opium in China, the British Government would not close the door. (ibid., c.514)

The conclusion to be drawn from this is that the initiative for a gradual reduction of imports of Indian opium would have to come from the Chinese. No evidence in the Foreign Office records supports Wolpert's contention that after the debate Morley urged Sir Edward Grey, Secretary of State for Foreign Affairs, to appeal to the Chinese government to seek more effectively to restrict opium imports and consumption. (Wolpert 1967, p.220)   No such approach was made at the time.

Representatives of the Chinese Ministry of Foreign Affairs first approached the British Minister to China, Sir John Jordan, in connection with this matter on 30 November 1906.   They desired to know whether his government would give sympathetic consideration and approval to a number of proposals designed to achieve the aims outlined in the Imperial decree of 2 September.   The most important of these was that imports of Indian opium be reduced by ten per cent each year from 1907, taking as a base the average quantity of Indian opium imported per annum during the years 1901-05.   Since this and other proposals directly effected the interests of India and the Crown Colonies, they were referred by the Foreign Office to the Indian and Colonial Office's for their observations.   There is no need to detail here the involved negotiations and complex issues that arose in relation to the gradual winding-down of the Indo-China traffic during the years 1906 to 1917.   Since the bearing which these had on the parallel development of an internationally organised programme for controlling the traffic in narcotics is of more immediate relevance, a brief summary will suffice.

The response of the Government of India to these and subsequent proposals advanced by the Chinese authorities in connection with the restriction of imports, was to draw out negotiations for as long as possible, make only those concessions which were politically necessary, maximise its financial returns from this source during the remaining years of the trade's decline, and minimise the impact of these and other negotiations on its exports of opium to other markets, and its sale of opium in India itself.   In this they were fully supported by officials of the far eastern Crown Colonies.   After lengthy negotiations between Jordan and Chinese officials, it was agreed in December 1907 that exports of opium from India would be reduced by ten per cent a year for three years from 1 January 1908:

> on the understanding that if during this period the Chinese Government shall have duly carried out the agreements on their part for reducing the production and consumption of opium in China, His Majesty's Government undertake to continue in the same proportion the annual diminution of the export after the expiration of the three years period of trial. (FO371/414/101)

Instead of reducing the extent of opposition to the Indo-China traffic, the Ten Year Agreement became the focus of increased agitation by British and Chinese anti-optimists, and was a source of continual friction between the British and Chinese governments.   The gradual reduction of imports of foreign opium over a ten year period, was a policy that could only be expected to work smoothly if the anti-opium campaign in China progressed exactly on schedule.   If it faltered, the Foreign Office, under pressure from the Government of India, would have had to insist that regular exports of Indian opium be resumed.   This would have been necessary because the agreement had not in fact repealed those provisions of the Treaty of Tientsin, and the Additional Article to the Chefoo Convention of 1886, which obliged the Chinese to import foreign opium. This, indeed, was one of its advantages, when viewed from the perspective of Indian officials. It would have placed the Foreign Office and British diplomats in an extremely difficult predicament, since it would have been virtually impossible to sustain such a policy in the face of the likely outcry in the Commons. In fact, the reverse occurred. Since poppy cultivation had been eradicated in many provinces after only two or three years, Chinese officials were prevented from effectively reducing consumption by the requirement that they do not hinder the distribution of that quantity of foreign opium imported under the terms of the agreement. It also meant that importers of Indian opium, most of whom were British subjects, were quite within their rights in insisting that British diplomats protest against any restrictions imposed by provincial officials on the wholesale and retail trade in opium. Consequently, they regularly lodged protests with central and provincial officials over treaty violations relating to opium, despite the fact that many were broadly sympathetic to the aims of the anti-opium campaign.

When the 1908 agreement came up for renewal in 1911, the Chinese authorities adopted an intransigent attitude, encouraged by the sustained and vociferous opposition of British and Chinese anti-opium societies to the conclusion of any further agreement. In China, demonstrations were accompanied by outbreaks of violence. So great was the opposition there that Jordan at times doubted that it would be possible to reach agreement with the Chinese authorities. Grey noted that reports received from consular officials indicated that it was likely that poppy cultivation would have ceased in all parts of China by the end of 1911. In these circumstances, he did not see how the importation of further Indian opium could be forced on the authorities. His senior advisors convinced him otherwise.

The agreement signed on 8 May 1911 made significant concessions to the Chinese. The most important of these was that the import of Indian opium would be excluded from those provinces which British consuls certified as being free from poppy cultivation. The ten per cent reduction in Indian exports to China would continue until the expiration of the agreement in 1917, or at such a date at which the whole of China was certified as being free of poppy cultivation. The Peking Daily News gave the following version of the reasons for the reluctant acquiescence of the Chinese authorities:

> The Chinese Government knew very well the wishes of the people and they would if they could refuse to ratify the Agreement. But they could not, for the simple reason that they knew whom they were dealing with. They could not get more than they did from a Government ... who so persistently insist upon the rights of British subjects which had been secured by ... an uncharitable war so many years ago. (18 July 1911)

The precise reasons for the Chinese government's compliance are not known. Either their diplomatic intelligence was poor, or submission to the demands of foreign powers had become so institutionalised that they failed to recognise the changed circumstances. It was probably a mixture of both. A perusal of Foreign Office records leaves no doubt that had the Chinese authorities abrogated the 1908 agreement unilaterally, and refused to allow any more imports of foreign opium, the British government would have had no alternative but to acquiesce in the situation. The outcry that could be expected at home, particularly in the Commons, would have given the Foreign Office little leeway for exerting any further pressure on the Chinese authorities. In 1912 the Indian government ceased its sales of opium for export to China. The problem of disposing of the large stocks that had been accumulated by merchant speculators at Shanghai and Canton continued to be a major bone of contention between Jordan and the Chinese authorities until 1917, when the Chinese purchased the remaining stocks and burned them publicly as a final gesture of defiance against rights which had been exacted in an 'uncharitable war'.

The effectiveness of the sustained pressure that had been brought to bear on the Foreign, India and Colonial Office's since May 1906 by anti-opium supporters and organisations, was undoubtedly an important factor in leading to the granting of significant concessions to the Chinese in the 1911 agreement. The return of a Liberal government and the anti-opium campaign mounted by the Chinese, spurred the movement into conducting a final assault on the trade. Rather than accepting the disappearance of the traffic at the expiration of ten years, anti-opium leaders intensified their efforts in an attempt to terminate the trade at an earlier date. The changed political situation placed them in a strong tactical position for exerting pressure on the relevant departments of state. When the issues had been joined in terms of abolition or continuation of the status quo, the Foreign and India Office's had little difficulty in neutralising the impact of anti-opium agitation, or deflecting criticism elsewhere. Once agreement had been reached on the eventual suppression of the trade, it was extremely difficult to devise convincing arguments to justify its continuation for any length of time. In the face of strenuous and largely successful efforts by the Chinese authorities to implement the anti-opium edict, the continuation of the traffic became less defensible than it had ever been. The Foreign Office was inundated with petitions from a variety of groups spread throughout the British Isles, all demanding the immediate cessation of the traffic. Public meetings were held in a number of cities during 1907. Many of the memorials, petitions and resolutions came, as they had in the past, from religious organisations. Others originated from the Central Liberal Association, a number of branches of the British Women's Temperance Association, the Scottish Anti-Tobacco Society and, of course, the various anti-opium organisations. The veteran campaigners sensed that after years of frustrated effort their goal was within grasp, and hastened to press home their advantage.

As the agitation intensified its scope widened. Until the 1906 debate, and the conclusion of the 1908 agreement, anti-opium crusaders had concentrated their efforts on issues relating to the Indo-China trade nearly exclusively. After the Commons passed a resolution describing the opium trade as 'morally indefensible', they directed their attention more freqently to the problem of opium consumption in the Crown Colonies. In May 1908, a resolution was passed in the Commons which urged the government to 'take steps to bring to a speedy close the system of licensing opium dens now prevailing in some of our Crown Colonies, more particularly Hong Kong, the Straits Settlements and Ceylon'. (Hansard, Vol.188, c.300). Although this issue was discussed in the Commons on a number of occasions between 1908 and 1912, few concrete measures were taken to meet the demands of critics.

As the number of countries featuring in the controversy increased, so did the number and type of drugs. Once the Chinese measures began to have some impact, importers, wholesalers and retailers sought alternative means of reaping profits from the long-established proclivities of Chinese smokers. A large variety of anti-opium remedies were already being marketed before publication of the imperial decree, most of which were found to be as habituating as the vice they were supposed to cure. The clamp-down on opium smoking increased the demand for such remedies spectacularly. Morphine was one of the most common ingredients. In 1892, according to the official returns of the Board of Maritime Customs, imports of morphine amounted to 15,761 ozs. Ten years later this had risen to 195,133 ozs.

Officials in the Crown Colonies and India perceived that the spread of morphine and cocaine addiction, could be used to advantage in diverting attention away from their financial dependence upon revenues collected from the sale of opium. If morphine and cocaine were shown to be greater evils than opium smoking, there would be some justification for proceeding cautiously with the introduction of restrictions on the trade in prepared opium. In 1909 the Governor of Hong Kong raised this matter with the Secretary of State for the Colonies. He suggested that since morphine was usually exported to China and Hong Kong from the United Kingdom:

> Those who are deeply interested in controlling the export of opium from India, and in restricting its consumption for smoking in the British Colonies, should investigate the conditions of the home trade in morphia with the Far East, and the extent of the participation of the United Kingdom in the profits of a trade which, in common with the highest expert authorities, I am convinced to be a source of the greatest danger to China. (FO415/1/2-3)

In March, the Governor of the Straits Settlements expressed the opinion to the Colonial Secretary that:

> Whatever may be the evils of opium smoking, the evils resulting from morphine and cocaine injection are immeasurably greater in intensity and extent, so far as the numbers physically and morally ruined are concerned. (ibid: 53-54)

He concluded by expressing the hope that His Majesty's Government would avail itself of any opportunity 'for arriving at an international agreement for restricting the trade in morphine and cocaine'. (ibid) Similarly, the Indian authorities repeatedly raised the problem of the spread of morphine and cocaine consumption in Burma and India in official communications. Seizures of cocaine had risen from 490,885 grains in 1907-08 to 939,685 grains in 1909-10. The greater portability of the drug in comparison with opium, made control of the illicit traffic more difficult. These facts, Indian officials argued:

> fully illustrate the difficulties of the situation in Burma (and India) ... In these circumstances we are concerned that our efforts towards suppression of the cocaine habit in this country will be infructuous unless something is done to restrict the export of the drug and its congeners from the chief manufacturing countries. (FO371/1073/86)

The contention that the evils attending morphine and cocaine consumption were greater than those associated with opium smoking or eating, were never supported by medical or any other kind of evidence. Their validity is not particularly relevant to the current discussion. What is of crucial significance is the fact that these officials had an incentive to direct attention toward the traffic in manufactured narcotics, in order to defend the vested economic interests of their administrations in the trade and consumption of raw and prepared opium. It is understandable that they should insist that in any international programme to control the availability of these substances, priority should be given to controlling the former traffic. Before exploring the impact which their views had on shaping the provisions of the International Opium Convention, it is necessary to examine those factors which persuaded officials of the American Department of State that it would be advantageous to assume responsibility for initiating such a programme.

3 Sino-American international relations 1895-1906: preliminary steps towards international narcotics control

In July 1906 Charles H. Brent, Episcopal Bishop of the Philippines, broached the idea of America assuming responsibility for coordinating national policies relating to the Far Eastern opium traffic, in a letter addressed to President Theodore Roosevelt.

> Recently ... the question of England's share in the opium traffic has been reopened in official circles in the old country. My experience on the Philippine opium investigating committee leads me to believe that the problem is of sufficient merit to warrant an endeavour to secure international action. From the earliest days of our diplomatic relations with the East the course of the United States of America has been so manifestly high in relation to the traffic in opium that it seems to me almost our duty, now that we have the responsibility of actually handling the matter in our own possessions, to promote some movement that would gather in its embrace representatives from all countries where the traffic and use of opium is a matter of moment.
>
> Why could we not hope to have an investigation on the basis of science as well as of practical observation of actual conditions in which England, France, Holland, China and Japan should take part with ourselves. The sole hope for the Chinese is concerted action. Foreign Relations of the United States 1906, pp.361-2.

Significantly, no action was taken immediately. In late September the Acting Secretary of State instructed the United States ambassador in London to raise the suggestion with the Foreign Office. This decision was justified in terms similar to those used by Brent:

> The Government of the United States has not hitherto been in a

position requiring it to make any official representations regarding the opium trade so far as it concerns other countries, because it is a trade which in no direct way concerned us. We have been heretofore neither producers, carriers, consumers, nor sellers of opium , so we have had no pretext whatever to open a discussion on the subject. Now that `we have the responsibility of actually handling the matter in our own possessions', as Bishop Brent says, the position is different, and we have full justification for approaching the other interested powers for our mutual benefit. (Adee to Whitelaw Reid, 27 September 1906, ibid, Vol.1)

Although the occupation of the Philippine Islands by the United States in 1898 meant that its colonial officials had to evolve a policy towards the extensive opium consumption of its Chinese population, it is clear from Acting Secretary of State Adee's letter that this localised matter was being used by the State Department only as a pretext. The underlying motives can be unravelled by examining certain issues, both domestic and external, which inclined American foreign policy makers to evolve, adopt, and implement, certain policies towards China during the years 1895-06, including those relating to opium.

FAR EASTERN INTERNATIONAL RELATIONS 1895-1906

Prior to the 1890s Chinese foreign policy had been directed towards two principal objectives: containment of the expansionist designs of the Western powers, and minimisation of the control they could exercise over internal affairs. Her diplomatic and commercial relations with foreign powers were governed by what historians refer to as the `treaty system', a term used to designate the collective impact of the separate treaties concluded between China and each foreign power. Their concurrent implementation had evolved into a `system' of international relations by virtue of the fact that nearly all of them included a `most-favoured nation' clause. This provided that if China were to grant any commercial, diplomatic or other concession in a future treaty with some other power, it would automatically be extended to those powers who had previously concluded treaties which incorporated such a clause. The treaty system was a by-product of the conflict that persisted throughout the nineteenth century between the European powers, who foresaw great commercial opportunities accruing from the opening up of the China market to the exploitation of their traders, and the Chinese authorities who endeavoured to resist such incursions. Since it was clear that concessions would not easily be obtained, the most-favoured nation proviso was a mechanism that ensured that each individual power would not have to exact them separately.

Until the mid-eighteen nineties China remained largely insulated from outside interference in her domestic affairs, primarily because the powers had placed definite limits on both the extent and nature of their intervention. Since British interests in China were perceived as primarily commercial, the Foreign Office pursued a policy aimed at preserving the territorial integrity of the empire, maintaining intact the authority of the internal bureaucracy, and increasing the opportunities for economic exploitation. (cf. Pelcovits 1948, p.85) Until the outbreak of the Sino-Japanese War in 1894, Britain exercised a controlling voice in far eastern international affairs, and the other powers were largely satisfied with the concessions that had been obtained. The underlying assumption was that few benefits would accrue from the acquisition of territorial concessions. Although one of the advantages of the treaty system was that the combined weight of the European powers and the United States was pitted against that of the Chinese authorities, it also acted as a brake on the designs of any one particular power, since the most-favoured nation provision precluded China from granting exclusive concessions. The status quo could only be maintained, however, as long as any power desirous of occupying Chinese territory, or obtaining exclusive concessions, believed that such a policy would be effectively resisted by the combined action of other powers. If one of them were successfully to implement such a policy, the likely result would be the gradual carving up of China into territorial concessions and spheres of influence. Other powers with commercial and strategic interests in that region would be bound to follow suit, and the Chinese were not in a position to resist such incursions. This is precisely what transpired in the years 1895-06.

The immediate catalyst of what has been characterised as the 'battle for concessions', was the acquiescence of the Chinese in demands made by Japan in April 1895, at the conclusion of the Sino-Japanese War. Under the terms of the Treaty of Shimonoseki, China was to relinquish to Japan the island of Taiwan and the southern appendix of Manchuria, known as the Liaotung or Kwantung Peninsula. (Maki 1961, pp.5-9) On the day the treaty was signed, the Russian foreign minister suggested to the British, French and German ambassadors, that they exert pressure on Japan to denounce these territorial claims. Although Britain refused to cooperate, the joint influence of the others was sufficient to ensure that the Japanese authorities acceded to their demands. (Bergamini 1972, p.226) France was the first member of the triplice to use her intervention 'in favour of China', to press forward her interests there. Under the terms of two Sino-Franco conventions, favourable alterations in the delimitation of the Chinese-Tongking frontier were agreed, customary tariffs on imports from Tongking were reduced, and French citizens were granted certain prior claims if the Chinese authorities should decide to exploit mines which were concentrated in Yunan, Kuangsi and Kwantung. In response, Britain demanded and received Chinese acquiescence in rectification of the Burmese frontier, and the extension of the Burmese railroad system into Yunan, should a suitable opportunity present itself. This became the regular pattern pursued by the European powers and Japan, resulting in the granting of exclusive commerical, industrial, financial and mining concessions during the ensuing decade. (Langer 1935, Vol.1, p.404)

Until 1897 the concessions exacted were primarily commercial and industrial, enabling the powers to exploit to greater advantage China's natural resources, whilst securing certain of their strategic interests. Although this constituted a significant transformation of the previous system of Sino-foreign relations, it was not until 1897 that inter-power rivalries shifted to include the direct occupation and control of Chinese territory. In November of that year German naval vessels steamed into Chiao-chou Bay, and their troops established a beachead in the province of Shantung. Once the Chinese recognised that opposition to their occupation from other powers would not be forthcoming, they had no alternative but to acquiesce in German demands. Germany was granted complete sovereignty within the leased territory of Kiaochow, and certain commerical and industrial concessions in the interior of Shantung province which effectively reduced it to a German sphere of influence. (cf. Schrecker 1971) These developments constituted an important turning point in Sino-foreign relations. Once the acquisition of territories, spheres of interest and influence, became acceptable to the powers, this could have no effect other than to stimulate further encroachments on Chinese sovereignty until such time as a new modus vivendi developed. The immediate Russian response was to demand a lease on Port Arthur. This they were granted in 1898, primarily because neither Japan nor Britain, to whom the Chinese appealed to counteract Russian pressure, were disposed to oppose the move. In compensation Britain received a lease on the port of Weihaiwei. (Langer 1935, Vol.2, p.485)

THE RHETORIC OF AMERICAN IMPERIALISM

The transition of the Far Eastern question from a 'state of quiescence to one of extreme activity', coincided with equally momentuous changes in the United States. With the ending of the Civil War, America entered upon a period of rapid industrialisation and urbanisation. The years 1885 to 1897, in particular, were characterised by almost unrelieved discontent as 'masses of Americans groped to escape the dominance of an uncompromising plutocracy - and groped in vain'. (Higham 1955, p.68) Opposition to the direction which these social and economic transformations were taking, found expression in the programmes advocated by supporters of Populist and Progressive causes. Both movements arose 'during a rapid and sometimes turbulent transition from the conditions of an agrarian society to those of modern urban life'. (Hofstadter 1955, p.7) Populism was primarily an expression of agrarian discontent, which crystallized in the People's or Populist Party of the 1890s, and the Greenback, Granger and anti-monopoly movements. The introduction of effective controls on the economic activities of the large industrial combines, the providing of 'cheap money', and the easing of land acquisition for purposes of agricultural expansion, were remedies advocated by farmers who were 'incensed at the mounting figures of farm foreclosures and a withering countryside'. (Mowry 1958, p.88)

Most Progressives, on the other hand, came from the 'solid middle class':

> Their resentment, if it arose from economic causes, came not from despair but from other feelings, from their sense of lessened power ... Their relative status and power in society had been going down consistently since the rise of the economic moguls following the Civil War. The gap between them and the Morgans and the Rockefellers had been steadily increasing, and their hopes for attaining the top of the economic heap were progressively dimming. (ibid, p.95)

Although Progressives frequently campaigned for or against the same things that the Populists did, their attention was riveted particularly on what they perceived as the corrupting impact of the burgeoning urban conglomerations. In domestic policy they fought campaigns against child labour, urban political corruption, the conditions prevailing in slaughterhouses, and urged federal control of the railways and the large trusts. (cf. Hofstadter 1955, p.176; Platt 1969, p.41; Leuchtenberg 1952, p.485)

The social turmoil of the post civil-war decade, particularly the economic depression of 1893-97, had a profound influence on shaping the attitudes adopted by important decision-makers and intellectuals towards foreign policy issues. The economic depression was one of the more important factors responsible for directing the attention of some members of the business and intellectual communities to the benefits that could be derived from overseas expansion. Prior to the downturn in the economy, a general sense of the inevitability of continuous and increasing prosperity prevailed amongst most of the former. Although in economic terms this depression was no more severe than those of the eighties, it occurred at a time when the effects of other dislocations attending industrialisation were felt particularly acutely. It is in this context of 'omnipresent anxiety and frustration', that the growth of an imperialist spirit in America has to be understood. (Young, M.B. 1968, p.4)

The considerations that initially prompted the adoption of a more forceful and interventionist foreign policy, were primarily strategic. Influential Americans who surveyed the world balance of power during the nineties, observed that the Western Hemisphere was surrounded by imperialist powers who had already carved up between themselves substantial portions of Africa and Asia. Many, such as Henry Cabot Lodge, the powerful senator from Massachusetts, were of the opinion that if these powers managed to stablise these areas, they would next turn their attentions to the Americas. Matters came to a head in 1895 when Britain claimed suzerainty over parts of Venezuela, and declared that the issue was no longer one that was subject to negotiation. Secretary of State Olney responded with an uncompromising despatch, informing the British government that the United States would not tolerate any intervention by a European power in the Western Hemisphere and, if necessary, would resist such an attempt by force:

> The result was an international sensation, and, ultimately, British agreement to submit to arbitration ... The immediate effects were at least twofold. One was the growing advocacy of prescriptive imperialism, a conviction that the United States should seize desirable areas before a rival power got them ... In addition some Americans came increasingly to incorporate imperialist assumptions into their thinking about their own nation's problems. (Healey 1970, p.28)

By 1899 'prescriptive imperialism' had led to the occupation of Cuba, Puerto Rico, Hawaii, the Philippine Islands and Guam.

Pari passu with these developments, a number of writers were laying the intellectual foundations which provided the cognitive framework within which America's Far Eastern policy during the ensuing decade and a half evolved. Particularly influential in this formulation were Alfred T. Mahan, Brooks Adams and Charles Conant. A more forceful and interventionist role in foreign policy, particularly in the Far East, was advocated on three principal grounds: economic, cultural and global-strategic. The first was a product of the assumption that the China market was potentially a major outlet for American capital investment and goods. The second emanated from a belief in America's civilising role, the need for her to take on her share of the 'white man's burden', a product of the amalgamation of 'American expansionism and British imperialism into an all-embracing Anglo-Saxon mission'. (ibid, p.29)

The third rationale was military-strategic in essence, a product of the assumption of responsibility for defense of the western hemisphere in the face of perceived expansionist aims of the European powers.

Economists and industrialists, as well as traders and financiers, advocated expansion on the basis of assumptions they entertained about the contributions this would make to the flagging economy. In searching for explanations for the economic depression, many opted for one or other variant of the 'glut theory'. Its most systematic exponent was Charles Conant, who, in a series of articles published between 1898 and 1900, argued that the source of the problem was rooted in 'the excess of saving, with the resulting accumulation of unconsumed goods'. Under the present social order, he maintained, 'it is becoming impossible to find at home in the great capitalist countries employment for all the capital saved which is at once safe and remunerative'. (1900, pp.10-12) The solution was to export capital, particularly to those countries 'which have not felt the pulse of modern progress'. (ibid, p.27) Similar views were widely held at the time.

The problem therefore resolved itself into determining which were the most suitable markets to cultivate. Many regarded China as a possible solution. China, with its countless millions, seemed a natural outlet for a society which was suffering from the ills of over-production and under-consumption and investment. Only 'such a vast market could absorb the surplus products of an industrial machine that, they thought, had satiated the domestic market and yet on whose full-scale operation the prosperity of the entire society depended'. (Young, M.B. 1968, p.2) The McKinley administration, however, initially expressed a disappointing lack of concern over the 'battle for concessions' that was raging in China. This was due primarily to its preoccupation with issues of hemisphere diplomacy, and the impending and actual conflict with Spain. The war and its outcome was one of the principal factors leading to a change in the administration's attitude.

Business circles felt that the securing of the Philippines would ensure preservation and expansion of American economic interests in China. Senator Beveridge declared ecstatically that the Pacific Ocean, the ocean of the commerce of the future, was America's. He concluded that 'the power that rules the Pacific, is the power that rules the world'. (Dulles 1946, p.105) Lodge was convinced the occupation was equivalent to the securing of the Eastern trade. Brooks Adams confidently predicted that the Philippines, 'rich, coal-bearing and with many fine harbours', would ensure that the China market would remain open to Americans and make her 'a greater seat of wealth and power than ever was England, Rome or Constantinople'. (Burton 1968, pp.96-97) Orville H. Platt, the influential and distinguished senator from Connecticut, was certain that their acquisition had been ordained by higher authority, and President McKinley, 'in prayerful judgement', concluded that the United States had no alternative but to acquiesce in their colonization, lest they fall into the hands of a nation less qualified to exercise power over the destinies of 'barbarous peoples'.

The administrations' decision to retain control of the Philippines was also influenced by 'questions of naval strategy and of the balance of Pacific power'. (Dulles 1946, p.103) In surveying the situation in Asia, Captain Alfred T. Mahan, an influential naval historian, had pointed out that China should not simply be regarded as a major outlet for America's economic surpluses, but as the centre of a region where a crucial battle between two forms of civilisation was destined to be joined. Accepting Brooks Adams' contention that the centre of world trade and power was shifting eastward, due to the decline of Britain as the dominant trading power, the industrialisation of the German states, and the potential economic transformation of Russia, he viewed the battle for concessions as one that was being waged between the 'land power' - Russia - and the 'sea powers', Britain, Japan and Germany. The land power would eventually seek to obtain access to the sea due to the 'obvious' advantages of sea over land commerce. (1898, p.62) The interests of the United States, he concluded, dictated that she join with other sea powers to prevent further Russian encroachments in Asia.

Other considerations played an important, albeit subordinate part, in the Weltanschauung of those concerned with problems of strategy and world power. In the eyes of many a progressive or conservative, active intervention in the Pacific and Far East would contribute much towards the preservation of certain qualities of American civilisation which, so they thought, were in danger of being submerged by the avaracious quest for wealth which had become an obsession amongst large sections of the population. To men of education and substance, 'the prospects were alarming ... a soft, self indulgent society of mollycoddles and money-grubbers would be short work for a warlike foe ... To a few iron souls, there was an obvious answer. The martial virtues came, they held, from Mars alone'. (Mowry 1958, p.88) Although this view did not command the support of many Americans, it evoked a favourable response amongst political leaders of the stature of Roosevelt and Lodge, influential intellectuals of the calibre of William James and James Bryce, and from the sociologist Franklin H. Giddings, who argued that an outlet must be found for the volatile manhood of America, lest it 'discharge itself in anarchistic, socialistic, and other destructive modes that are likely to work incalculable mischief'. (Healey 1970, p.108) These were alternatives which were unlikely to appeal to either progressives or conservatives.

In conclusion, it is clear that the separate elements of the developing imperialist world-view harmonized most adequately with each other when applied to the 'problem of Asia'. Morever, it was there that the theoretical presuppositions and practical goals of both progessivism and imperialism were most likely to be fulfilled. As Leuchtenburg has noted:

> Imperialism and progressivism flourished together because they were both expressions of the same philosophy of government, a tendency to judge actions not by the means employed but by the results achieved ... and an almost religious faith in the democratic mission of America ... since the United States was the land of free institutions, any extension of its domain was per se an extension of freedom and democracy. (1952, pp.500-01)

ECONOMIC INTERESTS: THE EXIGENCIES OF OPENING AND CLOSING DOORS

There was little in the actualities of the China market to substantiate the wild claims advanced by economic interest groups, and advocates of overseas expansion:

The most elementary facts contradicted the dream that China would, before long provide a large market. The first of these was that only a small part of China, the coastal cities and a few ports on the rivers were open to (Western) trade ... The lack of a transportation system restricted the influx of western goods ... Another formidable barrier stood in the way. Western goods fitted neither ancient Chinese preferences nor Chinese pocketbooks. (Varg 1968, pp.37-39)

The fact that these perceived interests were primarily 'mythical', did not deter the administration in Washington from taking energetic steps to protect them. Secretary of State John Hay launched the American diplomatic offensive in September 1899 by initiating a correspondence with all the major powers that had direct interests in China. These despatches, known as the Open Door Notes, were drafted by William Woodville Rockhill, a former Secretary at the Peking legation. In 1899 he was appointed as a consultant to the State Department on Pan American affairs, but was preoccupied for most of his time in advising Hay and Roosevelt on Far Eastern policy. China, in his opinion, had to be cajoled, guided and threatened by the Western powers in order to force her into complying with their 'reasonable' demands. Being particularly suspicious of the designs of the other powers, he considered it essential to arrest the battle for concessions so that their combined pressure could be brought to bear on China, 'compelling her to take the necessary steps for her own protection'. (Varg 1952, p.30)

After Hay had approved the substance of Rockhill's memorandum on this question, the notes were drafted and despatched to the powers. They focused principally on the customs question, suggested that no power should interfere with the vested interests held by one or more of the powers within its respective 'sphere of interest' or 'sphere of influence', that only the Chinese authorities should collect customs duties, and that no preferential harbour or railroad dues should be levied so as to favour the subjects of one power vis a vis those of others. (Notes reproduced in Maki, 1961, pp.12-15) The replies were evasive:

Great Britain agreed to the proposals only after the United States met her insistence that Kowloon be excluded by suggesting that no mention be made of this leasehold. Germany also agreed, but ... advised that she did not think it would be wise to press the powers for specific commitments. (Varg 1952, p.34)

France accepted the proposals but was careful to omit any reference to 'spheres of influence'. Italy and Japan accepted without qualifications, although the latter took the replies of other powers to be statements of intent, rather than firm commitments. Least satisfactory was the Russian response. She had 'specifically excluded leased territories, stating that it was for China to settle the question of customs duties in open ports and that Russia would claim no special privileges for her own subjects'. (ibid, pp.34-35. Replies of the powers reproduced in Malloy 1910, Vol.1, pp.244-60)

Despite the unsatisfactory nature of the 'commitments' given by the powers, Hay was sufficiently reassured by March 1900 to announce, what was obviously not true, that 'the nations addressed had replied favourably' (Vevier 1955, p.1) Like Rockhill, he was well aware of the fact

that the United States could ensure neither the territorial integrity of
the Chinese empire, nor the equality of commerical opportunity, in the
face of determined opposition from the other powers. Rockhill seems
simply to have devised `a verbal formula that would have the effect of a
self-fulfilling prophecy'. (Young, M.B. 1968, p.141) It is unlikely
that either Hay or McKinley had any clear policy for dealing with the
Far Eastern situation. They also did not appear to be interested in
inaugurating radical policies to be applied in that region: `Both
favoured the Open Door Notes because they sensed the need to appease
alarmed businessmen and missionaires and thought that the international
situation favoured a successful demarche'. (Neu 1967, p.6)

That the Notes had not achieved their objectives was soon apparent,
for during the spring of 1900 `it became evident that China, perversely
unaffected by Hay's brilliant diplomacy was following an independent
path towards convulsion and dismemberment'. (Young, M.B. 1968, p.136)
By the middle of the year the powers, now the `allied powers', were
cooperating in order to suppress the Boxer uprising. Whilst their
armies were preparing for the march on Peking, Russian forces had
already occupied much of Northern China. Hay felt sufficiently alarmed
to follow up the `notes' of 1899 with a circular to the powers in which
he announced that the United States aimed at a peaceful settlement of
the conflict, one which would preserve the territorial and administrative integrity of the empire.

The diplomatic response of the United States to the intensification of
the battle for concessions, differed substantially from that of other
powers. Whilst they encroached increasingly on Chinese territory at the
periphery of the empire, and extended their commerical, industrial and
other interests in the interior, the underlying objectives of American
policy remained essentially the same as prior to these developments.
They were directed at maintaining the territorial integrity and
sovereignty of China whilst simultaneously ensuring that any concessions
exacted by other powers would be extended to American citizens under the
provisions of the `most favoured nation' clauses included in pre-1895
Sino-foreign treaties. This, as Dennet notes, was the `tap-root' of
America's China policy, and was as old an objective as her relations
with Asia. (Dennet 1941, p.580; Neu 1967, p.5; Esthus 1966, p.6) It
was based on the premise that neither public opinion, nor Congress,
would support military intervention by United States forces to secure
American interests there. This was readily acknowledged by Hay. In
commenting upon Russia's refusal to relinquish her control over
Manchuria after the suppression of the Boxer rebellion, he noted that
`Russia knows as well as we do that we will not fight over Manchuria ...
If our rights and our opposition to Russia in the Far East were as clear
as noonday, we could never get a treaty through the Senate the object
of which was to check Russian aggression'. (ibid, p.9) It was this
constraint which lent American China diplomacy its distinctive style,
and accounted for differences in foreign policy strategy between her and
the other powers. The latter either shared a common frontier with,
possessed colonies bordering on, or occupied salients of China. They
could, and frequently did, advance or secure their interests there by
means of military intervention. Usually the threat of such intervention sufficed to ensure that the Chinese authorities bowed to their
demands.

Those responsible for formulating and implementing American policy could not reply on such leverage in attempting to advance strategic and economic interests. In order to achieve goals which were not significantly dissimilar from those of other powers, American diplomatic and State Department officials wielded 'verbal formulae', and relied on rhetorical flourishes to camouflage their lack of military and economic influence on developments then taking place on the Asiatic mainland. It was a strategy which relied on the deployment of symbols rather than of manpower and material resources. The objective was to secure goals as a by-product of having created a favourable 'diplomatic image'. A desired image, as Jervis notes, 'can often be of greater use than a significant increment of military or economic power'. (1970, p.6) The main advantage of such a strategy, if successful, is that objectives can be realised 'without paying a high price in terms of resources used, risks run, and other goals sacrificed'. (ibid, p.4)

Rockhill, in drafting the Open Door Notes, recognised that the perceived strategic and economic interests of the United States could only be secured in one or more of three ways: by the other powers voluntarily agreeing to refrain from annexing Chinese territory and establishing exclusive spheres of interest; by military intervention; or by the mediation of the Chinese authorities. It was unlikely that the first could be achieved, and certain that the second was not feasible. The third required that the Chinese authorities perceive United States policy as being animated by motives which differed substantially in character from those underlying the policies being implemented by other powers. These, ideally, should be interpreted as being of a 'disinterested' nature. It was also desirable that they should be convinced that United States policy was directed at securing the territorial and administrative integrity of the empire.

Prior to the eruption of the battle for concessions, the creation of such an image was not particularly important, since any concession secured by one power was automatically extended to others. Subsequently, American policy makers had to rely increasingly on such a strategy since 'most favoured nation' treatment no longer applied in the changed circumstances. That Rockhill clearly understood this is evident from the content of the memorandum he submitted to Hay accompanying his draft of the 'notes'. The proposals, he declared, 'have the advantage of insuring to the United States the appreciation of the Chinese Government, who would see in it a strong desire to arrest the disintegration of the Empire and would greatly add to our prestige and influence in Peking'. (Varg 1952, p.30) As the competition for concessions intensified during the first decade of the century, American policy makers were forced increasingly to rely on moral persuasion as a counter token to the military and economic leverage of the other powers. Although the cultivation of Chinese 'appreciation' paid few dividends in terms of economic goals secured, it was an important consideration, not only in Hay and Rockhill's Open Door policy, but also in the decision to adopt a moderate stand at the Peking Conference in 1900, and to remit the Boxer indemnity in 1904.

After the suppression of the Boxer uprising, diplomatic representatives of the 'allied powers' met in Peking in order to draw up terms to be submitted to the Chinese authorities as pre-conditions for the withdrawal of their troops. Most of the powers demanded the payment of large financial indemnities. There is general agreement amongst historians that during these negotiations Rockhill adopted a 'moderate' stand. He repeatedly expressed the view that the financial recompense being demanded was excessively high. The extent to which this was promoted by magnanimity is at best problematic. Varg emphasises that Rockhill's objective was to prevent any further undermining of the power and authority of the dynasty and bureaucracy, 'reasoning that if (China) could not defend herself or meet the demands of the indemnnity, the other powers would use this as a pretext to carve up the empire'. (1952, p.47) Dunnell notes in this connection that the American negotiators 'were always prepared to scale down ... demands in return for increased trading privileges'. (1901-02)

Rockhill's influence was also paramount in 1904 in convincing Roosevelt and State Department officials, that it would be expedient to return the monies received as an indemnity. The condition was that these would be used to educate Chinese students in the United States. Whilst he considered this to be a simple act of justice, since the amount of money that had been demanded from the Chinese far exceeded the cost of damages caused, State Department officials viewed the matter in a different light. William Phillips, Chief of the Division of Far Eastern Affairs, read Rockhill's account of the remission to mean that it would 'insure us a preponderating influence in the Empire'. Huntington Wilson, another official of this division, seeing the diplomatic possibilities, commented that the remission 'should be used to make China do some of the things we want. Otherwise I fear that her gratitude will be empty'. (Vevier 1955, p.63)

At the time that Rockhill made this suggestion, and Wilson perceived the 'diplomatic possibilities', it was becoming more imperative than ever that American foreign policy makers find some means of placating the Chinese and enhance their influence in Peking. Sino-American relations were approaching an all-time nadir because of a dispute over the emigration of Chinese citizens to the United States. The re-enactment of anti-Chinese immigration legislation by Congress provoked a vigorous attack on American interests in China. Led by Chinese nationalists, it culminated in a boycott of United States produce in China and elsewhere in the Far East. It was against this background of deteriorating diplomatic relations, a foreign policy strategy that was not backed by the exertion of military and economic power, a belief in the importance of the China market amongst important decision makers, and the Chinese anti-opium campaign, that State Department officials recognised the 'diplomatic possibilities' that could be reaped if the United States assumed responsibility for a concerted international approach directed at reducing consumption of opium in the Far East.

IMMIGRATION PROBLEMS

Chinese immigrants first arrived in California in the late eighteen forties, attracted there by plentiful opportunities for employment. Expressions of enmity towards the new arrivals were voiced soon after. Intense hostility towards orientals rapidly became an indelible part of the consciousness of many Californians:

> Throughout the state, for almost half a century, John Chinaman was buffeted from pillar to post. He was everywhere discriminated against; he was robbed, beaten and frequently murdered, and no punishment was meted out to his assailant; he was brutally and

unceremoniously ejected from whatever mining or agricultural
property he managed to acquire; in the courts he was classed lower
than the Negro or the Indian; and scores of laws were enacted for
the sole purpose of hampering him in his efforts to earn an honest
living. (Asbury 1968, p.143)

There is no need here to delve in depth into the causes of anti-
Chinese hostility. In part it was simply a product of crude
ethnocentrism, a reaction to a cultural group whose way of life differed
most from anything that they had previously encountered:

The clannishness of the immigrants and their retention of their own
way of life ... awoke discomforting fears among the people of
California. The Chinese made no effort whatsoever to adopt American
customs. Speaking their own language, wearing their own native
clothes, retaining the distinctive badge of the queue, eating their
own food, insisting on being taken back to China for burial, and
worshipping their own gods they remained completely alien to the
civilization which surrounded them. (Dulles 1946, p.85)

A particular bone of contention was the nature of their monetary
obligations to Chinese immigration associations. One of the
consequences of the abolition of the international slave traffic had
been its substitution by what was known as the 'coolie trade'. Chinese
unskilled labourers were induced to sign employment contracts under
whose terms they agreed to work in plantations in the West Indies and
Latin America, for a fixed number of years at a fixed rate of
remuneration. It was widely believed by Californians that the Chinese
were brought there under similar conditions. It was easy enough to draw
this inference from their behaviour:

Labourers who arrived in San Francisco had very little money, yet
their passages had to be prepaid; they were met at the wharves, went
directly ... to employment which seemed to await them; they appeared
to make no individual bargains, but to be guided by some Chinese
agent and when working in gangs often received their money through
such an agent. It was naturally inferred by casual observers that
(immigrant associations) had imported them and were holding them in
control until the cost of immigration were repaid. (Coolidge 1909,
p.51)

The intensity of anti-Chinese hostility tended to vary with fluctua-
tions in the economic cycle, and the electoral prospects of the
Republican and Democratic parties. The pervasiveness of anti-Chinese
hostility amongst working men constituted a useful asset in the hands of
overly opportunistic politicians. Many Governors of the state came to
consider the expression of anti-Chinese enmity as a prerequisite to
electoral success. The 1879 constitution forbade their employment by
corporations, debarred them from the suffrage, and imposed severe
restrictions on their places of residence in the state. Municipal
authorities had no desire to be outdone in the promulgation of anti-
Chinese legislation, and discriminatory ordinances of a harassing and
petty nature were introduced in many cities in the 1870s.

Much of this anti-Chinese legislation was either unconstitutional or
violated the provisions of Sino-American treaties, particularly those of
the 1868 Burlingame Treaty which:

secured, reciprocally, exemption from persecution or disability on account of religious belief ... and the privilege of residence or travel on the basis of the most favoured nation...and recognized the right of voluntary emigration, making the engaging in involuntary immigration by the subjects of either power a penal offense. (ibid, p.149)

It was evident to Californian politicians that effective measures against the Chinese could only be introduced after the negotiation of a new treaty, and by the introduction of federal legislation. To this end they next turned their attention. In 1876 the senate of California set up a committee to investigate the social and political effects of Chinese immigration. Its report stressed those factors most likely to appeal to anti-Chinese sentiments: prostitution, criminality, non-conversion, competition, and coolie slavery. Hardly any pretence of objectivity was maintained. Prior to its publication Congress had been petitioned to adopt a national exclusion policy. The Chinese, the memorial stressed, were an unassimilable element, who remained 'the same stolid Asiatics that have floated on the rivers and slaved in the fields of China for thirty centuries of time'. (Dulles 1946, p.85)

In response to the agitation, President Hayes despatched a commission to China to renegotiate the Burlingame Treaty. The reasons that prompted this decision are not particularly difficult to unravel. Coolidge, in what is still the standard work on Chinese exclusion legislation, convincingly has shown that that competition between the two main parties for the working man's vote in Californian and national elections was, in large measure, responsible for the introduction of discriminatory state legislation and the immigration exclusion acts. (cf. Stein 1978, pp.153-56 where the merits of an alternative perspective advanced by S.C. Miller are discussed) Eighteen-eighty, the year the commission was despatched to China, was no exception. As the electoral campaign rolled on, each party endeavoured to put forward the impression that it was no less hostile to Chinese immigration than its opponents.

The negotiations were concluded with the signing of the Sino-American Treaty of 1880. The most important part of the treaty relating to the immigration issue was Article I. This provided that:

Whenever in the opinion of the Government of the United States, the coming of Chinese laborers to the United States, or their residence therein, affects or threatens to affect the interests of that country, or to endanger the good order of the said country...the Government of the United States may regulate, limit or suspend such coming or residence, but may not absolutely prohibit it. The limitation or suspension shall be reasonable and shall apply only to Chinese who may go to the United States as laborers, other classes not being included in the limitations. (Malloy 1910, Vol.1, pp.237-38. Emphasis added.)

Whilst the commissioners were still negotiating, Congress was exercising its ingenuity in attempting to curb the 'terrible scourge' of Chinese immigration. During the life of the forty-seventh Congress, seven exclusion bills were introduced. The bill which eventually became the Restriction Act, 1882, provided for the suspension of immigration of skilled and unskilled labourers for a period of ten years. This did not satisfy many Californians who continued to press for even more stringent controls. In 1888, a year of presidential elections, the Scott Act was signed by President Cleveland. It increased the period of prohibition to twenty years, and prevented the re-entry of Chinese who had temporarily returned home. In 1892 a system of registration for Chinese resident in America was introduced under the terms of the Geary Law. In 1894 the Chinese Minister in Washington expressed his government's desire to enter into new treaty negotiations with respect to the immigration question. The outcome of the negotiations was the Sino-American Treaty of 1894. Its terms provided for the absolute exclusion of Chinese labourers for a period of ten years, except such registered labourers who had a lawful wife, child, parent or property in the United States. (ibid, Vol.1, pp.241-43) This legislation required re-enactment in 1904 if the policy of exclusion was to be continued.

Until 1904 the Chinese government had been relatively indifferent to the hostile treatment meted out to its citizens in the United States. At this time, however, it was less willing to brush aside the issue. On 3 March the Chinese Board of Foreign Affairs informed the United States Minister to China that, in accordance with Article VI of the 1894 immigration treaty, they were giving formal notice that it would 'terminate immediately upon the expiration of the period mentioned, and shall not continue for another period'. (Foreign Relations of the United States 1904, p.117) The Chinese pointed out that since the two countries were 'united by friendly ties', there should be no difficulty in negotiating a new treaty before the expiration of the current one on 7 December.

Roosevelt, however, was up for re-election in November, and was clearly unwilling to endanger his presidential hopes by pandering to Chinese sensibilities, as his message to Congress on the subject indicates:

> Not only must our labor be protected by the tariff, but it should also be protected so far as it is possible from the presence in this country of laborers brought over by contract, or of those who, though coming freely, yet represent a standard of living so depressed that they can undersell our men in the labour market and drag them to a lower level. I regard it as necessary, with this end in view, to re-enact immediately the law excluding Chinese laborers and to strengthen it wherever necessary in order to make its enforcement entirely effective. (Roosevelt 1904, p.546)

Whilst negotiations on the renewal of the immigration treaty were still pending, a meeting of a large group of Chinese who opposed its re-enactment met at Shanghai in May 1905. They resolved on a boycott of American goods unless the United States agreed to modify its immigration policy. The decision was communicated to various merchant guilds at twenty-two treaty ports. In due course they declared their intentions of following suit. Other groups declared their support. Students of the Anglo-Chinese College of Foochow detailed their complaints in a petition which they delivered to Rockhill, who had recently been appointed as the United States Minister to China.

The Shanghai merchants chose 20 July as the day when the embargo on American products would start. The press, particularly that of Canton, was instrumental in spreading support. Many doctors in Shanghai and

Canton refused to purchase American medicines:

> The Hong Kong World News reported that the gamblers of Canton were giving away Chinese cigarettes instead of American brands. The traditional `moon feast' felt the impact ... The women of Canton decided to make rice cakes in place of the usual `moon cakes', which required American flour. (Field 1957, p.70)

The motives of the diverse groups which supported the boycott, either actively or passively, were mixed. The government, although careful not to openly encourage it, tacitly approved of its aims. Moreover, due to the increasingly precarious nature of its authority, it could not afford voluntarily to submit to the unilateral decision of the American government to re-enact the exclusion laws. Some provincial officials failed to take action against the agitation because they supported its aims and desired to embarrass the central authorities. The students, the group most deeply committed to the new nationalism, were prompted by the desire to rid China of all imperialist encumberances, and a need to assert their own sense of dignity. Those merchants who supported the boycott did so out of sympathy with the Cantonese, who suffered most from the exclusion policy. (Varg 1952, p.60) Chinese communities overseas lent support. The boycott spread to Singapore and the Straits Settlements. In San Francisco the Chinese community expressed its support by raising funds to sustain it, as did the China Reform Association, a world-wide group of Chinese radicals dedicated to the overthrow of the Manchu dynasty.

Although the enthusiasm of merchants waned rapidly, its effect on Sino-American relations outweighed any economic significance it might have had. Most authorities consider that the latter was negligible. The agitation forced Roosevelt to modify somewhat his stand on this question. Although he continued to believe that it was not in America's interest that Chinese labourers should be permitted to migrate there freely, he now thought it necessary to ensure that everything possible should be done to prevent the harsh treatment of those Chinese permitted entry. He issued new instructions to the immigration authorities, ordering them to treat Chinese immigrants and visitors with greater circumspection than had hitherto been the norm. Having administered this palliative, he impressed upon Rockhill the desirability of his taking a strong line with the Chinese authorities. Rockhill's more aggressive approach bore fruit, and on 31 August 1905, a reluctant Manchu government issued a decree condemning the boycott and demanding that the provincial authorities take the necessary steps to stamp it out.

This did not immediately call a halt to the boycott. Some provincial officials refused to enforce it, on the grounds that hasty measures `would stir up a revolution, and it would be more difficult than ever to ward off calamity'. (Field 1957, p.85) Nevertheless, the economic effects declined rapidly with the dwindling of active mercantile support. By the end of August its influence on the volume of American trade was negligible. The diplomatic channels between the two countries, on the other hand, continued to reverberate with its implications until 1907. Matters were aggravated by a number of sporadic outbursts of violence against foreigners residing in China, particularly during the latter part of 1905. In October a mob killed five members of an American mission at Lienchow. The crisis came to a head in December, when an American admiral was mobbed after he had accidentally shot a Chinese woman whilst out hunting game. By this time Roosevelt was tiring of the Chinese agitation and decided to adopt a more forceful approach. On 23 December he issued instructions for two regiments to proceed to the Philippines in preparation for possible action in China. Military action would be contemplated if the imperial authorities failed to respond satisfactorily to American demands for an immediate suppression of the boycott, and the prevention of further outbreaks of violence against foreigners. During January and February, rumours of a second Boxer uprising gained widespread currency throughout the United States, and grandiose preparations were embarked upon by the army and navy in anticipation of a possible invasion of China or, at the very least, the occupation of a port there. The crisis was eventually defused in March with the publication of an imperial decree which complied with most of the demands made by the United States government. This ended the immediate diplomatic crisis over the question of immigration.

CONCLUSION: SINO-AMERICAN INTERNATIONAL RELATIONS AND THE OPIUM INITIATIVE

The operative word in the vocabulary of American historians who have surveyed Sino-American relations during the years 1840-1910, has been ambivalence. According to many, United States policy, particularly during the years 1898-1909, displayed this characteristic at every level:

> Generosity has been matched by insistence on retaining the old treaty system ... support for China in its efforts to free itself of the opium trade (was) accompanied by paternalism and a sense of superiority; and a hearty moral support was not matched by deeds. (Varg 1968, p.171. Emphasis added.)

Young notes a similar ambivalence in the attitudes of missionaries and their supporters:

> The missionary, whose commitment to China was total, found himself hating both country and people fully as much as he loved them. The parishioner, convinced of the special love he felt for China each time he dropped a coin in the collection box, was also in wholehearted agreement with those who kept Chinese emigrating to America. (Young, M.B. 1968, p.12)

Although there is certainly sufficient evidence to substantiate the contention that attitudes towards China and the Chinese were characterised by 'ambivalence', there is none to suggest that this was manifested in inconsistencies in the policies pursued by State Department officials and China diplomats. The discrepancy between what Fairbank refers to as the 'vigor' of 'verbal pronouncements and the 'limitations' of 'official actions', was a product of the constraints within which the foreign policy of the United States respecting China had to be conducted. (1971, pp.289-290) These had changed little since the eighteen-forties. Although it might appear that the forceful handling of the immigration crisis and, according to Young, anti-missionary outbursts after 1900, marked a change in American policy in that 'the government moved towards dispelling the impression that it was soft' on

China, the evidence to support such a conclusion is lacking. (Young, M.B. 1968, pp.170-171) In fact, the State Department could never have been accused of being 'soft on China'. It appeared to be so because unlike the other major powers, the United States had never had to exact economic or political concessions at the point of a gun. These were automatically extended to her citizens and diplomats once they had been secured by other powers, under the provisions of the 'most favoured nation' clauses included in Sino-American treaties. Once the other powers started to stake out 'spheres of influence' for themselves, or acquired territorial concessions, this provision could no longer be relied on to secure additional economic or political concessions. In order to persuade the Chinese authorities to take effective action against anti-missionary outburts, or to defuse the boycott agitation, verbal aggression had to be intensified. This cannot be taken to mean that American policy had moved from being less to more forceful in substantive terms.

In attempting to explain why these historians have characterised American policy as 'ambivalent', and have confused self-interest with 'generosity', 'moral support', and 'acts of international friendship', it is only necessary to seach for the frame of reference they have employed in arriving at such conclusions. It was not only the McKinley administration which, on the issue of China, 'began to define its policy in opposition to that of Russia'. (ibid, p.73) Just as the diplomats who manned American consular posts in China perceived the intrigues of the Russians or Japanese behind the failure of their endeavours to advance American economic interests, historians have employed the policies pursued by these powers as a 'contrast conception', in order to provide an evaluative framework within which to assess and analyse the policy of the United States. Only in such a context can the educational indemnity be viewed as an 'act of international friendship' (Israel 1971, pp.43-44), Varg be led to conclude that Rockhill's policy 'contributed a great deal to establishing a tradition of friendship between the two countries' (1952, p.130), Young come to believe that China came to view America as 'a special friend and special enemy' (Young, M.B. 1968, p.12), Dennet deduce that the United States desired 'justice' in Asia and aimed to remove any restrictions upon these ststes which would 'thwart their development as strong states' (p.508), and Tong single out the Open Door policy as evidence to substantiate his contention that 'any power that aimed to dominate China alone was to be opposed by the United States'. (1964, pp.284-285) Opposition, such as it was, was only verbal.

Although included in this literature are many references to America's 'special relationship' with China, acts of 'goodwill', 'friendship', 'moderation', and 'hearty moral support', reference is not made to the foreign policy makers of the other powers sharing these virtues. It is only the reluctance of these historians to equate America's foreign policy with that of Russia, Germany, Japan and Great Britain, that has enabled them to characterise it as 'ambivalent'. On the level of rhetoric it undoubtedly was. If, on the other hand, the policies actually pursued by United States diplomats are compared with those implemented by other powers, the conclusion is inescapable that American foreign policy-makers were no more inclined to indulge in acts of 'goodwill', 'international friendship', or 'hearty-moral support', than were their Russian, German, Japanese, French or British opposite numbers. American policy respecting China was conducted simultaneously on two levels: the verbal or rhetorical, and the real or substantive. It is only in terms of the former that it is possible to perceive any ambivalence. In attempting to arrive at some assessment of the motives that prompted the adoption of particular policy decisions, it is necessary to conduct an evaluation on both levels. It is essential to establish whether the verbal or the real is a more adequate explanatory guide. Political activities, as Edelman has emphasised, 'require the most exhaustive scrutiny to ascertain whether their chief function is symbolic or substantive'. (1964, p.43)

Until 1895 the United States did not have to rely on her own efforts to extend her perceived strategic, commercial and financial interests in China. The other powers, who unlike her could intervene directly to advance their own interests, served those of the United States whilst pursuing their own. Once they began to occupy salients of Chinese territory, and to stake out exclusive 'spheres of interest', the position of the United States became more precarious as the political options available to her decision-makers had not altered. At the same time, the context within which American Far Eastern policy was being conducted, changed significantly. The development of an imperialist ideology, and the acquisition of overseas territories, heightened concern amongst important sections of the political elite for the protection of American interests in China and the Far East. In these years, Americans 'somehow came to feel that having influence in Asia was a categorical imperative for a world power'. (Young, M.B. 1968, p.231) The paradox was that this changed attitude merely served to highlight the fact that the United States had few substantive interests in China, or other parts of the Far East, with the possible exception of the Philippines, which decision-makers could rely on to justify a more forceful foreign policy. If the United States was to 'take the lead' in the Far East, 'then it too would presumably have to lead the way in investments. These were the measure of a nation's influence in China, and, equally important, only a large stake in China could justify a strong policy'. (Varg 1968, p.125) In fact, the value of American trade with China dropped between 1860 and 1897 from 3 to 2 percent of her overall international trade. The trans-pacific trade was not particularly important. Similarly, American investments in railroad, mining and engineering projects in China were small in comparison with those of other powers. In was, as Dennett notes, 'the missionary and political interests of America in Asia which kept the Far Eastern problem before the American people, to even the slight degree in which it held their attention. (1941, p.580) The absence of sufficiently substantial economic interests to justify 'a strong policy', was reflected both in a withdrawal from involvement in this area, and in the nature of the foreign policy strategy adopted. There were a number of reasons for the former.

First, the turn of the century was accompanied by a new period of economic prosperity. As the decade advanced "more and more of its adventurous optimism flowed into reform. Progressivism gradually replaced imperialism as the central interest in the public mind ... The crusading fervor ... turned into a domestic struggle against the trust, the bosses, and the 'interests'". (Highman 1955, p.116) Bloomfield having examined the contents of five important American magazines in order to establish the major issues preoccupying their readers, concluded that during the first seven years of the decade, journalistic 'anxieties' focused on corruption 'in business, labor, and government'.

(1957, p.11; Peterson 1956, pp.15-16).

Secondly, some historians have exaggerated the extent of the commitment of influential decision-makers to imperialist policies, and the degree of their centrality in the climate of opinion prevailing in the eighteen-nineties and the first decade of the new century. Although in the sphere of foreign policy there was a significant shift away from a merely passive interpretation of the Monroe Doctrine, this change was confined primarily to issues connected with hemisphere diplomacy. The acquisition of possessions further afield, such as the Philippines and Guam, could be regarded as deviations from the 'new foreign policy' which was then in a state of crystallisation. It was much easier to justify intervention in Hawaii, Cuba, Puerto Rico and Panama in the context of the Monroe Doctrine, than it was in the Philippines, as Roosevelt, Lodge and others of imperialist inclinations were acutely aware. The fact that the United States adopted a more aggressive stance in affairs of hemisphere diplomacy, does not necessarily entail the corollary that a more forceful policy was also pursued in the Far East, as Beale, Neu, and Esthus, amongst others, appear to suggest. On the whole the United States was still profoundly isolationist:

The average American believed that foreign nations were corrupt, unstable, class-ridden, selfish, and trapped in a cycle of dynastic wars. His own country must beware of becoming caught in the same snares; it belonged spiritually as well as geographically to another hemisphere. The Monroe Doctrine epitomized the sense of separateness, and the determination to remain separate from Europe's entanglements. (Cunliffe 1972, p.240)

There are obviously serious difficulties involved in establishing indices which would be generally acceptable as criteria for determining whether a specific course of action can justifiably be considered as a deviation from earlier ones. Perhaps most useful to employ in the present discussion are those suggested by Jervis, namely, resources used, risks run, and other goals sacrificed. In terms of these criteria, it is difficult to come to any conclusion other than that if there had been a change in America's China policy, it amounted to a persistent withdrawal from previously held objectives. The commercial aspects of the 'open door' notes added no new principles or objectives to America's pre-1895 China policy. The Hay circular of the following year, in emphasising the need to preserve the territorial and administrative integrity of the empire, simply spelt out the prerequisites considered necessary to achieve the objectives outlined in the 'notes'. This principle was not new. The 1868 Burlingame Treaty had specifically pledged the territorial integrity of the empire, and had disavowed any intention on the part of the United States to interfere with China's internal affairs. The 'notes', in exempting leased territories from the application of the principles of equality of commercial opportunity, sacrificed this objective as did, even more blatantly, United States policy in connection with Roosevelt's mediation of the Russo-Japanese conflict. He was instrumental in bringing the war to a close, arranging for representatives of the two sides to conduct peace negotiations in the United States. The provisions of the peace treaty, the Treaty of Portsmouth, included the transfer to Japan of Russian concessions in North China. Roosevelt instructed Rockhill to make it clear to the Chinese authorities that they could not 'with propriety question the efficacy of this transfer or hestitate to allow the Japanese all the rights the Russians were exercising.' (Esthus 1966, p.116)

A third factor that accounted for withdrawal from involvement in Chinese affairs, was that after the Russo-Japanese War Roosevelt recognised the significance of Japan's emergence as a major Far Eastern power. He therefore sought to avoid conflict with her over American interests in Manchuria, Japan's 'sphere of influence'. This became more imperative later, with the deterioration of relations between the two countries as a consequence of the reaction of the Pacific coast states to Japanese immigration:

> Roosevelt was willing to sacrifice the open door and the integrity of China in favor of the strategic and economic interests of Japan in Manchuria in order to compensate Japan for discrimination in the United States against Japanese and the exclusion of Japanese laborers. (ibid, p.308; Neu 1967, p.319)

Finally, the lack of co-operation between the powers jostling for control in China, coupled with the restrictions on America's political options, meant that it was increasingly difficult for her foreign policy decision-makers to advance or secure United States interests in China in the face of renewed Chinese resistance to Western encroachments. Thus, at the same time that some influential Americans came to believe that the United States had important interests in Asia, the position of the United States in China was being increasingly undermined by policies adopted by other powers and the Chinese. The immigration dispute, the subsequent boycott and the hostility it generated, left her diplomats with few political levers with which to manipulate policy. At the time only two were available: the educational indemnity already discussed, and the 1906 opium initiative.

The 'opium problem' had been elevated into a position of prominence by British and American missionaries working in China. Within the ambit of their preoccupations it held a position of particular significance as an explanation for their lack of success. The Boxer uprising focused the public searchlight on missionary activities for a brief period. It led to some critical appraisals, and undermined the confidence of missionary societies in the evangelising policies they had been pursuing for some sixty years. It was in this atmosphere of mutual recriminations and search for explanations, that two American ex-China missionaries foresaw that the negotiations that would take place in Peking to settle conditions for the withdrawal of foreign troops, would afford an opportunity 'to bring international pressure to bear upon Great Britain to withdraw the treaty by which the opium traffic had been forced upon China since the opium war of 1840'. (Senate Document No.135, 58th Congress, 3rd Session 1905) A petition to this effect was circulated amongst missionary boards, presidents of colleges, authorized representatives of chambers of commerce, and other reform-minded organisations, before being forwarded to the President. The petitioners suggested that since the foreign powers 'will be urging a great extension of commercial privileges' they could most readily reciprocate 'what may be granted by China in this respect by giving her their powerful help in delivering her from the multiplied evils of the opium traffic'. (ibid) The State Department decided to take no action, on the grounds that it would be untimely for a 'friendly power' to raise such a delicate issue, given Britain's preoccupation with the Boer War.

In 1904 this question was brought to the attention of the State Department again, this time by the Rev. Wilbur F. Crafts, superintendent and treasurer of the International Reform Bureau. The exact nature of this organisation is not particularly important in the present context since its involvement in matters relating to the opium traffic was only temporary. The suppression of the traffic in and consumption of opium fell within the ambit of its other concerns, which centered largely on exerting pressure on colonial powers to introduce legislative and administrative controls to protect 'savage races' from the harmful effects of intoxicating liquors. During 1904 the bureau initiated a campaign directed at securing the release of China from the obligation to import Indian opium. It arranged for a hearing on the 1900 petition at the State Department. To the hearing, held on 19 November were invited representatives of all the missionary societies and members of the Native-Races Deputation, which included such stalwarts of moral reform as the Women's Christian Temperance Union, the National Temperance Society, and the Anti-Saloon League. The interest of all these organisations in the question of the Indo-China opium traffic was clearly incidental to their primary preoccupation with controlling the traffic in and consumption of intoxicating beverages. There is no record of the Department of State having taken any action at the time in connection with the matters discussed at the hearing. The next important development was Brent's letter to Roosevelt, in which the convening of an international investigatory commission was suggested. (cf. supra, p.27)

Bishop Brent's attitudes to questions relating to opium consumption and the Indo-China traffic, were most probably shaped by his experiences as a member of the Philippine Opium Commission. This was appointed by the Governor of the islands to investigate the opium situation there and in other parts of the Far East, prior to deciding upon a policy to be adopted to deal with the problem of opium consumption in the Philippines. (Report of the Committee Appointed by the Philippine Commission to Investigate the Use of Opium and the Traffic Therein, etc. Senate Document No.265, 59th Congress, 1st Session; A.H. Taylor 1969, pp.311-346; Musto 1973, pp.25-28) Taylor maintains that:

> The significance of the Philippine opium situation extended far beyond the Islands. Its great importance was in furnishing the United States with ample justification for interceding on behalf of China with the other powers having Oriental possessions. Thus, in 1906 ... the United States launched an international campaign to help rid China of the opium menace. (p.328)

The difficulty with this conclusion is that the Philippine Commission reported in June 1904. If the opium situation in the Philippines was such a crucial factor in determining the policy embarked upon by the United States in 1906, it is certainly not clear why the State Department did not respond positively to the proposals advanced by the Native Races Deputation in November 1904, only five months after the report had been published.

The reasons were twofold. Any programme directed at reducing the extent of non-medical consumption of opium in the Far East would require the active co-operation of the British and Chinese authorities. The British would have to cooperate because India was the major exporter of opium in that region. The Chinese, on the other hand, themselves produced vast quantities of the drug, and were the major consumers of opium. Until the publication of the imperial decree on 2 September 1906, there was no reason to assume that the authorities in either India or China were considering any changes in their policies concerning this traffic. Consequently, it would have been extremely unlikely that the British government would regard such an approach by the State Department as anything other than an unwarranted interference in a traffic in which the United States had no direct interests. Secondly, the central and provincial authorities in China derived large revenues from the taxation of opium, whether domestically produced or imported. Proposals emanating from the State Department which were directed at solving China's external and internal opium problems, could only be expected to be received favourably if the Chinese authorities themselves desired to pursue such a programme. Until September 1906, State Department officials had no reason to believe that a change in policy was then under consideration. It was only after the Chinese government had itself decided to take action in order to prohibit the consumption of opium for non-medical purposes, and to eliminate poppy cultivation, that the State Department decided to accept the proposals set forth in Brent's letter.

The central theme of the analysis to this point has been that the deterioration in Sino-American relations was the major consideration that predisposed State Department officials to favour the adoption of the diplomatic initiative outlined in Brent's letter. The convening of an international conference to discuss the Far Eastern opium traffic was simply another means of exercising some control over affairs in China. Such a step was made desirable by the decline in American influence there in 1905-07, stemming from the immigration controversy and the ensuing boycott. Contrary to the views of Lim (1969, p.162), Willoughby (1925, pp.14-20) and Taylor (pp.25-26), the 1906 initiative was not prompted by 'humanitarianism', 'friendship' or 'solicitude' for the Chinese. It was not an act of international charity: 'diplomacy demanded levers to manipulate policy'. Added leverage was essential due to the deterioration in Sino-American relations in this particular period.

Thus, a series of events and considerations, some of independent causal status, others interdependent, combined to lend initial impetus to the development of international cooperation in the sphere of narcotics control. China missionaries, backed by British anti-opium societies and American social movements preoccupied with issues of 'moral reform', had successfully identified and defined non-medical consumptioon of opium as a negative and undesirable practice, one that necessitated governmental and international intervention to extirpate it. Between 1900 and 1906, this negative assessment was translated into specific policy recommendations which were relayed to the State Department. Due to the internal-isation of certain precepts of an imperialist ideology that had been evolved in the United States during the eighteen-nineties, precepts whose origins were traceable to certain domestic developments, State Department officials and influential political leaders had come to believe that it was essential for the United States to exercise some degree of control over events then occuring in China. Their ability to do so had been undermined by significant changes in the pattern of Far Eastern international relations, and a dispute with the Chinese authorities over questions concerning the migration of their nationals to the United States.

Lacking any substantial economic or political backing which would justify pursuing a 'strong policy' in China, they could only hope to retain or increase American influence in Peking by implementing policies which did not entail the sacrificing of other goals, the taking of significant risks, or the employment of economic or military resources. Brent's proposal fell into this category. It was not dissimilar from recommendations made in the 1900 petition and raised at the 1904 hearing. A prerequisite for translating it into a concrete diplomatic demarche, was the initiation of the Chinese anti-opium campaign. This programme had been embarked upon for reasons that were connected with the increasing encroachment of foreign powers on Chinese sovereignty, the development of a nationalist movement in China, and the decline of the authority and power of the Manchu dynasty, all of which were directly related to each other. Without the missionaries, the consumption of opium for non-medical purposes would not have become a social problem when it did. In the absence of a deterioration in Sino-American relations during the first decade of the century the consumption of opium for non-medical purposes would not have become an international social problem, necessitating the introduction of a complex system of controls; at least not during the first decade of the twentieth century.

4 The Shanghai Conference and its aftermath

On 17 October 1906, the British Foreign Secretary, Sir Edward Grey, was asked by the American ambassador what view his government would take of a joint commission or investigation of the opium trade and the opium habit in the Far East, to be undertaken by the United States, Great Britain, France, the Netherlands, Germany, China and Japan. Grey replied that he would have to consult with the India Office, but that although any interference would involve a 'great sacrifice' of Indian revenue, 'that would not prevent the British Government from considering the question or incurring some sacrifice if it was clearly proved that the result would be to diminish the opium habit'. (FO371/22/110) At the beginning of November the India Office informed the Foreign Office that they favoured participation in such an investigation if the other powers mentioned agreed to this proposal, and if, 'as regards China, the inquiry extends to the production of opium in China as well as to the imports of foreign opium'. (ibid 152)

Although there is little documentary evidence to show why Grey and Morley felt obliged to respond in the affirmative to the American proposal, it is likely that they were influenced by the hostility of the majority of Liberal M.P.'s to the traffic. It is relatively certain that if it became known that either had refused to participate in what was, after all, only an investigatory commission, this would have prompted some of their number to take further steps to bring the trade to an immediate end. Furthermore, it is reasonable to suppose that senior officials at the India Office may have perceived that such an investigation had certain merits. Both they and the authorities in India were aware that it would be impossible to continue to force the Chinese to import Indian opium in the face of successful efforts to stamp out poppy cultivation and opium smoking. Their strategy throughout the period 1906-1917 was to delay the impact of such measures

50

on the Indian economy and budget.

John Morley's views on the opium traffic were not free of ambiguity. Although originally regarded by leading anti-opiumists as a staunch opponent of the trade, as Secretary of State for India he interpreted his responsibilities as requiring that he ensure that those of radical persuasion should not 'gratify their philanthropy at the cost of India'. (Morley Papers, MSS.Euro.D.573, 29/6/1906) Even if he had been swayed by the cogency of their arguments, he would still have found it difficult to impose such a policy on the Indian authorities. He had to contend not only with their sustained resistance to any rapid decline in exports of opium to China, but also with the opposition of his senior officials to such a policy, particularly that of his Personal Private Secretary, Frederick Arthur Hirtzel, and the Permanent Under Secretary, Sir Arthur Godley. (cf. Hirtzel Papers, 28/5/1906) Both acted for most of the time as spokesmen for the Government of India:

> Although Morley was firm and active enough a minister to see to it that Godley in fact no longer 'ruled India', the Permanent Under Secretary nonetheless served as Minto's foremost agent in Whitehall for four-fifths of Morley's tenure ... Even after retiring, thanks to the influence he exerted over older members of Morley's council, Godley's conservatism helped to counteract Morley's liberalising influence. (Wolpert 1967, p.53. Viscount Minto was Viceroy of India)

It must have been obvious to such experienced officials that an investigatory commission which included all those powers with economic interests in the traffic in opium, would highlight the fact that the trade in opium between India and China was only part of a much wider problem. Moreover, since all the invited powers, with the exception of Germany, themselves derived large revenues from this traffic, it would not be easy to arrive at an acceptable regional agreement relating to this question. Since international conferences are ordinarily conducted in accordance with the principle that all recommendations must be unanimously agreed upon, the proposed commission would be unable to pass resolutions whose terms went beyond what the power most hostile to the objectives of the inviting power would be willing to accept. The handling of these issues by way of multilateral negotiations, would also tend to divert attention away from the possibility of achieving the same objectives by way of bilateral agreements, or by the unilateral action of the participating powers. Rather than expediting a solution to the opium problem in the Far East, acceptance of the American proposal could reasonably be expected to delay matters considerably.

Detailed American proposals were received in May 1908 after all the invited powers had agreed to participate. Shanghai was suggested as the meeting place, the commission to convene early in the following year. It was suggested that:

> each Commission should proceed independently and immediately with the investigation of the opium question on behalf of their respective countries with a view - 1. to devise means to limit the use of opium in the possessions of that country; 2. to ascertain the best means of suppressing the opium traffic, if such now exists among their own nationals in the Far East; 3. to be in a position, when the various Commissions meet in Shanghai, to co-operate and

offer jointly or severally definite suggestions of measures which their respective Governments may adopt for the gradual suppression of opium cultivation, traffic and use within their Eastern possessions, and thus to assist China in her purpose of eradicating the evil from that Empire. (FO371/423/30. Emphasis added.)

The significant points to note are: (a) the participants were to investigate the opium problem only in their Far Eastern possessions; (b) the only dangerous drug under consideration was opium; (c) one of the primary objectives of the commission was to devise means of assisting the Chinese authorities achieve the aims of their anti-opium campaign. There is no suggestion that the opium problem would be regarded as anything other than an issue which had ramifications in relation to one particular geographical region.

Holderness, an official at the India office, objected to the proposals on two grouds. Firstly, that they anticipated the possible outcome of the commission's deliberations before it had met, since they implied that the traffic was an evil which should be extirpated, a viewpoint which was not necessarily shared by all the invited powers. Secondly, the original intention had been to investigate only the inter-state traffic in the Far East, whereas the detailed proposals stipulated that the commissions would investigate the opium question within their own possessions as well. (Lim 1969, p.180) He suggested that prior to their departure for Shanghai, representatives of the participating powers should investigate fully the opium situation in their own countries. Their governments would then be in a position to implement the commission's recommendations without undue delay. Foreign Office officials considered that these objections were well taken, and the American ambassador was informed accordingly. (FO371/423/125)

The outcome of the objections raised by the India Office, was that the scope of the commission's activities had been widened considerably. If the preliminary investigations of the delegates were to include a detailed study of the opium problem in areas outside the Far East, and their deliberations pointed to the desirability of suppressing opium consumption in the Far East, it would be extremely difficult to confine a system of control to that region alone. The India Office, in its desire to leave open-ended the question of whether the consumption of opium was an 'unmitigated evil', had manoeuvred the participating powers into an all-or-nothing situation. If it was concluded that the effects of opium consumption were relatively harmless, there would be no need for a system of inter-state control, in the Far East or elsewhere. On the other hand, if controls were required, the commission's terms of reference dictated that their scope would be global.

THE COMMISSION

The commission met between 1 and 26 February 1909. It was attended by representatives from Austria-Hungary, China, France, Germany, Russia, Great Britain, Italy, Japan, the Netherlands, Portugal, Persia, Siam and the United States. Turkey, a major producer and exporter of opium, declined the American invitation.

Fittingly, the American delegation was headed by the man who had originally suggested the convening of an investigative commission,

Charles H. Brent. He was ably reinforced by Drs. Charles D. Tenney and Hamilton Wright. Tenney, Secretary to the United States Legation at Peking, was an ex-missionary who strongly opposed the Indo-China traffic and the consumption of opiates for anything other than medical purposes. The most important member of the delegation, and the one who had the greatest impact on the subsequent developmennt of both American and international narcotics control, was Wright. He had been asked to represent the United States primarily because of his experience in tropical medicine. Having worked for a number of years in the Straits Settlements, it was assumed that he had some acquaintance with problems stemming from addiction to opiates and its treatment. According to his own account, his appointmment was a product of fortuitous circumstances. In the course of passing 'the time of day' with an acquaintance who was a correspondent of the <u>Chicago Tribune</u>, he was asked whether he would like to be a member of an opium commission about to be appointed by Roosevelt: 'I saw at a glance that it was bound to be a large and extensive bit of work and I said that certainly I would like to be a member'. (Musto 1973, p.31)

Immediately after his appointment he set about collecting information on the opium problem in the United States. As an <u>ad hoc</u> employee of the State Department, he was in a much stronger position to collect relevant information and exert pressure on departmental officials than were his fellow commissioners, Brent based in Manilla, and Tenney in Peking. It is also probably fair to say that he took the matter more seriously. He was more diligent in acquainting himself with various facets of the problem, and by the time he arrived in Shanghai he had a more thorough grasp of the issues. On the basis of the information he had collected in the United States in connection with the extent of opium consumption there, and his familiarity with the problem in the Far East, he concluded that the only effective way to tackle the trend towards an increase in the extent of opium-addiction in the United States and elsewhere, was by pursuing a policy of strict prohibition. In his view, the only legitimate use of these drugs was for medical purposes. This was 'the principle which ran throughout the American resolutions' submitted to the commission. (Taylor 1969, p.67) Whilst this was a viewpoint that was shared by both Brent and Tenney, it was Wright who wielded the greatest influence in determining the strategy adopted by the American delegation, partly because Brent was elected to chair the proceedings.

Great Britain sent five delegates: Sir Cecil Clementi Smith, a former governor of the Straits Settlements who headed the delegation; James Bennet Brunyate, Acting Financial Secretary to the Government of India; Robert Laidlaw, M.P., who was appointed to represent the interests of the anti-opium campaigners; William Lyon Mackenzie King, representing the dominion of Canada; and Sir Alexander Hosie, nominally consul-general at Tientsin, but in practice acting commercial attache to the Peking legation. Despite the fact that Laidlaw and King (Cook 1969, pp.36-37) were both reputed to be staunch opponents of the traffic in opium, this orientation, as far as can be ascertained, was not manifested by the British delegation in its handling of the negotiations and discussions at the conference. Clementi Smith was obviously the dominant member of the delegation. Throughout the negotiations he consistently opposed the adoption of any resolutions which could be anticipated to have the effect of reducing the revenues derived from the traffic by Britain's Far Eastern colonial administrations.

The exchanges and bargaining between the delegations of the United States, Britain and China dominated the proceedings. Most of the negotiations on substantive resolutions took place between the former two, the American delegates frequently arguing the Chinese case. The Netherlands, Portugal, France and Persia had economic interests at stake which were not dissimilar from, though not as extensive, as those of Great Britain. Consequently, their representatives tended to endorse the views advanced by the British delegates, and the deliberations turned into a direct confrontation between the positions adopted by the British and American delegations. The representatives from Austria-Hungary, Italy and Siam took little part in the proceedings. Germany had no significant stake in the Far Eastern traffic, and although her representative tended to side with the American and Chinese delegations, the absence of important interests in the trade reduced his influence.

In the handling of the negotiations Clementi Smith adopted a defensive strategy, aimed at securing the status quo, and the neutralisation of any attempt to steer the commissioners towards the adoption of resolutions which implied a negative assessment of the traffic in, or consumption, of opium. This necessitated, firstly, opposition to attempts made by the Chinese and Americans to discuss matters relating to the Anglo-Sino Ten Year Agreement which stipulated a reduction in exports of Indian opium to China. Despite assurances given by officials of the Chinese Ministry of Foreign Affairs to Jordan that their delegates would not raise issues relating to Sino-British agreements concerning the opium trade, the Viceroy of Liankiang did so in the course of opening the conference. He claimed, with complete justification, that the attempts of his government to suppress opium consumption were 'hampered by existing treaties'. (Report of the International Opium Commission 1909, Vol.1, p.10) He expressed the hope that the conference would use some of its time to 'thrash out' the question, and provide some means whereby such clauses could be removed from Sino-foreign treaties. The issue was later taken up by Tenney, who introduced a resolution which stipulated that 'every nation which effectively prohibits the production of opium and its derivatives ... except for medical purposes, should be free to prohibit' its importation. (ibid, p.5) After a lengthy, heated, and ill-tempered debate, during which Tenney had to be ruled out of order by the chair, the resolution was quashed on the grounds that the commission was not an appropriate forum for discussing questions pending between the British and Chinese governments.

There was one other issue that arose prior to consideration of the substantive resolutions which, if not neutralised by the British delegation, could have had serious repercussions on British interests in the traffic. On the 18th the Chinese delegate proposed that a committee of five delegates be appointed to consider and report on medical aspects of the opium question, a suggestion that was immediately endorsed by Tenney. An adverse decision by such a committee, if ratified by the commission, would have seriously undermined the position adopted by India and the Crown Colonies in relation to the consumption of opium. One of the mainstays of the case they had advanced for more than a century, was that no adverse medical effects accompanied the regular consumption of opium, however administered. The Indian authorities had convinced the Royal Commission on Opium that opium eating in moderation was beneficial, and that opium smoking was no more harmful than the temperate consumption of alcoholic beverages. Any verdict to the contrary, was likely to be more damaging in its consequences than a condemnation of the ten year agreement. Tenney's resolution, had it been adopted, would not have effected immediately the trade in opium between India and China. It did not imply that opium itself should be prohibited for other than medicinal purposes. The same applied to the Commons resolutions of 1906 and 1908. All these resolutions, even if they had been implemented, would have had little bearing on the extensiveness of opium consumption in India and the Crown Colonies. On the other hand, the collection of government revenues from the traffic could only be justified if it was assumed that opiate consumption, by whatever method, had no harmful physiological, psychological or social consequences. If it was acknowledged that it did have such ill-effects, the question would no longer be that of whether the Indian and colonial opium traffics should be wound up, but how rapidly and by what means.

Clementi Smith opposed the resolution on grounds that the commission was not competent to assess medical aspects of the questions before it. He was supported by the French delegate, who argued that the subjects to be dealt with by the commission were determined in correspondence between his own and the American government, and that in it there was no reference to medical aspects of the problem. He had, he said, been instructed not to deviate from the programme outlined in the American proposals, particularly since any of the commission's proposals might effect the budget of French Indo-China. Despite Wright's contention that there were three physicians in the ranks of the commissioners who were qualified to investigate medical aspects of opiate consumption, a British amendment which commended this matter to the attention of the governments of the participating powers, was adopted by seven votes to six.

The United States delegation introduced eight resolutions. In addition to the one put forward by Tenney, which was referred to earlier, seven were suggested by Wright. In his preliminary remarks, he implied that the commission had already 'concluded that the traffic in opium for other than necessary uses ought not much longer to continue'. (ibid, p.44) His first resolution was aimed at restricting its use to medical requirements, 'at once or in the near future'. (ibid, p.46) Clementi Smith's objections were predictable. He took exception to the preamble which implied that all those represented at the conference were of the opinion that the use of opium should be confined to medical practise, when in fact this only applied to the delegates from the United States, China and Canada. There were, he argued,

> other countries to whom the opium question presents itself under
> wholly different conditions. Either they have not accepted the view
> that the use of opium can or should be strictly confined to medical
> purposes, or, if they look forward to prohibition as the ultimate
> goal, they are still so far from its attainment that the proposition
> enunciated in the resolution could not be a practical guide to their
> action in the near future. (ibid, pp.49-50)

He stressed the difficulties that would be encountered in enforcing such a policy in India, dwelling on the problem of policing effectively such a vast and geographically dispersed population, and drawing attention to the position of Native States, suggesting that the Government of India was unable to dictate to their rulers what they should or should not produce. In his view, the attempt to implement such a policy would constitute 'despotic interference with a national habit'. Most of these arguments were of ancient origin; some, such as the one concerning the difficulties of enforcement, were valid; others, particularly the one relating to the Native States, were deliberate deceptions, successfully advanced because none of the delegates were sufficiently well-briefed on this matter. After a further exchange with Wright, Clementi Smith summed up with the statement that the British delegation 'were not able to accept the view that opium should be confined simply and solely to medical uses'. (ibid, p.50)

The views expressed by both sides in relation to this question set the pattern for all subsequent resolutions submitted by Wright. Of the eight presented by the American delegation, none was accepted until after it had been substantiallly amended by the British delegation, some were defeated, and others had to be withdrawn. From the lengthy discussions that took place in connection with the above resolution, it was apparent to most of the delegates that a considerable amount of time would be taken up if disagreements between the two sides were settled in plenary session. At the suggestion of the French delegate, some of the more contentious American resolutions were negotiated at a meeting between the two delegations. The amended resolutions were then referred back to the full commission and were, without exception, unanimously adopted without any further discussion.

The commissioners adopted nine resolutions. Four had application only to China and those powers who had treaty relations with her. Number 1 merely recognised the 'unswerving sincerity of the government of China in their efforts to eradicate the production and consumption of opium'. Numbers 7, 8 and 9 urged all governments possessing concessions or settlements in China to take 'effective action toward the closing of opium dens in the said concessions and settlements', enter into negotiations with the Chinese government 'with a view to effective and prompt measures being taken in the various foreign concessions and settlements ... for the prohibition of the trade and manufacture of such anti-opium remedies as contain opium or its derivatives', and 'apply its pharmacy laws to its subjects in the consular districts, concessions and settlements in China'.

No 2 recommended that each delegation move its own government 'to take measures for the gradual suppression of the practice of opium smoking in its own territories and possessions, with due regard to the varying circumstances of each country concerned'. (Emphasis added.) Clementi Smith, whilst agreeing that the practice was one 'which should be done away with', had objected to the absence in the original American resolution of any appreciation of the fact that 'you would require in different countries ... different systems by which to carry out the objectives in view'. His main concern was to ensure that any resolution dealing with this matter should place emphasis on the need to suppress the practice gradually, no doubt so that the impact of implementing it would have an equally gradual effect on the revenues of the Crown Colonies. Consequently, the final resolution which emerged from the Anglo-American meeting included the reference to 'gradual' suppression and 'varying circumstances of each country concerned'.

The original intent of the American version of resolution number 3 was diluted in a similar way. The final resolution specified that:

the use of opium in any form otherwise than for medical purposes is held by almost every participating country to be a matter for prohibition or careful regulation; ... each country in the administration of its system of regulation purports to be aiming, as opportunity offers, at progressively increasing stringency. In recording these conclusions the International Opium Commission recognises the wide variations between the conditions prevailing in the different countries. (Emphasis added.)

The British delegation insisted that the resolution include reference to `careful regulation', and, once again, `wide variations' in conditions prevailing in the different countries.

One of Wright's other resolutions was accepted with what appeared to be only minor amendments to its operative clause. This stipulated that it was `the duty of all countries which continue to produce opium, its alkaloids, derivatives and preparations', to prevent at ports of departure the(ir) shipment ... to any country which prohibits the(ir) entry'. (ibid, p.47) Clementi Smith suggested that the words `which continue to produce opium, its alkaloids, derivatives and preparations' should be omitted. He persuaded the Americans that the alteration would put pressure on all countries, not only the producers, to prevent the exportation of the drugs to countries which prohibited their importation. Although the amendment was advanced on the grounds that it would strengthen the original intent of the resolution, the reverse was likely to be the case, as Clementi Smith and Brunyate were undoubtedly aware. The original version placed the onus of responsibility on a small number of producing countries, and would have made control of exports much easier to monitor. The amended version facilitated the exporting of these drugs from producing countries, to countries prohibiting their import, via other non-producing countries with limited or no import restrictions. The reduction in Indian opium exports was having precisely this effect. The high prices prevailing or anticipated in China encouraged speculators in opium to divert opium there from other markets. Wright, who was not sufficiently familiar with the conditions of the Indo-China trade, accepted the amendment.

One of Wright's resolutions stressed that `strict International Agreements are needed to control the trade in and the present or possible future abuse of morphia and its salts and derivatives by the people of the Governments represented in the International Opium Commission'. (ibid) Clementi Smith did not feel able to accept it in that form, and proposed an alternative, number 5 of the final resolutions. This recognised that `the unrestricted manufacture, sale and distribution of morphine already constitute a grave danger'. It went on to stress the need for the introduction of `drastic measures' to control the spread of the habit. In contrast to Wright's version, Clementi Smith's provided that such controls should be taken `by each Government in its own territories and possessions'. Whereas the British formula places the burden of control on the respective governments of the participating powers, and leaves the matter there, Wright's necessitated the convening of an international conference to hammer out an acceptable agreement. It was in the interest of India and the Crown Colonies to prevent, if possible, any further meetings of this nature. Whatever their outcome, it was predictable that the imposition of additional restrictions on their internal and external trade in opium were likely to be demanded.

Resolution number 6 simply commended to the governments of the participating powers the desirability of conducting scientific enquiries into the medical aspects of opium and its products, and of anti-opium remedies.

In the light of British objectives and interests in the traffic, the agreed resolutions, even if implemented, were unlikely to have any significant impact on the financial situation of the Far Eastern colonial administrations. Although some of the resolutions were quite wide-ranging in scope, they were phrased in such a way that they were open to a multiplicity of interpretations. The inclusion of such ambiguous phrases as 'gradual suppression', 'progressively increasing stringency', 'as soon as they may deem it possible', 'reasonable measures', and 'varying circumstances' or 'conditions', was intentional: 'Equivocal language is used to cover up disagreement on issues which must be included for some reason in a larger settlement or must be dealt with as if there was an agreement'. (Ikle 1964, p.15) Of all the resolutions, number 5 was the most positive in that it urged the introduction of drastic measures to control the manufacture, sale and distribution of morphine, and other derivatives of opium 'as may appear on scientific enquiry to be liable to similar abuse and productive of like ill effects'. These measures, however, were to be enacted and enforced by 'each government in its own territories'. There was, in any event, nothing that the British, or other delegations representing powers with an interest in the opium traffic, could take exception to in this resolution. In fact, a plausible case could be made for the argument that it was in the interest of Far Eastern colonial administrations to introduce such measures if they had not already done so. The spread of the consumption of morphine and other opium derivatives threatened to reduce revenues derived from the sale of opium prepared for smoking, and from the licensing of opium shops and divans. From the perspective of these powers, particularly that of Great Britain, the final resolutions constituted a pseudo-agreement: 'a pact which is all formality, which does not record any new settlement'. (ibid, p.21) One foreign office official described the commission as a farce, and the resolutions as 'pious wishes for steps to be taken which have long ago been adopted in this country and its dependencies'. (F0371/616/28-29)

From the perspectives of the American and Chinese delegations, the outcome of the negotiations was far from satisfactory. Of the eight resolutions submitted by the Americans, four had to be withdrawn. These sought to restrict the consumption of opium to medical uses, to condemn the trafficking in opium as immoral, and to obtain support for concerted international action to control the abuse of opium, its derivatives and preparations. To these can be added two Chinese resolutions that had to be withdrawn and were endorsed by the American delegates: one attempting to establish a committee to report on medical aspects of opium consumption and addiction, and a second relating to the ten year agreement. Of the remaining four American resolutions, three were amended in such a way as to defeat their original purpose: one attempting to confine the consumption of opium to 'legitimate medical practices', another calling for interstate co-operation in regulating a state's internal opium problem, and the third enjoining the prompt 'stamping out' of opium smoking. Only one resolution, corresponding to number 4 of the final resolutions, was passed with what appeared to be only a minor amendment. The Chinese fared no better. The resolutions they submitted had either to be withdrawn or they were amended in such a way as to render them ineffectual. None of the final resolutions could be unambiguously interpreted in such a way as to ensure that, if implemented, they would materially effect the addiction problem, in China or elsewhere.

The failure of Wright and Tenney to wrest substantial concessions is attributable to a number of factors. It should have been apparent, both to those State Department officials who helped to arrange the conference, and Wright, that any radical change in the attitudes of most of the participants was likely to emerge from a meeting of this sort. The participants had been invited on the grounds that they had important economic interests in the Far Eastern commerce in opium, or because they had treaty relations with China which placed them in a position of being able to exert some influence on the extent of opium consumption in certain parts of that country. It was extremely unlikely that those powers with a financial stake in the traffic would agree to the passing of resolutions which would seriously threaten these interests. From the perspectives of these powers, all the American resolutions appeared to require radical changes in policies which they had pursued over extended periods of time. Wright's moralising attitude, and his preoccupation with seeking 'ultimate' solutions, did not help. He prefaced the introduction of the resolutions with the statement that 'opium was a pernicious article ... which the wisdom of Governments should carefully restrain from consumption'. In the second resolution he attacked the principle of obtaining revenues from the production of opium, its alkaloids and derivatives, and sought to confine their use to 'legitimate medical practice'. Neither the premise, nor the objectives, were acceptable to most of the participating powers.

This uncompromising approach was ill-conceived given the weakness of the American bargaining position. As Schelling notes:

When the agreement must be reached on something that is inherently a one-man act, any division of the cost depends on compensation. The 'agenda' assumes particular importance in these cases, since a principal means of compensation is a concession in some other object. (1960, pp.31-32)

The Americans and the Chinese had nothing to compensate the other powers with, and the moralising attitude evident in the resolutions only served to alienate the British delegates. Although, in substantive terms, the Chinese and Americans had little to offer those powers with significant economic interests in the traffic as a quid pro quo for concessions on their part, Wright's diplomatic inexperience led him, paradoxically, to over-estimate the strength of the British bargaining position:

Most bargaining situations ultimately involve some range of possible outcomes within which each party would rather make a concession than fail to reach agreement at all ... Any potential outcome is therefore one that either party could have improved by insisting ... The final outcome must be a point from which neither expects the other to retreat ... These infinitely reflexive expectations must somehow converge on a single point, at which each expects the other not to expect to be expected to retreat. (ibid, p.70)

Wright's approach to the handling of the negotiations gave him little leeway for establishing where Clementi Smith's 'final point' was situated in relation to the alternative agreements it may have been possible to conclude. There is no question that Clementi Smith would have preferred to make some concessions on the substantive resolutions, rather than reach no agreement at all. It was essential to ensure that anti-opium supporters in Britain, China and the Crown Colonies, could not be given grounds for subsequently arguing that the achieving of an accord was prevented by the obstructionist tactics of the British delegates.

Although Wright can be faulted for adopting a rather amateurish approach during the negotiations, Clementi Smith and officials of the Far Eastern Department at the foreign office, were guilty of equally serious misjudgements. The outcome of the commission's investigations could only be considered a success if the matter was allowed to rest there. The British delegates had ensured that the final resolutions would be rendered ineffectual by couching them in equivocal language. This was a double-edged tactic, and Wright was quick to place his own interpretation upon them. In the report he submitted on the conference, he claimed that the resolutions amounted to a unanimous condemnation by the participants of the 'opium vice', which it was agreed 'must cease'. Resolution No.3, he submitted, 'practically denounces the use of opium for other than medical purposes'. He also argued that it was recognised by the participants that it was necessary to convene a further conference to conventionalise the reslts of the commission's investigations. (Senate Doc.377, 61st Congress, 2nd Session 1910, pp.69-70) Most of these claims were patently false, but such a construction could be placed on some of the resolutions if they were read without reference to the official report of the proceedings.

The attitude of foreign office officials to the commission, in the years immediately preceding and succeedings its convening, was one of near total indifference. They failed to appreciate that any recommendations it made, however innocuous, could be used to reopen the issues at some later date. For, as Ikle notes:

> The amount of agreement reached and the residual disagreements left do not encompass the entire outcome of negotiations. In addition, there may be latent effects which impinge on the course of subsequent negotiations. Even if a conference ends without any specific agreement ... the issues dealt with may be permamently altered. The effect of negotiation is latent, since it materialises only if a future conference leads to an agreement on the same issues. (1964, p.22)

In the long run it may have been more advantageous for the securing of British interests in the opium traffic, to have made minor concessions at Shanghai, thereby precluding the possibility of the same issues becoming the object of future international negotiations.

LATENT EFFECTS: THE ROAD TO THE HAGUE

Wright and Brent departed from Shanghai with the conviction that, though the results had been inconclusive, 'the way was prepared for a conference that will have plenipotentiary powers'. (Davidson Papers 1909, 03 Opium) Soon after his return to the United States, Wright began to exert pressure on State Department officials to take the necessary steps to convene such a conference. The chief of the Far Eastern Division was far from enthusiastic. (Musto 1973, p.308) Wright therefore appealed directly to the Secretary of State, Philander C. Knox. He argued that:

> our move to help China in her opium reform gave us more prestige in China than any of our recent friendly acts towards her. If we continue and press steadily for the conference, China will recognise that we are sincere in her behalf, and the whole business may be used as oil to smooth the troubled water of our aggressive commercial policy there. (ibid, p.39)

Musto maintains that Knox was receptive to this argument, and told Wright to 'go ahead', as the commercial policy he had pressed upon American diplomats in China had received unfavourable publicity in the nationalist press, and was fiercely resented by Chinese officials.

Wright's proposals for the agenda of such a conference were received by the British foreign office in September 1909. The items which it was suggested might suitably be discussed by the conference were:

(a) The advisability of uniform international laws and regulations to control the production, manufacture, and, distribution of opium, its derivatives, and preparations.

(b) The advisability of restricting the number of ports through which opium may be shipped by opium producing countries.

(c) The means to be taken to prevent at the port of departure the shipment of opium, its derivatives, and preparations to countries that prohibit, or wish to prohibit, or control their entry.

(d) The advisability of reciprocal notification of the amount of opium, its derivatives, and preparations shipped from one country to another.

(e) Regulation by the Universal Postal Union of the transmission of opium, its derivatives, and preparations through the mails.

(f) The restriction or control of the cultivation of the poppy, so that the production of opium would not be undertaken by countries which presently do not produce it, to compensate for the reduction being made in British India and China.

(g) The application of the pharmacy laws of the governments concerned to their subjects in the consular districts, concessions and settlements in China.

(h) The propriety of re-studying treaty obligations and international agreements under which the opium traffic is at present conducted.

(i) The advisability of uniform provisions of penal laws concerning offenses against any agreements that the Powers may make in regard to opium production and traffic.

(j)   The advisability of uniform marks of identification of packages
        containing opium in international transit.

(k)   The advisability of permits to be granted to exporters of
        opium, its derivatives, and preparations.

(l)   The advisability of reciprocal rights of search of vessels
        suspected of carrying contraband opium.

(m)   The advisability of measures to prevent the unlawful use of a
        flag by vessels engaged in the opium traffic.

(n)   The advisability of an international commission to be entrusted
        with the carrying out of any international agreement concluded.
        (FO371/616/32)

The initial reaction of foreign office officials was one of
incredulity and hostility. Alston, senior clerk of the Far Eastern
section of the department, thought that since there was no limit to the
political ardour of Americans respecting this issue, it was a pity that
'it was not possible to administer opium in strong doses to the United
States Government when they get on the opium warpath'. In the preamble
to the detailed proposals, it had been argued that international co-
operation in this sphere was essential if the United States Government
was to achieve certain domestic objectives. The United States, it was
pointed out, already prohibited the importation of prepared opium. It
was likely that restrictions would be introduced in the future to
control the manufacture of opium, its derivatives and preparations, as
well as controls on the availability of Indian hemp and cocaine. Alston
was not impressed with the cogency of the argument. His view was that
if it were considered necessary to impose restrictions on imports of
these substances to the United States, this would more appropriately be
achieved by an exchange of notes between the relevant governments. A
further conference, in his opinion, was not likely to prove more
successful than the previous one. Given the range of subjects suggested
for discussion, which it was hoped may be further 'varied and enlarged',
it was likely that the deliberations would be 'interminable'. He was
convinced that the India and Colonial Offices would join with the
Foreign Office in 'deprecating the necessity for another move in the
matter at this early date', particularly since there were 'other and
worse evils existent than the opium habit'. (ibid, pp.28-29) At the
same time he felt that it would be extremely difficult to refuse the
invitation without having 'ulterior motives ... attributed to us, the
country mainly interested in the opium trade'. (ibid,p.30)

The Colonial Office had sent a copy of the American proposals to
Clementi Smith for his observations. In his reply, he stressed that the
Crown Colonies had already gone a considerable way towards implementing
the recommendations of the Shanghai Commission. Opium divans had been
suppressed and greater control was being exercised over the traffic in,
and consumption of opium. The convening of a conference at this
juncture was premature, and would have a 'hampering and most
embarrassing effect' on those charged with the administration of these
territories:

If there was one point more expressed by the Shanghai Commission
than another it was that owing to the entire absence of uniformity

in regard to the different nationalities in the countries in which opium is consumed, it was not practicable to make regulations applicable to them all for the control and ultimate suppression of the opium habit. (ibid, p.35)

Although there was, in his view, no need for any further meddling with the opium traffic, there might be a case for co-operation between the powers with respect to the manufacture and distribution of morphine, and other similar 'highly deleterious drugs, the abuse of which had far graver results than that of opium'. His fiercest criticism was directed against item (h) of the tentative programme:

It cannot be necessary for me to dilate on the inexpediency of allowing any matter of that kind to come under the consideration of an international conference. The interests and responsibilities of this country are far greater in regard to the subject matter than those of any other country that would be represented at such a conference, and I have little doubt that His Majesty's Government will not be prepared to submit the propriety of any treaties and agreements they have entered into for discussion by any tribunal that may be formed. (ibid)

The Colonial Office adhered strictly to the views outlined by Clementi Smith in the years preceding the conference.

The government of India's reply was received towards the end of May 1910. Their objections were not dissimilar from those raised by Clementi Smith. The holding of a conference at this moment in time would be premature. The Shanghai Commission's resolutions were an acknowledgement of the principle that uniform laws were not applicable to the handling of this particular problem, due to the varying circumstances of each country. International treaties between China and Britain should not be allowed to come under discussion at an international conference. It was also argued that the export of opium from India to other countries could easily be controlled under the provisions of existing legislation. In the government of India's view:

a principal object of the proposals appears ... to be not co-operation in matters of legitimate joint concern, but the establishment of an international censorship in matters of purely individual concern ... the proposed conference if it keeps within its proper limits will, we think, find little scope for its activities. (FO371/847/44)

Grey believed that, whatever the merits of the views advanced by the government of India and the Colonial Office, it would be difficult for Britain to stand out alone and obstruct the convening of the proposed conference. He pointed out, however, that it was for them to have the 'deciding voice', as they would have the 'inconvenience either of accepting or resisting the wishes of the majority at the Conference'. (ibid: p.23734)

After receipt of the government of India's observations, it was decided to convene an interdepartmental conference to consider the question in detail, so that a response to the American proposals could be formulated. The meeting was held on 12 July 1910. It was attended by representatives of the India and Colonial Offices, and the Board of

Trade, under the chairmanship of the Foreign Office representative. The consensus was that the objections raised by the government of India were well taken. At the same time, it was recognised that 'a point-blank refusal would, for political reasons, be difficult'. (ibid, p.406) It was agreed that if the conference was held, it was essential to ensure that the problems associated with the abuse of morphine and cocaine be adequately dealt with. The India Office had stressed the importance of this issue in its covering letter to the Government of India's response to the American proposals. It was pointed out that 'in the spread of the morphine habit and its disastrous effects the Shanghai Commission found the greatest menace to the success of China's efforts and grave danger to the Eastern possessions of other countries'. (FO371/846/129) Although this was a misconstruction of the commissioners conclusions, they considered it necessary to 'restore' this question to the 'prominent position which the Shanghai Commission rightly assigned' it, in any subsequent conference.

The intention of the India office, and the Indian and colonial authorities, was to shift the focus of attention away from the Far Eastern opium traffics. Since the representatives of the Board of Trade and the Foreign Office accepted this viewpoint, the committee concluded that one of the pre-conditions to accepting the Americans invitation should be that 'the other participating powers are willing that the Conference should thoroughly and completely deal with the question of restricting the manufacture, sale and distribution of morphia ... and also with the allied question of cocaine'. (FO371/847/406) As for the other items of the 'tentative programme', it was agreed that:

> His Majesty's Government consider that (the subjects for discussion) should be those indicated in the recommendations of the Shanghai Commission, and they must take exception to the items numbered (h), (l), (m) and (n) ... These they are not prepared to discuss ... It might also be pointed out to the United States Government that in item (a) of the programme, the epithet 'uniform' is opposed to the express findings of the Shanghai Opium Commission. The Commission recognised that the production, manufacture, and distribution of opium could not be subjected to uniform laws. (ibid)

The objections to the discussion of international agreements concerning the Far Eastern opium traffic (h), and to the appointment of an international commission (n), were predictable, and wholly congruent with the stand adopted by the British delegates during the deliberations of the Shanghai Commission. Opposition to the discussion of reciprocal rights of search and seizure was undoubtedly based on more general considerations. It was unlikely to be agreed to by any of the invited powers, since it raised controversial questions concerning territorial rights and freedom of passage on the high seas.

Since the strategy adopted at Shanghai had failed to ensure that proposals for concerted international efforts to control the abuse of opium would be removed from the diplomatic agenda, the Indian and colonial authorities decided to fall back on the commission's recommendations as the starting point for any further negotiations. The American proposals were directed disproportionately against the traffic in opium. Of the fourteen proposals, seven dealt exclusively with this substance, whilst six others mentioned its derivatives and preparations as well. There was no reference to cocaine. Moreover, since they did not include any reference to the desirability of restricting the uses of any of these substances to 'legitimate medical purposes', it was predictable that their implementation would reduce the volume of the opium traffic, without necessarily effecting that of the trade in its derivatives and preparations. Consequently, the Indian and colonial authorities, ably backed by their controlling departments in London, sought to establish that the Commission's greatest concern had been with the growth of the latter, and the spread of morphine and cocaine addiction. The inclusion in the agenda of items relating exclusively to the trade in, and consumption of, manufactured narcotics and cocaine, would increase the difficulties of achieving an international accord, and strengthen the bargaining position of India and the Far Eastern possessions of the European powers. At Shanghai the German and Japanese delegates had consistently supported resolutions submitted by the Chinese and Americans. Germany, however, was the major manufacturer of cocaine, and second only to Britain as a producer of morphine. The bulk of both substances were exported to the Far East. Japan, on the other hand, was the major Far Eastern entrepot for morphine, and her traders were heavily involved in the clandestine traffic in this drug, particularly in Manchuria. It was reasonable to expect that both countries would resist attempts to elevate issues concerning these drugs to positions of prominence in any international negotiations they would be willing to take part in. At the very least, their enthusiasm for supporting proposals that would endanger the interests of India and the Crown Colonies in the closely allied traffic in opium, would be dampened considerably.

From the receipt of the American proposals, up until the convening of the conference, the Indian and colonial authorities repeatedly drew attention to this question. They thereby ensured that both the Board of Trade and the Foreign Office continued to attach to it the importance that they considered it deserved. It was particularly important to demonstrate the interdependence between the abuse of opium and that of its derivatives and preparations. In March 1910, the Governor of the Straits Settlements pointed out to the Colonial Office that attempts made by his officials to curb addiction to opium, in accordance with the recommendations of the Shanghai Commission, were proving counter-productive, as the 'raising of the price of opium ... militates strongly against our efforts to combat morphine'. In spite of the efforts of police and revenue officers, 'and the systematic banishment of professional injectors and dealers' in morphine and cocaine, 'we are, I regret to say, making no real progress toward an effective diminution of the evil'. (FO415/1/53-54) The Indian authorities repeatedly raised the problem of the spread of morphine and cocaine consumption in India and Burma. Seizures of cocaine had risen from 490,885 grains in 1907-08 to 939,685 in 1909-10.

The Foreign Office reply to the American invitation and proposals was sent in September 1910. The letter followed along the lines of the recommendations of the inter-departmental meeting. It was stressed that the British government was as concerned as that of the United States that effect should be given to the resolutions of the Shanghai Commission, and would be prepared, 'at the proper time', to participate in a conference for the furtherance of this objective. In order to ensure that the deliberations were productive, it was essential that the participants completed detailed enquiries in their own countries and possessions of the problems likely to be raised by implementing the

Shanghai Commission's recommendations. A pre-condition for British participation was that questions concerning the traffic in morphine and cocaine would be thoroughly discussed. In addition, items (h), (l), (m) and (n) of the original proposals would have to be omitted from the agenda. In short, the letter attempted to convey the impression that the British government was extremely reluctant to participate in a further international conference on these issues, and would do so only if the emphasis in the original proposals was altered significantly. (FO415/2/95-96; FO371/848/p.28753)

The reply of the American ambassador was received in early October. He accepted the desirability of the participating powers having completed exhaustive enquiries prior to the convening of the conference. The Netherlands government, which was making the necessary preparations for the convening of the conference at The Hague, had been informed accordingly, and would bring this to the attention of other invited powers. He pointed out that although the question of cocaine had not been discussed in plenary sessions at Shanghai, it had been a topic of discussion in the informal meetings that took place. In the view of the government of the United States, Resolution number 5, which dealt with morphine, 'indicates a willingness on the part of the interested governments to include cocaine in the category of menacing drugs, and that a cordial co-operation of the Powers may be secured to place it under the same drastic restrictions that are needed in the case of morphine'. (FO415/2/107) Other governments had advanced either proposals or reservations, and it was the intention of the Department of State to have them 'collated, printed and ready for circulation on the meeting of the conference'. (ibid)

This was not exactly what foreign office officials had had in mind. First, there was no reason to believe that because the delegates at Shanghai had passed a resolution calling for the introduction of 'drastic measures' to control the manufacture, sale and distribution of morphine, that they would do so again at The Hague. The possibility of entrusting the monitoring of the implementation of the recommendations to an international agency, had not been envisaged at Shanghai, as it was by item (n) of the American proposals. Secondly, cocaine was neither a derivative nor preparation of opium. Some of the powers with an interest in the commerce in this substance had not participated in the Shanghai proceedings, or been invited to attend the proposed Hague conference. Far more important was the issue of the agenda. If this was to be decided on at the conference itself, it would weaken the bargaining position of those powers who objected to the inclusion of some of the items outlined in the American programme. It would obviously be easier to ensure that they were not raised at the conference if this was made a pre-condition for accepting the invitation. If the conference drew up the agenda, negotiations on this issue would become part of the overall bargaining situation. Obtaining concessions in this sphere might have to be traded against the granting of concessions in relation to substantive issues.

The India Office pointed out that the American reply appeared to be based on the premise that Great Britain had already agreed to take part in the proceedings, 'the provision contained in Sir Edward Grey's letter being regarded by him apparently as a proposal rather than a condition of the assent of His Majesty's Government'. (FO415/2/126) On their suggestion, a further letter was sent to the United States ambassador requesting clarification as to whether the relevant assurances would be forthcoming. He replied that the Netherlands government would issue a supplementary note to the invited powers, in which the British objections would be detailed. (ibid, p.161) Subsequent correspondence on these matters indicates that insistence on omission of certain items from the agenda was dropped. The sole pre-condition for British participation remained the obtaining of assurances from other invited powers that they would be willing to agree in advance to the placing of severe restrictions on the traffics in morphine and cocaine. In April 1911, the Netherlands Minister of Foreign Affairs informed the Foreign Office that the German, Japanese and Portuguese governments were not as yet prepared to give such assurances. The Netherlands government desired to know whether the conference should be postponed until 1912. The India and Colonial Offices recommended that the conference be postponed until such time as the relevant British conditions were accepted. Grey informed the United States ambassador in May that he was sure that the Secretary of State would understand that 'until Germany, Japan and Portugal, who are amongst the most important participating Powers, are agreed to the necessity for placing effective restrictions on the sale and exportation of morphia and cocaine, and are able to furnish the necessary data, the conference could not accomplish what is desired and expected of it'. He added, that 'as soon as these countries are in a position to comply with the conditions referred to, His Majesty's Government will be only too happy to take part in the conference'. (F0415/2/132) In August, the Ambassador informed the Foreign Office that France, Germany and Japan had agreed to meet these conditions, and that an affirmative reply from Portugal was expected shortly. (F0371/1073/p.30763) At the request of the Dutch authorities the conference was to be opened in December 1911.

On 21 November representatives of the Foreign, Colonial and India Offices, and the Board of Trade, met to draft the instructions that would be issued to the British delegates. In the document it was stressed that they should ensure that issues relating to the traffics in morphine and cocaine be discussed thoroughly, and should refuse to discuss items (h), (1), (m) and (n) of the original American proposals. Two additional matters must be excluded from consideration by the conference: (1) All treaties between Britain and China; (2) Any resolution 'specifically affecting the domestic regulation of the production and use of opium and cognate questions of internal administration in India, or any other portion of the British dominions'. Finally, the delegates were informed that their powers to enter into any agreement were not plenary, but ad referendum. (F0371/1076/308)

5 The Hague Conferences

The British delegation was headed by Clementi Smith.   Due to ill-health
he was unable to return to The Hague after a recess lasting between 22
December and 18 January 1912. Leadership of the delegation then fell to
Sir William Meyer.   He was well qualified to safeguard the financial
interests of the Indian authorities in the opium trafffic.   Having
joined the Indian Civil Service in 1881, he served in Madras until 1898
when appointed Deputy Secretary of the Finance Department of the
Government of India, a post which he held until 1902.   After a three
year spell as Indian Editor of the Imperial Gazetteer of India, he spent
a year as Financial Secretary of the Government of India before his
appointment to the newly created post of Secretary of Military Finance,
a position he occupied until 1913.

The Foreign Office was represented by William G. Max Muller.   Jordan
had suggested his appointment on the basis of his familiarity with the
opium situation in China.   Since his arrival there in 1909 he had
conducted most of the negotiations with the Chinese authorities
concerning issues relating to the Indo-China opium traffic, and the
anti-opium campaign.   He was probably more sympathetic to the
predicament of Chinese officials than any other member of the Foreign
Office who was involved in formulating policy on these issues.   For
instance, in a report he drew up in 1909 on the progress of the anti-
opium campaign in China, he stressed that there was no `gainsaying the
fact that China has not an entirely free hand in dealing with the opium
question, and that she is to a certain extent hampered by existing
treaty rights in taking measures for the regulation of the opium trade'.
(FO371/616/246) This, and similar statements, were excised from those
portions of the report which were eventually published as a Blue Paper.
In consequence of his previous experiences in China, and his having
represented the Foreign Office at the three conferences held at The

Hague to draw up the convention, and settle the questions of ratification, adhesion and implementation, he came to be regarded as an expert on the subject. His views were frequently sought prior to any decisions being taken on issues relating to the international traffics in 'dangerous drugs'.

The fourth delegate was Sir William Collins. He was selected in order to redress the predominance of delegates with vested departmental interests in the matters under consideration. A physican by training, he had specialised in ophthalmology, but maintained throughout his career an interest in medical and social aspects of addiction to alcohol and other substances. He was also an author and politician. He had served as a member of the Royal Commission on Vaccination between 1889 and 1896, was Chairman on the L.C.C. during 1897-98, M.P. for West St. Pancras 1906-10, and Chancellor of the University of London in the years 1907-09 and 1911-12. He attended all The Hague conferences on opium, and continued to maintain an interest in the question both during and after the war.

The United States delegation included Brent, Wright and H.J. Finger, a Californian pharmacist. Since Brent was elected to chair the proceedings, leadership of the delegation passed to Wright.

The other powers represented at the conference were Germany, China, France, Italy, Japan, the Netherlands, Persia, Portugal, Russia and Siam.

THE CONVENTION

The convention is divided into six chapters. Chapters I and II deal with raw and prepared opium respectively. Chapter III covers medicinal opium, morphine, cocaine, and their derivatives and preparations. The articles included in Chapter IV relate exclusively to China and those contracting powers having treaty relations with her, which place them in a position to adopt certain measures directed at assisting the Chinese authorities to achieve the objectives of their anti-opium campaign. Of the two articles in Chapter V, one enjoins the contracting parties to examine the possibility of enacting laws or regulations making the illegal possession of all the substances mentioned in the convention liable to penalties, whilst the other provides that the contracting powers shall communicate to each other the texts of laws, regulations, etc., and statistical data relating to the traffics in the substances mentioned in the convention, via the Netherlands Ministry of Foreign Affairs. Some of the most complex articles of the convention are included in Chapter VI, titled Final Provisions. These spell out the conditions for ratification, bringing the convention into force, and the adhesion of powers not represennted at the conference.

The articles included in the first two chapters gave rise to little dissent. All the resolutions relating to raw opium were submitted by the British delegation. They did not go far beyond the recommendations of the Shanghai Commission, and were unlikely to seriously effect the interests of India and the Crown Colonies in the traffic. Articles 2, 3 and 4 enlarged upon the principle underlying resolution number 4 of the Commission, namely, that it was 'the duty of all countries to adopt reasonable measures to prevent at ports of departure the shipment of opium ... to any country which prohibits the entry of opium'. (Report of the International Opium Commission 1909) These measures were now to include (a) the limitation of the 'number of towns, ports, or other places through which the importation of raw opium shall be permitted' (Article 2); (b) the prevention of the export of raw opium to countries which have prohibited its entry, and the control of exports to countries which had limited its importation (Article 3); (c) the special marking of packages containing raw opium destined for export (Article 4); (d) the confining of the right to import or export the drug to duly authorised persons (Article 5) Most of these provisions had already been introduced by India and the Crown Colonies. The implementation of those which had not, would entail minimal disruption to their existing methods of regulating the traffic. Article 1, which stipulated that 'efficacious laws or regulations for the control of the production and distribution of raw opium', should be introduced by the contracting parties, did not go beyond what was provided for by resolution number 3 of the Shanghai Commission.

Later on in the proceedings, the Persian delegate introduced a resolution which provided for the gradual suppression of the production of opium containing less than 9 per cent of morphine. To this end, it enjoined the confining of poppy cultivation to government monopolies initially, and total prohibition within a period of eight years. This was a circuitous attempt to restrict the consumption of opium to medicinal purposes. Turkish and Persian opium, both of which contained more than 9 per cent of morphine, were not considered particularly palatable by either smokers or eaters of opium. In replying to this resolution, Sir William Meyer argued that his government did not consider that it was desirable to confine the consumption of opium exclusively to medical uses. It was defeated by 9 votes to 2, only the United States delegate rallying to support its mover. The British delegates concluded that it was 'tolerably certain that this mischievous resolution, the intention of which was to strike at Indian opium, was due to the suggestion of Dr. Hamilton Wright, since it is within our knowledge that (he) had himself previously drafted a resolution to the same effect'. (FO371/1331/165, hereafter referred to as Report. (This report was signed by only three of the delegates, Sir William Collins insisting that certain alterations be made prior to its publication, consisting for the most part in the expunging of remarks which were critical of the motives of some of the other delegates. Regarded by the Foreign Office as confidential, it had only a limited circulation.)

The resolutions concerning prepared opium gave rise to a slightly greater degree of controversy, primarily because of the attitude adopted by the Portuguese delegate. The Netherlands delegation had introduced a resolution stipulating that the participating powers 'agree to prohibit the importation and exportation of prepared opium'. The Colonial Office interpreted this to mean that 'each power should undertake to manufacture, by itself or through its agents, only such amounts of prepared opium as is required for consumption in its own territories, including in that term colonies or protectorates'. (FO371/1077/62) This would have, as was pointed out in an accompanying memorandum, no effect on the Crown Colonies, since various restrictions were already being imposed on its exportation to other countries. The Foreign Office therefore instructed the British delegates to vote for a motion worded: 'Each of the participating Governments binds itself to prohibit the importation and exportation of prepared opium respectively from and to the territories of the other Powers'. (ibid, p.63) The Portuguese delegate moved an amendment to the Dutch resolution, inserting the word 'gradually' after the word 'prohibit'. This was defeated. Later, with the aim of placating the Portuguese delegate in order to ensure that the acceptance of more important substantive and procedural resolutions would not be jeopardised, the Americans introduced another resolution relating to this question. After being amended by the Chinese and British delegates, it now read, in part: 'those nations which are not yet ready to prohibit the exportation of prepared opium at once, shall prohibit such exportation as soon as possible'. (Report, p.165) This was tagged on to the Dutch resolution, and the composite features as Article 7 of the convention. It had the effect of defeating the original intention of the Dutch resolution since the phrase 'as soon as possible' was somewhat unspecific. However, since Portugal was the only dissenting power, and the resolution's relevance was primarily confined to the exporting of prepared opium to China from Macao, all of which originated from India, it was within the power of the British authorities to adopt measures to reduce exports to the Portuguese colony. In 1913 an agreement was concluded between the two powers which restricted exports of opium from India to Macao. (For the text of the agreement cf. FO371/1599/p.25556)

The other articles in Chapter II were passed without opposition. All were of American origin. Article 6, which enjoined 'the gradual and efficacious suppression of the manufacture, the internal traffic in and use of prepared opium in so far as different conditions peculiar to each nation shall allow', was identical in intent with the second of the Shanghai resolutions. Article 8 provided that those countries which as yet were not ready to prohibit the exportation of prepared opium, should place restrictions on its exports to those countries which controlled or prohibited its importation. These restrictions were identical to those provided for in relation to raw opium.

The articles included in Chapter IV, relating exclusively to China and those powers who had treaty relations with her, or foreign concessions and settlements there, were all introduced by the Chinese delegates. These had been the subject of joint discussions with the British delegation, and had been worded in accordance with its recommendations. They closely parallel the resolutions of the Shanghai Commission on the same issues. Article 15, which provided that China and the powers should take steps to prohibit the smuggling of the drugs dealt with by the convention into each others territories, was similar to resolution No.4 of the commission. It was, in any case, a composite restatement of what had already been agreed in respect of the drugs mentioned in Chapters I-III. It merely added that such measures should be concerted with the Chinese authorities, something that Britain and some of the other powers were already doing. Article 16 stipulated that China should promulgate pharmacy laws, and that the Treaty Powers should consider the possibility of applying these to their own nationals who resided in China. This differed somewhat from the equivalent shanghai resolution, number 9. The latter provided that the powers should consider enforcing the pharmacy laws operative in their home countries to their foreign settlements and concessions in China. The regulations likely to be formulated by the Chinese would probably be more restrictive, but there was no guarantee that the powers would find them acceptable.

Article 17 was more restrictive than the corresponding resolution of the commission, number 7. The former committed the signatories to take measures to restrict opium smoking in their leased territories, settlements and concessions, and to suppress, pari passu with the Chinese authorities, opium divans and similar establishments. The Shanghai resolution, in contrast, had only provided that these measures should be undertaken by the powers 'as soon as they may deem it possible'. Article 18, which enjoined on the powers the gradual closing of opium shops, pari passu with similar measures being undertaken by the Chinese authorities, had not been included in the recommendations of the commissioners, due to objections raised at the time by the French delegate. On this occasion objection was raised to its inclusion. Article 19 stipulated that the powers who had post offices in China should take steps to prohibit the illegal importation of the drugs mentioned in the convention via the mails.

That section of the convention relating to the regulation of specific drugs which gave rise to the greatest degree of controversy, was Chapter III. This detailed the nature of the controls to be applied to the manufacture, sale, distribution, exportation and importation, of medicinal opium, morphine, and its derivatives and preparations, and cocaine. All the resolutions relating to these drugs were originally introduced by the British delegates. They expected that the main opposition would be offered by the German delegation. Germany, in the words of the Report:

> has a practical monopoly of cocaine production; and the German delegates, holding that they had a satisfactory system of domestic control, were reluctant to embark on further measures that might, as they put it, simply sacrifice a lucrative German industry for the benefit of outside countries not represented at the Conference. They observed, too, that the convention as a whole would have to be ratified by the Reichstag, and that measures in restriction of trade were likely to provoke considerable opposition. They held that foreign countries should look after themselves by tightening their customs and police control, or otherwise. (p.166)

Since opposition from this quarter was anticipated, the British delegates had gone out of their way to placate the German delegates on other issues. (cf. Stein 1978, pp.354-355) Max Muller who had had a meeting with the chief German delegate, 'an old friend' of his, gained the impression that it would be extremely difficult to obtain the assent of German delegates to the resolutions it was intended to submit in relation to these substances. He informed the Foreign Office that German officials "don't understand action based on humanitarian motives and the delegates here evidently consider that the Reichstag would understand it still less when called on to enact legislation to restrict German traders in 'the legitimate business of poisoning Hindoos and Chinese'". (F0371/1076/461) In an attempt to prevent these resolutions becoming the subject of protracted discussion in plenary session, a series of private meetings were held between the members of the two delegations. The British delegates were of the opinion that this was necessary since it was essential 'to endeavour to carry the German delegates with us, for if Germany were out-voted on any important point, she might very likely decline to accept the convention's stipulations, and her example might render adhesion of outside Powers problematic'. (Report, p.166)

The proposals that formed the basis of these discussions had been worked out at a meeting held between representatives of the Foreign Office, Board of Trade, and Customs and Excise. They recommended that with respect to medicinal opium, morphine, cocaine and their respective salts and preparations: (1) 'All manufacturers and dealers in morphia and cocaine should be required to take out a licence'. (2) 'All such manufacturers and dealers will be required to keep a record of all transactions in such drugs, including the names and addresses of all persons from whom they obtain or to whom they sell them and the quantity involved in each transaction. This record shall be open to inspection and verification by a Government officer'. (3) 'It is advisable to prohibit the sale of these drugs except to those persons authorised to purchase the same by licence or otherwise'. (4) 'The customs shall be empowered to detain imported consignments, except in transit, of the above drugs until satisfied that the consignee is a licensed manufacturer or dealer or a person duly authorised to receive the drugs'. (5) The export of these drugs would only be permitted if the exporter could produce an authorisation provided by the importer that he was permitted by his own government to import these substances. (FO371/1076/366; B.T. 11-14/C1000/19/C9657-1911)

The first and third of these proposals were acceptable to the German delegates. In relation to the second, they were willing to agree to the stipulation that licensed manufacturers and dealers in these drugs should be obliged to keep records of all transactions. They held, however, that this condition should not be applied to medical prescriptions or to sales by duly licensed pharmacists. It was also their view that each individual power should determine whether these records be open to inspection by government officers. In regard to (4):

the Germans were emphatically opposed to anything which would impose specific obligations on their Customs Department, pointing out that the circumstances of their country, with its extended frontiers and enormous railway systems, would render such action oppressive. It was agreed ... that each Government should take steps, in accordance with its commercial conditions, to prevent the importation of morphine and cocaine, save when consigned to persons authorised to receive the drug. (Report, p.166)

They objected to (5) on the grounds that the conference included the representatives of twelve powers only, 'and that it was at present quite unknown how far outside Powers would adhere to its proposals'. (ibid) Accordingly, it was agreed that the proposal should only apply in respect of exports 'to the territories of the other participating governments'.

All the objections raised by the German delegates were taken into consideration by the British delegation prior to submitting their amended proposals to the conference. Even though they had the effect of weakening the original proposals, their implementation would have formed the basis of a relatively stringent system of controls. Certainly, they were more far-reaching than any entertained on the same issues by the Shanghai commissioners. In any event, there was no alternative but to accede to German demands:

We had ample opportunity of ascertaining the views of other delegations in regard to controlling the trade in these drugs, and

as to what measures to that end they would be able to accept. The
series of resolutions which we presented under Chapter III must
therefore be taken as indicating not the limit of control which we
desired to have introduced in the trade, but rather the maximum
amount of control which we could expect countries represented here
to accept unanimously. (Clementi Smith to Foreign Office,
FO371/1077/124)

With minor amendments of a verbal character, the British proposals were
carried prior to adjournment of the conference for the Christmas recess.

Their adoption turned out to be but a temporary resolution of the
problem. Firstly, Board of Trade officials raised objections on the
grounds that they did not go far enough. Their view was that:

Should the convention become operative, and certain trading
countries fail to adhere to it, there would apparently be no
restriction on exports from the convention countries to such non-
adhering countries so that exports of morphia, cocaine, etc., which
were sent to the East via such countries would be checked in the
importing countries only, and the object of this portion of the
proposed convention which is understood to be to check the trade in
these drugs in these countries of export as well as in the countries
of import, would seem to be to that extent defeated.
(FO371/1330/154)

The attitude of Board of Trade officials with respect to this matter,
and later in relation to the proposed ratification and adhesion
articles, was that it was pointless to introduce an elaborate system of
controls in Britain, and in those other countries which brought the
convention into force, unless it could be ensured that there were no
loopholes that enabled some manufacturing countries to continue
funneling these drugs into the clandestine traffic in the East. They
desired to ensure that no other signatory would enjoy an unfair
advantage because of its failure to respect the spirit of the agreement
as well as its letter. There is no evidence available to suggest that
these officials were unduly perturbed by the fact that the introduction
of such restrictions would adversely effect the interests of British
firms engaged in the manufacture of the substances covered by Chapter
III. They merely desired to ensure that if the implementation of this
part of the convention should prove to have such effects, the burden
should be equitably distributed between all manufacturing countries.

The main obstacle to reaching an agreement in relation to these
substances proved to be the attitude adopted by the German delegation
upon the reassembling of the delegates after the recess. They suggested
some important modifications to the proposals they had earlier agreed
to. These, they argued, were now necessary since it had been pointed
out to them in Berlin that 'the matters with which these articles dealt
were, for the most part, within the sphere not of the Imperial
Government or legislature, but of the individual States. The Bundesrat
was accordingly not likely to put before the Reichstag, or the latter to
ratify, articles which would thus encroach upon State autonomy'.
(Report, p.173) The modifications which they now required to the
original proposals necessitated further meetings between them and the
British delegates. For the purposes of clarity, and due to their
centrality in the subsequent system of international narcotics control

which was introduced towards the end of the second decade of the century, the finally agreed articles included in Chapter III are reproduced below.

Article 9

The Contracting Powers shall enact pharmacy laws and regulations in such a way as to limit the manufacture, the sale and use of morphine, cocaine and their respective salts to medical and legitimate uses only, unless existing laws or regulations have already regulated the matter. They shall co-operate amongst themselves in order to prevent the use of these drugs for any other purpose.

Article 10

The Contracting Powers shall use their best efforts to control, or to cause to be controlled all those who manufacture, import, sell distribute and export morphine, cocaine and their respective salts, as well as the buildings where such persons exercise that industry or that commerce.

To this end the Contracting Powers shall use their best efforts to adopt or to cause to be adopted the following measures, unless existing measures have already regulated the matter:

(a) to limit the manufacture of morphine, cocaine and their respective salts to the premises and localities alone which shall have been authorised to this effect, or to keep themselves informed as to the establishments and places where such drugs are manufactured, and to keep a register thereof;

(b) to demand that all those who manufacture, import, sell, distribute and export morphine, cocaine and their respective salts shall be provided with an authorisation or a licence to carry on these operations, or shall make an official declaration thereof to the competent authorities;

(c) to demand of these persons that they register on their books the quantities manufacured, the importations, the sales or any other transfer and exportations of morphine, cocaine and their respective salts. This rule shall not apply necessarily to medical prescriptions and to sales made by the duly authorised pharmacists.

Article 11

The Contracting Powers shall take measures to prohibit in their internal commerce all transfer of morphine, cocaine and their respective salts to all non-authorised persons, unless existing measures have already regulated the matter.

Article 12

The Contracting Powers, taking the differences in their conditions into account shall use their best efforts to limit the importation of morphine, cocaine and their respective salts, to authorised persons.

Article 13

The Contracting Powers shall use their best efforts to adopt, or to cause to be adopted, measures to the end that the exportation of morphine, cocaine and their respective salts from their countries, possessions, colonies and leased territories to the countries, possessions, colonies and leased territories of the other contracting powers, shall not take place except in case the persons for whom the drugs are intended shall have received authorisations or permits granted in conformity with the laws or regulations of the importing country. To this end every government may from time to time communicate to the governments of the exporting countries lists of the persons to whom authorisations or permits to import morphine, cocaine and their respective salts shall have been granted.

Article 14

The Contracting Powers shall apply the laws and regulations for the manufacture, importation, sale or exportation of morphine, cocaine and their respective salts:

(a) to medicinal opium;

(b) to all preparations (official and non-official including the so-called anti-opium remedies) containing more than 0.2% of morphine or more than 0.1% of cocaine;

(c) to heroin, its salts and preparations containing more than 0.1% of heroin;

(d) to every new derivative of morphine, cocaine or their respective salts or to any other alkaloid of opium which might after generally recognised scientific investigations give rise to similar abuse and to result in the same injurious effects.

After prolonged discussions, the British delegates agreed to substitute the words 'will use their best efforts' for the previous formulations of 'will limit' or 'will require', as in final articles 10, 12 and 13. In the context of the explanation given by the German delegates for the need to modify the articles in this way, such changes were significant. They considerably undermined the intent of the original formulation. It would now be open to the German authorities to argue that any failure on their part to implement the provisions of these articles was due to their inability to compel the individual States to pursue particular policies, despite a desire on their part to implement these measures. In addition to this general weakening of the proposed system of control, the Germans demanded some additional changes. Amongst the clauses included in the original proposals was a stipulation to the effect that the manufacturing of morphine and cocaine should be confined to premises that had been specifically set aside for these purposes. The Germans now objected to this, and the British had to yield to their demand that the manufacture of these drugs be confined to 'authorised' premises and localities, or that the authorities should simply 'keep themselves informed as to the establishments and places where such drugs are manufactured, and keep a register thereof'. (Article 10, clause a) Whereas previously they had agreed that producers and dealers in these substances should be required to obtain a licence authorising them to engage in such commerce, they now insisted that an authorisation should suffice or, alternatively, that those involved in this trade should 'make an official declaration thereof to the competent authorities'. (Article 19, clause b) This more or less nullified the objective of the original proposal.

Board of Trade officials were perturbed by these developments. In a telephone conversation Stanley informed one of the clerks of the Far Eastern Department of the Foreign Office, that unless the Germans could be induced to change their minds, 'we may have to reconsider the question of signing the convention'. Walter Langley, a senior Foreign Office official, attempted to impress upon Stanley that it was essential to find a solution to this difficulty, 'as it will not do for us to wreck the conference and get into hot water both with the United States and the anti-opium party'. (FO371/1330/176) The Board's objections to the proposed amendments were that they would create a situation:

> in which Great Britain would be uder an obligation to impose restrictions on the manufacture and importation of morphine, whilst Germany would be able to escape the imposition of restrictions of similar stringency on cocaine, a drug which, as all the available information goes to show, has produced, and is producing, far more pernicious effects than morphine on the inhabitants of our Indian and other Eastern possessions and colonies. (ibid, p.232)

This was also the reason why the Board was so insistent that an attempt be made to induce the Germans to accept their proposal that exports of drugs to consignees in non-signatory countries, should depend upon their producing an authorisation that their importation was permitted by their government: 'either in accordance with the stipulations of the convention or with local laws or regulations, which, in the opinion of the customs authorities, are equally stringent'. This they were not willing to entertain. They pointed out to the British delegates that only twelve powers were represented at the conference, and that:

> it would be impossible ... for such a limited number of Powers to set up as regulators of the traffic to the rest of the world, or for country (A), within the convention, to set itself up as a judge of the character of the internal regulations of country (B), outside it. (ibid, p.193)

The British delegates were of the opinion that these objections were well founded, and would be supported by the conference as a whole. Accordingly, it was agreed that the proposal only apply to exports from the countries, possessions, colonies and leased territories of a contracting power, to those of other signatories. (Article 13)

The real underlying problem was not that of the relative weakening of the original proposals by German amendments, nor, for that matter, their precise content, but that of obtaining the adhesion of powers not represented at the conference to the final draft of the convention. However drastic the measures provided for in it, or the laws or regulations introduced by contracting powers in their own countries or possessions, their impact would be negligible unless the major commercial powers not represented at the conference could be induced, first to ratify and then implement it. If this could be achieved, modification of the conventions' provisions, either by an exchange of notes, or by way of subsequent conferences, would most probably not be too difficult to bring about. Moreover, once the most important commercial powers with economic interests in the production and manufacture of these drugs put the convention into force, they could concert efforts to restrict supplies of raw materials and manufactured articles to non-signatories. The Netherlands delegate, commenting on the implications of the refusal of Servia and Turkey to adhere to the convention during one of the sessions of the Third Hague Opium Conference, noted that:

> Whilst it was true that they would be able to produce morphia, cocaine ad other drugs, and to sell them within their territories without any restriction ... they would not be able to sell any of these substances in the countries which had introduced the legislation required by the convention, and this situation would prove to be disadvantageous to the countries which remained outside the convention. (FO371.1927/328)

At the first Hague conference there were too few potential signatories to make this appear to be a feasible solution. Many of the participants, particularly Germany, were unwilling to implement an agreement which would have the effect of restricting the commerce of its citizens in these substances, without their being any likelihood that the objectives which its proponents hoped for would be achieved. The main fear of the German authorities, and Board of Trade officials, was that the only result of their implementing the convention prior to securing the adhesion of non-participating powers, would be the transfer of the manufacture and commerce in these drugs to the nationals of these countries. Consequently, the most crucial negotiations at the conference were those relating to the drafting of the effectuating articles of the convention; those concerned with ratification, coming into force, and denunciation. The aim of the United States delegates was to ensure that the agreement arrived at would be brought into force with minimum delay by the contracting powers, or at least a sufficient number of them to achieve an effective regulation of the drugs in question. Despite the fact that the delegates devoted a considerable proportion of their time to devising a formula which would be acceptable to all the participants, they found it impossible to agree on a solution to this problem. It was in fact necessary to call two further conferences, known as the Second and Third Hague Opium Conferences, held in July 1913 and June 1914 respectively, for the sole purpose of examining the possibility of bringing the convention into force and ensuring the adhesion of non-signatories. Neither was successful, with the result that prior to the outbreak of the First World War none of the signatories had done so. It is unnecessary to explore these complex negotiations here since an alternative means of achieving this objective was agreed at the Paris Peace Conference in 1919. (For a detailed discussion of the Conferences, cf. Stein, 1978:366-373)

CONCLUSION

It is apparent that there were some major differences in the strategies adopted by British officials at the Shanghai and Hague conferences. In the first place, the latter was taken seriously while the former was not. This was reflected in the thoroughness of the preliminary preparations that were undertaken in each case. Prior to the Shanghai conference there had been very few exchanges of notes concerning the meeting between the inviting power and the Foreign Office, and even less with the Foreign Office of the host country. There were also few inter-departmental exchanges and no inter-departmental meetings. Preparations for the Hague conference had, in contrast, been thorough, and policy had been worked out in some detail over an extended period of time.

These differences in approach are in large measure traceable to the expectations held by officials as to the likely long-term impact of any agreements reached on the interests they were representing. It was clear that any accord reached at Shanghai would only be of the nature of a voue, and would not commit the participating powers to any particular course of action. The outcome of the Hague conference was likely to be the conclusion of an international agreement, and Foreign Office officials anticipated that it would commit both the Home and Colonial governments to introduce detailed legislative and/or administrative measures to implement its provisions. Consequently, the implications of the various proposals that were likely to be included in the agreement had to be worked out in greater detail. This was reflected in the inclusion in the policy formulating process of departments which previously had not been consulted on matters relating to the traffic in opium, particularly the Boards of Trade and Customs and Excise.

The broadening of the consultative process and the anticipated change in outcomes, heralded a shift in the relative influence of the departments hitherto involved in the decision-making process. Prior to receipt of the American proposals, the Foreign Office had played a subsidiary and largely mediating role, acting throughout on the assumption that since it was the interests represented by the Indian and Colonial Offices that were largely at stake and that it was up to them to take the important decisions. Even during the period of preliminary negotiations there was still a marked tendency on the part of Foreign Office officials and Grey to fall back on this argument.

The division of responsibility between the Foreign and India Offices in the handling of internal and external problems associated with the Far Eastern opium traffic, particularly matters related to the Indo-China trade, had been of considerable advantage to the Government of India. It meant that it was extremely difficult to bring pressure to bear on those who were directly responsible for promoting the traffic, and whom derived immediate and tangible benefits from its continuation. Representatives of the Government of India did not have to negotiate directly with the Chinese or American authorities, respond to Parliamentary critics, or the anti-opium organisations. They were always shielded from a direct confrontation by either the Foreign or India Offices. Foreign Office officials, for their part, never queried the arguments advanced by representatives of the Government of India in justification of the policies they were pursuing, accepting them always at face value. Although this situation continued for many more years, the transformation of the issue from a regional to a global one, altered the role of the Foreign Office vis a vis some of the other home departments.

The strategy of the Indian and Colonial authorities in directing attention away from the traffic in opium towards the problems associated with the development of a clandestine trade in morphine, its salts and preparations, and cocaine, although largely successful in achieving its main objective, altered the role they played in the determination of policy. So long as the main problem was that of controlling the traffic in prepared and raw opium, the Indian and Colonial authorities could be expected to exercise direct supervision over all facets of the commerce in the drug themselves. Once they acknowledged that they could not influence the commerce in, and consumption, of their congeners, the implication could only be that the ambit of control would have to be widened.

In the short-run this paid off for a number of reasons. First, it meant that attention would no longer be directed solely at the Far Eastern traffic in opium. Once they had convinced Foreign Office officials of the need to consider the traffic in raw and prepared opium in conjunction with the traffic in and consumption of manufactured opium-based drugs and cocaine, any concerted international effort to regulate the trade would necessarily be concerned with controlling the traffic in opium as only one of many separate, though interrelated problems. Inevitably this would reduce the attention that could be devoted to any one particular tributary of the international trade in narcotic drugs. The success of this strategy was clearly reflected in the limited amount of time devoted to questions concerning the Far Eastern traffic at the conference, and in the nature and scope of the measures adopted for regulating the traffic in raw or prepared opium, in contrast to those accepted as being necessary to control the traffic in and consumption of morphine, cocaine, etc. Article 9 of the convention, which was not considered to be controversial by the delegates, stipulated that the contracting powers should enact pharmacy laws and regulations 'in such a way as to limit the manufacture, the sale and use of morphine, cocaine and their respective salts to medical and legitimate uses only'. (Emphasis added.) No similar provision was included in those chapters of the convention relating to raw or prepared opium. In fact, it is possible to argue that resolution number 4 of the Shanghai Commission went further than the provisions relating to the identical drugs included in the Hague Convention, inasmuch as the former stressed that 'the use of opium in any form otherwise than for medical purposes is held by almost every participating country to be a matter for prohibition or for careful regulation'. (Emphasis added.) The measures agreed by the conference relating to morphine, cocaine, etc., were much more detailed and stringent than those provided for under Chapters I and II. There are no requirements relating to the internal controls to be applied to the cultivation, distribution or manufacture of raw or prepared opium, in contrast to the detailed measures allowed for in relation to all facets of the manufacture and trade in the drugs dealt with under Chapter III.

This change in the focus of attention also paid off because it made the achieving of an overall international policy for the regulation of the traffic in opiate-narcotics more difficult. Once the Foreign Office made it a condition of concluding an agreement relating to the Far Eastern traffic in raw and prepared opium, that this should also provide for the regulation of morphine, cocaine, etc., it increased the number of powers who were likely to be directly affected by such policies, and made it less likely that a satisfactory solution could be reached. This is precisely what happened at The Hague conference. Although there was little difficulty in arriving at a mutually acceptable series of proposals relating to the Far Eastern opium traffic, these could not be brought into force because of the difficulty of reaching an accord with respect to the effectuation of the measures agreed in connection with the drugs covered by Chapter III. In order to break this impasse, Hamilton Wright had suggested that the convention should be split into two parts, one dealing with raw and prepared opium, and the other relating to the other drugs under consideration. His thinking was simple; on the former issues all delegates were in agreement, whereas with respect to the latter there were fundamental differences of opinion. According to this plan, normal ratification procedures would apply to that part of the convention dealing with raw and prepared opium, and the preferred German scheme would apply to the other drugs. (Lowes 1966, p.177) This solution was not acceptable to the British delegates, who throughout the conference insisted that in order to be effective, controls would have to be applied to all branches of the traffic. Undoubtedly, there were good reasons for assuming that this argument was valid since, as noted earlier, the success of the Chinese anti-opium campaign and the restrictions introduced elsewhere in the Far East, had been accompanied by an increase in the consumption of manufactured drugs of addiction.

It would, however, be wrong to attribute the reasons for British insistence on the interrelationship of the two issues solely to this latter set of circumstances. Although it was nominally the responsibility of Foreign Office officials to direct and formulate policies relating to questions of international drug control, during this phase of their development they continued to act mainly in an intermediary capacity. Previously, in matters relating to the international traffic, they had negotiated with China and other powers on behalf of the Government of India and the Far Eastern Crown Colonies, as they nominally did at the Shanghai conference. When the authorities of the eastern dependencies successfully manoeuvred the Foreign Office into linking a solution to the Far Eastern question with the control of the commerce in manufactured drugs, the immediate effect was to transfer the responsibility for monitoring the traffic in all drugs to the European powers and the United States, since colonial administrators had no authority to enter into international negotiations of their own accord. This increased the influence of the home departments at the expense of the Indian and Colonial authorities, a sacrifice that officials of the latter were willing to make since it diverted attention away from their continued financial dependence upon the traffic in opium; at least in the short-run. It did not result in the Foreign Office developing an independent approach to questions of international drug control, since the vacuum was quickly filled by officials of the Board of Trade. At the time of The Hague conference it was they who exerted direct control over the way the negotiations were handled by the British delegates, particularly in relation to the articles concerning morphine, cocaine, etc., and the effectuating clauses.

Inasmuch as the main purpose of both the Shanghai and Hague conferences was the devising of means to gradually suppress opiate consumption in the Far East, both can be adjudged failures. Between 1906 and 1914 various measures were introduced to this end in Hong Kong, Ceylon, the Straits Settlements and the Federated Malay States. All of these measures had been introduced primarily in response to the Chinese anti-opium campaign. It is beyond doubt that they would have been implemented regardless of American endeavours to secure an international agreement directed at regulating the traffic in opium. Paradoxically, although the original purpose of the American initiative of 1906 was to secure international accord in the cause of regulating the Far Eastern traffic in opium, the Hague Convention was a direct product of the failure to arrive at an agreement on this question. The most stringent controls foreshadowed in the convention were those which were directed at curbing all phases of the traffic in manufactured narcotic substances. In comparison, those parts of the convention relating to raw and prepared opium, envisaged the introduction of a relatively lax system of control over manufacture, distribution and consumption. Whether they would be introduced by the colonial authorities depended upon whether they considered that the practices of opium-smoking and opium-eating were unsuited to the `conditions peculiar' to their indigenous populations.

The reasons for the failure to reach an unambiguous agreement directed at curbing the extent of opium consumption in the Far East were threefold:

(1) the importance of the opium trade in the economies of the Far Eastern colonial territories, particularly in India;

(2) the autonomy of the government of India; and

(3) the handling of negotiations relating to all aspects of the opium traffic, both regional and international, within the low level policy decision-making process.

Although the economic importance of the opium trade explains the intensity of opposition of the authorities in India and the Crown Colonies to attempts to suppress it, it does not account for their success in minimising the impact of the Shanghai and Hague conferences, and the anti-opium movements, on the traffic in this drug. Probably the single most important factor that contributed to their success, was the division of responsibility for overseeing British opium policies in the Far East between the Foreign, India and Colonial Offices. Despite the fact that the latter was consulted on all issues appertaining to the Shanghai and Hague conferences, its influence lay primarily in determining the opium policies of the Crown Colonies. Questions concerning the Indo-China traffic were largely outside the orbit of its concerns. Although the views of its officials, and those of the authorities in the Crown Colonies, had a significant bearing on the way in which the problem of morphine and cocaine consumption was handled, most of the more important inter-departmental negotiations were conducted between the Foreign and India Offices. This was not necessarily detrimental to the interests of the Crown Colonies, since these coincided with those of the Government of India.

From a strictly constitutional point of view, the officials of the Government of India were accountable for their actions to the Secretary of State for India in Council, and ultimately to the cabinet and parliament. The former was empowered to make certain decisions, or issue orders to the Governor-General, later Viceroy, without reference to the council. These related to such matters as `the levying of war or making of peace, or the treating or negotiating with any Prince or state, which virtually gave effect to Cabinet decisions'. (Lovett 1932, pp.206-10) On all other matters the Council of India had to be consulted. Orders relating to expenditure and loans required the concurrence of a majority of its members. During the first two decades of the twentieth century, members had to be appointed from amongst the ranks of those who had served or resided in India for at least ten years, providing they had not left that country more than ten years prior to taking office. Although their powers were primarily consultative, and they had no authority to veto decisions of the Secretary of State, the fact that the overwhelming majority of them had been senior members of the Indian civil service meant that any changes in the status quo would have to be introduced in the face of serious opposition from both the authorities in India and the Council of India.

Their conservatism was reinforced by that of senior officials at the India Office. They consistently endeavoured to ensure that the authorities in India were given a relatively free hand to administer their domain with a minimum of interference from the House of Commons, the Cabinet or Secretary of State. This was particularly noticeable during Morley's tenure of office, since he, unlike many of his predecessors, took the view that 'imperial affairs required the constant surveillance of parliamentarians in order to temper at least the abuses of despotism in those colonial areas which, according to his rigid ... criteria, were unsuited for democratic institutions'. (Koss 1969, p.84) During Minto's viceroyalty he frequently attempted to intervene in the administration of Indian affairs, but with little success. His struggle with the 'Simla and Anglo-Indian bureaucracy was indeed made difficult because of the bureaucratic 'expert' advisors and ultraconservative Council of India, so firmly entrenched all around him in Whitehall itself'. (Wolpert 1967, p.52) Both the Permanent Under-Secretary and his Principal Private Secretary regularly attempted to dissuade him from pursuing policies that were not to their liking.

The inevitable result of this bifurcation of political and administrative responsibility, was that the home authorities exercised virtually no control over events taking place in India. In fact, little had changed since the days of the East India Company; India was still governed by 'benevolent' despots who answered to no-one but themselves. The autonomy of the Indian bureaucracy, and the isolation of a reforming Secretary of State, such as was Morley, was reinforced by the indifference of the Commons to foreign affairs in general, and Indian affairs in particular. The main reason for this during the Liberal administrations of 1906-14 was that most members were preoccupied with important domestic issues. As Gosses has noted, Labour and Liberal members had an unusually great 'acquaintance with' and 'interest in economic and social questions; international problems, on the contrary, were quite strange to most of these members ... in such an assembly no government need fear from their supporters serious criticism of its foreign policy'. (1948, p.88) The Liberal Cabinets rarely occupied themselves with foreign affairs. Lloyd George notes that:

> During the eight years that preceded the war, the Cabinet devoted a ridiculously small percentage of its time to a consideration of foreign affairs. This was partly ... due to the political conditions under which we worked. The 1906-14 Governments and Parliaments were engaged in a series of controversies on home affairs, each of which raised more passion than any dispute between the rival political parties within living memory. (1938, Vol.1, pp.27-28)

What was true of foreign affairs applied in equal measure to those of India: 'It was always to a 'scanty and listless audience' that the great Ministers had expounded the mysteries of the Indian empire'. (Das 1964, p.67)

In these circumstances of deeply entrenched conservative bureaucrats in Whitehall and India, and the indifference of members of the Commons to foreign and colonial affairs, the ease with which the Indian and colonial authorities could prevaricate with respect to questions concerning the Far Eastern opium traffic is understandable. In this, and other matters, the former took the view that the task of the Secretary of State was to represent their interests in the Cabinet and Commons, justifying their past actions, and sanctioning those policies which they considered it necessary to implement in the present and future. Every intervention in Indian affairs by Whitehall or Westminster was steadfastly resisted and always resented. In the opinion of the administrators of the Indian empire, only they were sufficiently familiar with conditions there to take the necessary decisions. Typical of such attitudes are those expressed by Sir John Strachey, a member of the Government of India for nine years, and later a member of the Council of India for ten. In his view:

> More than one instance could be quoted in which serious injury to India had been caused or threatened by interference of the House of Commons in matters in regard to which the great majority of its members are profoundly ignorant, but out of which some temporary political advantage was apparently to be gained, or which possessed some special interest for the always numerous body of doctrinaires and fanatics. (1903, p.71)

Anti-opiumists and their supporters outside the Commons were always regarded as falling within the category of 'doctrinaires and fanatics'.

Since neither the Colonial nor India Offices were inclined to exert consistent pressure on their subordinates in the Far East, the only other administrative department potentially in a position to persuade them to sever their economic dependence on the traffic in opium was the Foreign Office. It was responsible for conducting all bilateral and multilateral negotiations relating to the international traffic. As such, it could be presumed to be in a tactically advantageous position vis a vis other interested departments. The record reveals that it rarely endeavoured to convince them of the desirability of doing so. Essentially, Foreign Office officials saw their role as that of intermediaries: between India and China in relation to questions concerning the Indo-China traffic, and between the United States, India and the Crown Colonies respecting the international traffic. This does not mean that they were in any sense neutral. There is no doubt that they did their utmost to promote the interests of India and the Crown Colonies in the opium traffic. The Foreign Office minutes are replete with statements by virtually all officials who were involved in formulating policies on these questions, which indicate that they wholeheartedly supported the position adopted by the colonial authorities. Nevertheless, until at least 1917-18, they adopted an essentially passive role in connection with all issues concerning the traffic in opium and other narcotic substances.

The main reason for their acquiescence in the policies advocated by the Indian and colonial authorities, was that they did not consider that any 'British' interests - as distinct from Indian or colonial - would be adversely affected by doing so. Their handling of these matters indicates that they adhered to the view that questions concerning the Indo-China and international traffics lay largely outside the ambit of their main responsibilities. This was reflected in the fact that the burden of defending these policies in the Commons usually fell to the parliamentary spokesmen of the India Office. In the nine debates on the subject between 1880 and 1907, the Secretary of State for India, or his parliamentary deputy, answered for the government on six occasions, the Under-Secretary of State for Foreign Affairs twice, and the Prime Minister once. One of the norms governing inter-departental relations in Whitehall is that the officials of one administrative entity do not attempt to persuade those of another to pursue a particular course of action, unless they can show that the issues involved fall within their own sphere of responsibilities. Since Foreign Office officials did not consider that questions concerning the Indo-China traffic effected Britain's external interests, they had no grounds for attempting to persuade the India Office to reverse the policies being pursued by the Indian authorities.

In point of fact, a plausible argument could be made for the case that British interests were adversely effected by the policies being pursued by the government of India. Jordan noted in 1913 that the trade 'undoubtedly causes grave prejudice to British interests'. (FO371/1924/266-267) That this was rarely appreciated by Foreign Office officials was partly a product of the way in which decisions were reached.

Decisions relating to a particular policy area are rarely evolved by Whitehall departments as an end product of a deliberative process in which all conceivable outcomes are established, by taking into consideration the possible inter-relationship of variables that might have some bearing on the issue, and simultaneously assessing their impact on other policy objectives. Compartmentalisation is, as Wallace notes, the Whitehall norm:

> In the real world, operating under the constraints of limited time and resources, a considerable degree of compartmentalisation of issues into 'commercial', 'cultural', or 'defence' questions, is clearly essential ... (this enables) policy-makers to isolate particular issues from the broader questions of bilateral and multilateral relations, and so to negotiate on those specific issues without directly raising issues in a different compartment. (1975, p.18)

Furthermore, it is, as Heclo and Wildavsky suggest, a mistake to regard the formulation of some overall strategy as a precondition for making policy decisions. Strategy is, in fact, the end product of the decision-making process. It is a by-product of countless minor decisions, many of which have been taken without reference to their possible impact on earlier decisions:

> The call for strategy is, in reality, a plea for preference ordering among conflicting policies and objectives. Finding examples of strategy is difficult because the purpose of the government process is to arrive at the hierarchy of values that is implied in meshing a

85

series of long-term objectives so that short-term actions can be taken to help them achieve them. If a Government were to set out at the beginning a consistent order of priorities under which future choices would be decided, there would be little left for anyone to do. (1975, pp.362-363)

Despite the undeniable merits of this argument, it is advisable, nonetheless, to distinguish between strategies which can be said to apply to some 'overall' or 'comprehensive', political or administrative objective, and those relating to more circumscribed policy areas. Insofar as Heclo and Wildavsky are referring to 'economic', 'domestic' or 'foreign policy' strategies, these simply do not, as they say, exist.

It is, nevertheless, still plausible to speak of a Treasury strategy relating to inflation, a Home Office strategy on parole, and the strategy pursued by the Foreign Office in connection with issues affecting Anglo-German relations in the decade prior to the First World War. The need for such a distinction arises because whether or not decisions taken in relation to a particular policy area are informed by some interrelated principles, which may loosely be referred to as a strategy, is not simply a product of the compartmentalisation of the decision-making process, resulting from constraints of time and resources. The perceived importance of a particular policy area partly determines whether decisions relating to a particular issue which falls within it, will be taken in the context of some 'middle-level' strategy. Questions concerning the Far Eastern opium traffic fell within the parameters of a policy area which was not considered to be particularly important in the context of other Foreign Office concerns. This, and the fact that the issue was not considered to be important in its own right, accounts for the acquiescence of Foreign Office officials in policies advocated by the colonial authorities. Issues relating to Anglo-Sino relations and the opium traffic had low priority, primarily because they were both managed within the low level policy decision-making process. Low policy issues are those:

in which few political values and few domestic interests are seen to be at stake: detailed and routine transactions between friendly governments, regular conversations with distant countries, technical agreements on matters to which governments attach little political significance, and so on. Policy here is close to administration. (Wallace 1975, pp.11-12)

Decisions concerning the Far Eastern opium traffic were, with rare exceptions, handled by Foreign Office officials as if they were low level policy issues. Day-to-day decisions, and there were many more of them throughout the period 1906-17 than commented upon in earlier chapters, were taken by the clerks of the Far Eastern Department and sanctioned by the superintending Assistant Under-Secretary. Only infrequently were matters referred higher up the hierarchy. Grey only intervened in a crisis situation, as he did with respect to the problem of opium stocks that had accumulated at Shanghai. On only one occasion throughout his long tenure did he enter into private correspondence with Jordan in connection with issues relating to the opium traffic. (Grey Papers, FO800, Vol.44, pp.143-45) Moreover, when he did intervene, this was usually only to approve suggestions that had been put forward by his officials.

All the senior officials who handled negotiations in this policy area had been with the Foreign Office for many years prior to 1906. Francis Campbell joined the Foreign Office in 1871, Walter Langley in 1878, and Beilby Alston, senior clerk of the Far Eastern Department since 1907, in 1890. Campbell was the expert on Asiatic affairs during the years 1906-10, and he ran the Far Eastern Department with a minimum of interference:

> When major issues arose, Grey was, of course, consulted, but on a whole range of minor, daily business, Campbell settled matters directly with the minister or ambassador concerned. (Steiner 1969, p.107)

Without exception these officials shared the attitudes held by the Indian authorities on all questions concerning the Far Eastern opium traffic. Since these issues fell for the most part within the category of 'minor, daily business', the briefs that Grey read on the subject reflected this approach to the subject. He was never presented with a choice of options. The bureaucratic hierarchy only perceived one solution to every issue that arose, and this usually was extracted from the views contained in the lengthy and tendentious despatches of the government of India. Since, as Barber points out, 'civil servants usually establish the parameters in which decisions are made', identifying the options and providing 'the sifted information which supports or questions these options', it is not surprising that Grey made vey few inroads on established departmental policy in this area. (Barber 1976, p.59) An additional factor was that, for most of the first decade of the century, Chinese affairs were considered to be of only 'secondary importance'. (Steiner 1969, p.80)

Because policy concerning the Far Eastern opium traffic was managed within the low level policy decision-making process, Foreign Office officials were quite prepared to let the India and Colonial Offices deal with these issues themselves. One of the more important consequences arising out of this was that the British delegations to the Shanghai and first Hague conferences, were headed by Clementi Smith, who was clearly primarily preoccupied with protecting the interests of India and the Crown Colonies in the opium traffic. In doing so he had no qualms about disregarding entirely the instructions issued by the Foreign Office, or placing on them unwarranted interpretations. Despite the fact that prior to the Shanghai conference Grey had stated categorically that there were no grounds for preventing a discussion of the Anglo-Sino opium understanding of 1907, he managed to obtain support of other delegations for declaring its consideration ultra vires. (For Grey's views cf. FO371/614/452) Similarly, there was nothing in his instructions that prevented the medical aspects of the question from being discussed, nor any basis in fact for his assertion that he had no powers to agree to a resolution calling for a subsequent conference.

Although it may appear that a shift in the policy pursued by the Foreign Office occurred between the two conferences, manifesting itself in the insistence that any agreement reached must include stringent provisions relating to the traffic in manufactured narcotic substances, this was not in fact the case. The inflexible stand taken by the Foreign Office on these questions, was adopted at the behest of the India and Colonial Offices, and the Board of Trade, for reasons that have been discussed earlier. Foreign Office officials had no independent policy relating to these issues, any more than they had on questions appertaining to the Indo-China traffic. Because of this it was relatively easy for officials of the Colonial and India Offices to convince them of the 'greater importance' of evolving means of regulating the traffic in manufactured narcotics, thereby minimising the likely impact of any international agreement on the traffic in raw and prepared opium. The ease with which this was accomplished was facilitated by the fact that Foreign Office officials could be presumed not to be in a position to assess the merits of the arguments put forward in support of this shift in emphasis. This applied particularly to the contention that the consumption of manufactured narcotics was accompanied by more deleterious physical, social and moral effects than was the consumption of raw or prepared opium. Remarkable though it may seem, no evidence was ever brought forward to substantiate this claim. The authorities in India and the Crown Colonies, the officials of all the British administrative departments that were involved in formulating policies on these questions, and the delegates to all the opium conferences, regardless of the countries they were representing, simply assumed that there was substance to this claim. The merits of the case are not important in the present context. The most important consequence that stemmed from its acceptance was that the outcome of two international conferences, originally proposed with the intention of regulating the Far Eastern traffic in raw and prepared opium, was the conclusion of a convention whose most stringent provisions were directed at controlling an entirely different traffic.

Great Britain ratified the convention on 15 July 1914. This step was purely formal in character. Under the terms of Article 24 the date on which its provisions were to be brought into force was to be the subject of subsequent negotiations. By 1915 little progress had been made beyond that achieved when the first Hague conference closed at the end of January 1912. Although a considerable number of powers had signed the convention, and a few had ratified it, there was still no agreement as to when it would be brought into force. German officials had insisted on the adherence of Turkey as a pre-condition of their ratification, and as the latter had refused no further progress was possible.

Until the signing of the Hague Convention in 1912 it is possible to discuss the development of international drug controls without making reference to the provisions that existed in Great Britain for controlling the availability of the drugs specified in the convention. Officials of all departments involved in negotiations preceding its signing, considered that its primary objective was to control the extent of consumption of these substances in the Far East. This was reflected in the fact that none of the departments responsible for monitoring the implementation of the 'poisons laws' in Great Britain were included in the interdepartmental negotiations that took place. During the First World War this situation changed, as problems connected with regulating domestic consumption of opiate-narcotic substances increasingly meshed with those associated with curbing the international traffic. The following chapters detail developments that took place in Britain during these years, and the impact they had on the evolution of international drug controls.

6 Soldiers and prostitutes: narcotics control during the First World War

At the end of August 1915, Sir John Jordan sent the Foreign Office a memorandum prepared by the Consul-General at Shanghai. It concerned the smuggling of opium into China by crew members employed aboard ships belonging to the Ben and Blue Funnel lines. Both vessels were owned by the British firm of Alfred Holt & Co., then the largest carriers in the China trade. Chinese customs officials had on a number of occasions found sizable quantities of the drug hidden in caches aboard these ships. As a consequence of subsequent court hearings their departure from Chinese ports was frequently delayed. Jordan, who obviously expected the war to be a short one, recommended that steps be taken to curb this contraband traffic with the cessation of hostilities. The company, for its part, pointed out to the Foreign Office that despite the fact that it was illegal under the provisions of a Royal Proclamation of 10 November 1914, to export opium, cocaine, their alkaloids and preparations, except under licence, it was 'almost impossible ... to stop this smuggling as the very lax regulations with regard to opium in this country place enormous difficulties in the way of preventing opium from being taken on board our ships in Birkenhead and other loading ports.' (FO371/2317/206) Although it was now necessary to obtain a licence from the War Trade Department before these drugs could be taken out of the country, there were few effective restrictions on the internal commerce in these drugs. It was therefore relatively easy for seamen to purchase them ashore, and then later arrange to conceal them aboard British ships.

The availability of these drugs was regulated under the provisions of the Pharmacy Acts of 1868 and 1908. Under the terms of the former a poison was defined as any substance described in the attached schedule. The only section of the act specifically concerned with regulating the handling of poisons was section 17. This stipluated that:

It shall be unlawful to sell any Poison, either by Wholesale or Retail, unless the Box, Bottle, Vessel, Wrapper, or cover in which such Poison is contained be distinctly labelled with the Name of the Article and the word Poison, and with the name and address of the Seller of the Poison; and it shall be unlawful to sell any Poison of those which are in the First Part of Schedule (A) to this Act, or may hereafter be added thereto under Section Two of this Act, to any person unknown to the Seller, unless introduced by some person known to the Seller; and on every sale of such Article, the Seller shall, before delivery, make or cause to be made an Entry in a Book to be kept for the Purpose stating ... the Date of the Sale, the Name and Address of the Purchaser, the Name and Quantity of the Article sold, and the Purpose for which it is stated by the Purchaser to be required, to which Entry the signature of the Purchaser and of the Person, if any, who introduced him shall be affixed.

The Schedule attached to the act was divided into two parts. Those substances listed in part I could only be sold if all the stipulations referred to above were complied with. Those specified in part II could be sold provided the vendor attached a label to the container in which they were dispensed which signified that it was a poison, and included on it the name and address of himself and the purchaser. There was no requirement that the Poison Book be signed. Opium, crude or in tincture, extract or powder, and cocaine, were included in this part of the schedule.

These provisions proved to have little impact on the retailing of preparations containing 'poisonous' substances. The safeguards provided for were, as a future Secretary of the Pharmaceutical Society noted, of a mechanical nature. (Linstead 1936, p.2) Once the specified rituals had been carried out, that is, the Poison Label had been affixed to the container, and the Poisons Book signed when appropriate, the would-be consumer could return to the vendor as frequently as he desired and obtain virtually unlimited supplies of the drugs in question. Serious defects in the provisions of the act prevented it from being used as an effective means of curbing the extent of consumption of substances included in the schedule. First, the House of Lords ruled in 1880 that its provisions did not apply to corporate bodies. This defect was only remedied in 1908, under provisions of the Poisons and Pharmacy Act of that year. No less serious was the fact that a medical prescription was taken as evidence by chemists that the substances specified therein were required for bona fide purposes. Once the consumer had managed to obtain a medical prescription there was nothing to prevent him or her from getting it filled repeatedly. A Dr. Wood pointed out that as the law stood, 'there is apparently nothing to prevent any person who obtains possession of a prescription from procuring by its aid enough poison to kill a community ... By this means drug habits go unchecked, and deadly poisons can be procured wholesale'. (The Lancet, 1904, Vol.1, p.215) In the course of an inquiry into the death of a woman who had died from an overdose of morphine, the coroner established that the drug had been obtained on the basis of a prescription issued by a doctor whose death had occurred some ten or eleven years previously. The chemist had regularly supplied the drug to the daughter of the deceased, and having seen the prescription on a number of occasions had ceased to ask for its presentation. (ibid, Vol.2, p.784) Omitted from the act was any direct mention of proprietary medicines containing substances listed as poisons in the schedule. These were considered to lie outside its scope until a series of cases brought by the Pharmaceutical Society before the courts in the eighteen-eighties determined otherwise. Their sale subsequently, however, was only subject to the fulfilling of the less exacting provisions relating to substances included in part II of the schedule of poisons.

By far the most serious deficiency in this system of control, concerned the methods allowed for in order to secure compliance with its terms. This task was left largely to the Council of the Pharmaceutical Society. It was entrusted with the task of bringing prosecutions against vendors who failed to comply with stipulations relating to the sale of poisons.

The Society had neither the staff nor the financial resources to undertake the task of enforcing the regulations, particularly since violations were widespread. Most of the prosecutions were brought against vendors who were not entitled to sell poisons in the first place. These can be interpreted as an attempt by officials of the Society to secure the financial interests of registered members of the profession. Given that additions to or deletions from the schedule were made upon the basis of proposals originating from the council of the Society, and that a significant proportion of the revenues of their members accrued from the sale of these substances, few additions were made. Even if the Society had at its disposal the necessary financial resources, and the incentive to ensure full compliance, the absence of any restrictions on the activities of manufacturers and wholesalers, would have made the task of preventing illegal transactions virtually impossible.

Under the provisions of the Poisons and Pharmacy Act 1908, opium and all preparations containing more than one percent of morphine were moved from part II to part I of the schedule. Cocaine was added to part I after August 1905. There can, however, be little doubt that the statutory controls in force until 1916 proved to be of little hinderance to those desiring to procure preparations containing opium, morphine or cocaine. Reports in the medical and pharmaceutical journals on inquests and police prosecutions attest to the ease with which these substances could be obtained virtually by anyone. A coroner in Cheshire, in summing up after the jury had returned a verdict of accidental death on a man who had died after an unqualified dentist had injected him with an excessive dose of cocaine, stated that he was unable to find any statute which prohibited any person, regardless of whether they possessed medical or dental qualifications, from administering anaesthetics or any other drug. (The Lancet, 1913, Vol.II, p.1821)

In this context, the prohibition of unlicensed exports of opium, under the terms of the Royal Proclamation of 1914, was unlikely to seriously impede the activities of those desiring to smuggle opium out of the country. At the end of February 1916, the Foreign Office received a lengthy memorial from Alfred Holt & Co. In considerable detail they described the difficulties they faced due to an increase in opium smuggling by their employees to China, the United States, Canada, Australia and the Far Eastern Crown Colonies.

They habitually employed aboard their ships a large number of Chinese seamen and firemen who apparently regularly carried the drug from the United Kingdom to foreign ports which had large Chinese settlements, despite precautions that were taken to prevent this. This was, they argued, causing them and other companies sailing to such ports considerable problems:

> The firm have in consequence been frequently compelled to pay fines or dues imposed by the Chinese authorities or by the Courts in China and elsewhere ... Their ships are delayed while search is made ... and if opium is found, as it often is, the port authorities refuse to grant the ship's discharge until a fine is paid, or legal proceedings taken against the owners in the Courts ... legal proceedings against the Chinese firemen are not, and are not likely to be, effective. It is in the first place very difficult to convict any particular man of having hidden opium in a coal bunker, or ash injector, or crank pit, or other places to which all have access. (F0371/2650/61-62)

In their view the only solution was to tackle the problem at its source:

> So long as it is possible for the principals in England to acquire large quantities of opium for export, so long will it be possible for small parcels to be smuggled ... (we) would therefore urge upon His Majesty's Government the necessity of altering the law, so that the contraband trade may be stopped in its early stages. (ibid)

They suggested that all opium imported into the United Kingdom should be documented, that wholesaling should be confined to qualified chemists, medical practitioners, and other persons or bodies who may be specifically licensed to handle it, and that heavy penalties be imposed on those who violated such provisions.

Copies of the memorial were sent to the Home and Colonial Offices, and the Boards of Trade and Customs and Excise. The Colonial Office, in agreeing with the recommendations, suggested that an inter-departmental conference be convened to discuss them. The Home Office noted that it would be essential to supervise, possibly control, the sale of opium by wholesale merchants, since 'At present the Chinese smugglers in Liverpool and elsewhere seem to have no difficulty in buying all the opium they want from the wholesale merchants in London'. (F0371/2650/133) It was also essential to make it an offence to prepare opium for smoking, or be in possession of such opium. The police would have to be granted powers to seize all plant, books, opium, etc., associated with such production. One of the questions which had to be resolved, was that of deciding the type of statute under which such activities should be regulated:

> The most convenient way of dealing with the question would be a Regulation under the Defence of the Realm Act (DORA), which would give power to control dealings in opium, etc. similar to the power which has been given for controlling dealings in war material ... The difficulty of dealing with the question in this way is that its bearing on the "Defence of the Realm" is neither very direct nor important. It would have to be justified on the grounds that opium is an article required for war purposes; that its exportation has been prohibited by Royal Proclamation; and that the smuggling traffic causes serious difficulties and delays to our overseas trade. (ibid, p.134)

One of the advantages of proceeding in this way was that it would be a lot easier to neutralise opposition from pharmacists, chemists, druggists, and their professional associations. It was they who throughout the nineteenth century had impeded the introduction of controls on these drugs. (cf. Stein 1978, pp.440-461)

The overcoming of opposition on the part of these groups was helped by the extensive publicity given in the press during the first six months of 1916 to cocaine and morphine consumption by British and Allied soldiers in France. In February The Times carried a report on the trial of a pharmacist and a Mr. Branch, both of whom were prosecuted for contraventions of the Pharmacy Acts. According to the prosecutor, the pharmacist had on 20 December 1915, inserted an advert in The Times "recommending 'as a useful present for friends at the front' a small pocket case containing medicines in the form of thin sheets or 'lamels'. Mr. Branch ... replied to the advertisement and obtained a case of lamels, two of which were morphine hydrocholoride and cocaine". (11 February) On the same day the paper reported the sentencing of two persons by Folkestone magistrates to six months hard labour for selling cocaine on three separate occasions to Canadian soldiers. In the course of the hearing it was claimed that in one camp alone there were known to be forty cases of addiction to the drug. Two days later, the News of the World followed up these cases, and reported on another that had been heard at Bow Street Police Court. The defendant had been charged with unlawful possession and sale of cocaine. The magistrate, in dimissing the case on grounds that there was no evidence that the defendant had actually acquired the drugs illegally, or sold them, stated that he 'sincerely hoped that the result of this case would lead to a speedy and drastic alteration of the law with regard to the sale of poisons'. The prosecutor declared that the use of cocaine 'constituted a grave social evil, which the authorities did not have in their minds when the Defence of the Realm Act was passed'. (14 May 1916) In February, under the heading 'Dopey' Soldiers, the Daily Mail reported that:

The Canadian Military authorities have experienced a great deal of trouble owing to a number of men obtaining cocaine ... For some time past the Assistant Provost-Marshall has been trying to find out the source from which Canadian soldiers were getting large quantities of cocaine ... The habit of taking cocaine made it useless to try and control the men, who were unreliable and it very often resulted in insanity. If a soldier acquired the habit he was useless for the Army from that day. (11 February 1916)

In pursuance of an article which appeared in The Times on 31 December, the Metropolitan Police conducted enquiries into allegations made by the Y.M.C.A. authorities that 'soldiers who have returned from France with their accumulated pay in their pockets have been waylaid outside Victoria and Euston railway stations and robbed'. The soldiers, it was claimed, were picked up by prostitutes, and after being 'doped' were robbed. Reports from police superintendents confirmed that soldiers were frequently robbed by prostitutes, but suggested that whilst they were often under the influence of strong spirits, it was unlikely that they had been 'drugged'. (Mepol.2/1968)

It is obviously impossible at this late date to ascertain the validity of the reports that appeared at this time in the press, or statements made by some magistrates and medical practitioners. An article in The Lancet stressed that:

> Although most of the sensational stories concerning the growth of the drug habit in the army can be safely discounted, it is evident ... that there is a considerable demand among soldiers, both officers and men, for morphine and cocaine ... what is still more important to observe is that this sale of morphine is being conducted in a manner which is perfectly lawful. (1916, p.476)

The military authorities reacted to the publicity by issuing, in May, an Army-Order-in-Council under the Defence of the Realm Regulations (Consolidation) 1914. It stipulated that henceforth:

> No person shall sell or supply any article specified in the Schedule to the Order to or for any member of His Majesty's Forces unless ordered for him by a registered medical practitioner on a written prescription dated and signed by the practitioner ... and marked with the words 'Not to be Repeated' and unless the person so selling or supplying shall mark the prescription with his name and address and the date on which it is dispensed. (The Times, 12 May 1916)

The drugs included in the schedule were: barbitone, codeine, diamorphine, Indian hemp, opium, morphine, sulphanol and its homologues and all other salts, preparations, and derivatives prepared therefrom or therewith. Whilst affecting only one section of the population, these restrictions were more drastic than any previous measures that had regulated access to drugs in the United Kingdom. Members of the medical profession had been advocating similar restrictions for decades, but had met with strenuous opposition from chemists, druggists and their professional associations. They therefore welcomed these measures, and suggested that the time was opportune to 'demand that a measure now applied to one section of the community should, through an Emergency Act of Parliament, be made applicable to all sections'. (The Lancet, 3 June 1916: 1133) The introduction of the Order was justified by the military authorities on grounds that addiction to the substances concerned had a detrimental effect on military efficiency and discipline.

There were other considerations which could be used to justify the curbing of illegal transactions in these drugs, particularly in opium. It was necessary to ensure that there were sufficient supplies of opium to meet the extensive military requirements for the drug. Soon after the outbreak of war, the editorial writer of The Lancet noted that Britain had increasingly become dependent upon imports of manufactured drugs from Germany: 'Practically the whole range of synthetics useful as antiseptic, antipyretic, and analgesic agents are of German manufacture, and besides these are the alkaloids, the salicylates, and the whole of the potash salts'. (22 August 1914, p.528) With the cutting off of supplies prices rose steeply. By September the price of cocaine, used extensively at that time in dentistry as an analgesic, had doubled. (ibid, 19 September 1914, p.773) Opium was the raw material from which morphine, its salts, derivatives and preparations were manufactured. With the shift of the centre of gravity of the war from the Eastern back to the Western front in 1916, the increase in casualties was reflected in a substantial increase in demand for opium-based analgesics, particularly morphine. Imports of raw opium rose from 566,834 lbs. in 1913 to 951,713 in 1915. Prior to the war most of the opium imported into the United Kingdom was of Turkish origin, due to its high morphine content. (Morphine content in percent: Turkish = 12-18; Persian = 8-16; Indian = 4-8.5. Pharmaceutical Journal, 1906, p.680) As this source was cut off during the war, imports from Persia and India had to be increased substantially. This took time, and as their morphine content was lower, greater quantities had to be imported to produce the same quantity of morphine. Consequently, it was important to ensure that illegal exports of the drug be minimised.

The interdepartmental meeting suggested by the Colonial Office to consider what steps should be taken to meet the request of Messrs Alfred Holt & Co. for a change in the laws governing the sale of opium, met on 19 June 1916. It was agreed that the only effective way of preventing illicit transactions in opium was to control its distribution from time of import. Their recommendation was that the importation of raw, medicinal or prepared opium should be prohibited, except to licensed importers, under Section 43 of the Customs (Consolidated) Act, 1876. All persons dealing in these drugs would henceforth have to keep a record of all transactions, which would be open to inspection by authorized persons. Sales should be restricted to registered medical practitioners, dentists, pharmacists, veterinary surgeons, persons licensed under the Cruelty to Animals Acts, and others specifically licensed to purchase it. It was also agreed that no person would be permitted to prepare opium for smoking, or deal in or have in his possession such opium. Since the prevention of smuggling was largely a police matter, the Home Office should assume responsibility for introducing and monitoring the implementation of the necessary legislation. (HO45/Box 10500/119609-126) No recommendations were made in respect of morphine, cocaine and allied drugs. Sir Malcolm Delevingne, then an Assistant Under-Secretary at the Home Office, noted that if action against the illicit transactions in cocaine were to be effective, 'something much stronger than the provisions of the Pharmacy Acts is wanted ... There is no doubt about the urgent need for controlling the sale of morphia too'. (ibid)

The Times devoted a leading article to the question of cocaine consumption on 13 July 1916. It advocated making its sale and possession an offence 'punishable with a substantial term of imprisonment, without the option of a fine', on grounds that the 'moral and physical effects of its abuse are inevitable and disastrous'. There can be no doubting that the restrictions that were subsequently introduced on the sale, possession and consumption of cocaine were a direct product of the publicity given to the matter in the press. No restrictions were introduced in respect of morphine. Those relating to prepared and raw opium were introduced for the reasons advanced by Alfred Holt & Co. in their memorial to the Foreign Office.

The regulations relating to cocaine and opium were published by Royal Proclamation on 18 July 1916. The most important are:

Regulation 40B, Defence of the Realm Act

(1) If any person sells, gives, procures, or supplies, or offers to sell, give, procure, or supply cocaine to or for any person, other than an authorised person, in the United Kingdom, he shall be guilty of a summary offence against these regulations unless he proves that the following conditions have been complied with:

(a) the cocaine must be supplied in accordance with a written prescription of a duly qualified medical practitioner and dispensed by a person legally authorised to dispense such prescription:

(b) the prescription must be dated and signed by the medical practitioner with his full name and address and qualifications, and marked with the words 'not to be repeated', and must specify the total amount of cocaine to be supplied on the prescription, except that, where the medicine to be supplied on the prescription is a proprietary medicine, it shall be sufficient to state the amount of the medicine to be supplied. (Provided that in the case of prescriptions issued for National Health Insurance purposes on the form provided by the Insurance Committee, the medical practitioners' address, qualifications and the words 'Not to be repeated' need not be inserted on the prescription).

(c) cocaine shall not be supplied more than once on the same prescription except in pursuance of fresh directions duly endorsed on the prescription by the medical practitioner by whom it was originally issued, and signed with his name in full, and dated:

(d) the name of the person, firm, or body corporate, dispensing the prescription, the address of the premises at which and the date on which it is dispensed, must be marked on the prescription:

(e) the ingredients of the prescription so dispensed, with the name and address of the person to whom it is sold or delivered, shall be entered in a book specially set apart for this sole purpose and kept on the premises where the prescription is dispensed, which book shall be open to inspection by any person authorised for the purpose by a Secretary of State.

(2) If any medical practitioner gives a prescription for the supply of cocaine otherwise than in accordance with the foregoing provisions, he shall be guilty of a summary offence against these regulations.

(3) If any person manufactures, or carries on any process in the manufacture of, cocaine without a licence from a Secretary of State, or otherwise than in accordance with any conditions attached to the licence he shall be guilty of a summary offence against these regulations.

(4) If any person, other than an authorised person or a person licensed to import or to manufacture cocaine, has in his possession any cocaine, he shall be guilty of a summary offence against these regulations unless he proves that the cocaine was supplied on and in accordance with such a prescription as aforesaid.

(5) If any person sells any proprietary article into the composition of which cocaine enters, in a package or bottle which has not plainly marked on it the amount of percentage of cocaine in the

article, he shall be guilty of a summary offence against these regulations.

(7) If any person prepares opium for smoking, or deals in or has in his possession any opium so prepared, he shall be guilty of a summary offence against these regulations.

(8) Every person who deals in cocaine or opium shall keep a record, in such a form as may be prescribed by a Secretary of State, of all dealings in cocaine or opium effected by him (including sales to persons outside the United Kingdom) and if he fails to do so he shall be guilty of a summary offence against these regulations; every such record shall be open to inspection by any person authorised for the purpose by a Secretary of State.

(9) If any person holding a general or special permit from a Secretary of State to purchase or to be in possession of any drug to which this regulation applies fails to comply with any of the conditions subject to which the permit is granted, he shall be guilty of a summary offence against these regulations.

(10) If any authorised person is convicted of any offence under this regulation or under any proclamation regulating the import or export of cocaine or opium, a Secretary of State may direct that he shall cease to be an authorised person for the purposes of this regulation.

(11) For the purposes of this regulation –
The expression 'authorised person' means a duly qualified medical practitioner, a registered dentist, a registered veterinary surgeon, a person, form or body corporate carrying on the retail business of chemist and druggist under and in accordance with the provisions of the Pharmacy Act, 1868, as amended by the Poisons and Pharmacy Act 1908, a person carrying on such business in Ireland under and in accordance with the provisions of the Pharmacy Act (Ireland) 1875, as amended by the Pharmacy Act (Ireland 1875) Amendment Act 1890, a licentiate of the Apothecaries' Hall in Ireland, or a person holding a general or special permit from a Secretary of State to purchase or to be in possession of the drug in question;
The expression 'cocaine' includes all preparations, salts, derivatives, or admixtures prepared therefrom or therewith and containing 0.1 percent (one part in a thousand) or more of the drug, or any solid or liquid extract of the coca leaf containing 0.1 percent or more of the drug;
The expression 'opium' means raw opium or powdered or granulated opium;
Cocaine or opium in the order or disposition of any person shall be deemed to be in his possession.
(HO45/10813/312966/X/L 01925; items in brackets added later as amendments to the Regulations.)

The most severe restrictions were applied to transactions in opium. In October 1917, further restrictions were applied in relation to prepared opium. Subsection (7) of Regulation 40B was amended so that it now read:

If any person—

(a) prepared opium for smoking; or

(b) deals in or has in his possession any opium prepared for smoking; or

(c) being the occupier of any premises permits those premises to be used for the purpose of the preparation of opium for smoking or the sale or smoking of opium prepared for smoking; or

(d) is concerned in the management of any premises used for any of such purposes as aforesaid; or

(e) has in his possession any pipes or other utensils for use in connection with the smoking of opium or any utensils for use in connection with the preparation of opium for smoking; or

(f) frequents any place used for the purpose of opium smoking; he shall be guilty of a summary offence against these regulations.

(Statutory Rules and Orders, 1917)

The regulation was directed at a practice reputed to be confined to persons of Chinese extraction.

Cocaine would now only be available on medical prescription. The detailed stipulations relating to the form that prescriptions should take, were directed at preventing forgery and the consumer from obtaining unlimited quantities of the drug on the same prescription form, a practice that had for many years been subjected to severe criticisms in the medical press. At the time of their introduction these regulations were the most severe in force in relation to any substance. They were later applied to other drugs under the provisions of the Dangerous Drugs Act 1920. In July 1918, the Home Secretary gave notice that the definition of cocaine in Regulation 40B had been amended to include ecgonine, its salts and derivatives. (The Times, 9 July)

Imports of opium, powdered, granulated, prepared, or any solid or semi-solid mixtures containing it were, from 11 December 1916, permitted only under licenses issued by a Secretary of State. Similar restrictions were applied to cocaine, including all preparations, salts, derivatives or admixtures prepared therefrom or therewith and containing 0.1 percent or more of the drug. Exports of opium, its preparations and alkaloids was prohibited, except under licence, in accordance with the provisions of a Royal Proclamation dated 28 July 1916.

The general consensus seems to have been that the system of controls was effective in substantially restricting the illicit traffic in, and consumption of cocaine. A Home Office memorandum noted that:

The reports (from police forces) ... show that the Regulation is working smoothly ... In a number of cases it is reported that the effect has been negligible as cocaine and opium were so little used before ... Attempted infringements are few in number and in most cases are not, perhaps, intentional ... References to persons known or suspected to be victims of the cocaine habit, or opium takers, are exceedingly few. (HO45/Box 10813/312966)

It is impossible to ascertain whether the extent of cocaine consumption has declined, or had merely become more clandestine, particularly since it is unknown how frequently it was consumed for non-medical purposes prior to the enactment of these regulations. Imports of cocaine and its salts declined substantially, from a peak of 66,603 ozs. in 1915, to 15,814 in 1918, and then to 6,608 in 1921. (Annual Statements of Trade of the United Kingdom) It is possible that the fall in legitimate imports was met by an increase in smuggling. This is very unlikely given the extent of controls imposed on all imports during the war, and the lack of any evidence suggesting that customs authorities or the police were aware of any illicit trafficking in the drug. This, at least, was the case until the latter months of 1918.

Most of the prosecutions reported in The Times relating to infringements, were for attempting to export opium illegally, management of premises which were used for opium smoking, and being in possession of prepared opium or opium smoking utensils. Many of those prosecuted were of Chinese extraction, and resident in the Limehouse area of London, or in Liverpool. The penalties imposed were usually light, consisting of fines, less frequently short terms of imprisonment, and occasionally deportation. Some magistrates were reluctant to impose heavy penalties on Chinese defendants for their indulgence in what was a Chinese national habit. (cf. The Times, 21 December 1918)

Towards the end of 1918, reports of an increase in the consumption of cocaine and other drugs began appearing in the press, fanned to some extent by the interest aroused by certain trials then taking place in London. The Daily Mail noted that the 'pernicious practice' of drug taking had been increasing amongst certain sections of the population for at least two years. In the view of its reporter, the practice was being encouraged by the casual approach to the administration of narcotics in French military hospitals, and the laxity of controls in Great Britain:

> Back again in England, the soldier remembers the transitory bliss of the drugged sleep and forgets the aftermath. Paraldehyde is almost impossible to obtain in England and veronal very difficult, but there are opium and cocaine to be had ... Nurses in hospitals have little difficulty in procuring quantities of anything from cocaine to heroin. Chorus girls invite acquaintances to take a 'sniff' and the unsuspecting person does so 'for the fun'. (21 December 1918)

The most extensive coverage of allegations of cocaine and opium consumption, and the trials concerning these practices, was given by the News of the World, which for five months devoted many pages to discussing the subject. According to a report which they published on 15 December 1918:

> There are harpies in the West End and the East End who batten and grow fat by pandering to the cravings of victims of the drug habit, who make enormous sums by selling the drugs to them, receiving pounds for shillings-worth; and these modern vampires supply the drugs taken at the doping parties which are now a feature of West End life. These orgies are of the most disgusting character.

Reports on so-called 'dope-parties' were not new. In 1902 the British Medical Journal drew attention to an article that had appeared in one of the 'popular weekly journals' which reported on 'Morphine Tea Parties given by Women':

> The fashion, which is said to have originated in Paris, consists of the formation of what may be termed a morphine club. A number of ladies meet about 4 o'clock every afternoon, tea is served, servants are sent out of the room, the door is locked, the guests bare their arms and the hostess produces a small hypodermic syringe with which she administers an injection to each person in turn. (22 February p.473)

This picture of staid society women rolling up their sleeves to receive their daily indulgence, is most probably a product of the author's imagination. Neither then, nor in 1918-19, when frequent references to 'drug parties' and 'orgies' were made, did any reporter intimate that he had actually attended such gatherings. Nevertheless, suspicions that the better-off and bohemian elements engaged in such activities, persisted. The News of the World maintained that:

> cocaine parties have long been a feature of the life followed by certain sections of the professional classes in the West End of London ... There are houses and flats in the West End where men and women barristers, politicians, actresses, music-hall artists and others, meet for a dose of cocaine and a night of revelry. (15 December 1918)

The medical correspondent of The Times accounted for the rise of a drug-taking cult in London in terms of the sudden release of the emotional stresses of war: 'We have all been living furiously ... now that a period of calm succeeds to the storm the call for other means of excitement becomes more insistent. The apostle of the cocaine cult finds many disciples, for he offers a new release from time and circumstances'. (16 December 1918) Allegations concerning the drugging of soldiers were revived. This time the culprits were the vendors of 'cocaine cigarettes'. The victims were colonial and American soldiers passing to and from the fighting fronts: 'The most pitiable sights were witnessed daily in the Strand, Piccadilly, Leicester Square, and in the vicinity of railway stations - soldiers and sailors, after a meal or a drink, suddenly collapse into a state of semi-unconsciousness'. (News of the World, 22 December 1918)

The editors of the Pharmaceutical Journal, with an eye to the potential repercussions of such publicity in leading to increased governmental controls on the trade in these and similar drugs, expressed the opinion that the daily and weekend press were making a 'clap-trap ado about the alleged rifeness in the West End of London of vicious indulgence in cocaine, opium and other narcotics'. (14 December 1918, p.228) In their view, the abuse of narcotics was limited and adequately controlled by the DORA regulations and the Pharmacy Acts. This 'outburst of pseudo-hysteria', as they characterised the matter, was prompted by revelations that came to light in the course of an inequest on Miss Florence Leonora Stewart, a twenty-two year old actress, professionally known as Billie Carleton. On the 27 November 1918, she had gone to the Victory Ball at the Royal Albert Hall, where she was, according to one report in the press, 'amongst the gayest and brightest of that historic festival'. In the early hours of the morning she had returned to her flat at Savoy Court Mansions. There she had entertained some friends to a light breakfast before going to bed. Later on in the day the maid found her dead. The inquest revealed that death had been due to an overdose of cocaine. Whether Miss Carleton was as successful an actress as press coverage made her out to be at the time, is difficult to ascertain at this late date. At the inquest and the subsequent trials of some of her associates, she was portrayed as a young and attractive woman with 'thousands' of admirers, who had been led astray by unscrupulous drug traffickers.

Although it had been known for many years that there were people who were addicted to cocaine and other narcotics, to which the frequent reports in the daily press of accidental deaths due to overdoses attested, medical journals attributed responsibility for these cases to the ineffectiveness of the provisions of the Pharmacy Acts. There was no suggestion that members of the public were being deliberately ensnared by drug pedlars, with the exception of reports of the 'doping' of soldiers in 1916. At the inquest of Billie Carleton, certain 'facts' were disclosed which did not fit into this interpretive framework. According to one report, the coroner's inquiry revealed an almost unbelievable state of affairs: "Young women and men have frankly confessed to being drug-takers - the drugs indulged in being cocaine and heroin. So far as it has gone, the inquiry into the death of Billie Carleton has shown that in the West End of London, in the quiet seclusion of luxurious flats, the 'most disgusting orgies' take place." (News of the World, 5 January 1919) The nature of these orgies was described by the prosecutor in the trial of Mrs. Ada Ping You, an Englishwoman married to a Chinaman, who was accused of supplying Miss Carleton with prepared opium:

> After dinner the party adjourned ... to the drawing room of the flat and having provided themselves with cushions and pillows placed them on the floor, and sat themselves thereon in a circle. The men divested themselves of their clothing and got into pyjamas, and the women into chiffon nightdresses. In that manner they seemed to prepare themselves for the orgy. There were about five or six of them. Miss Carleton arrived later at the flat from the theatre, and she, after disrobing, took her place in this circle of degenerates. In the centre of it Mrs Ping You officiated. She had an opium tin and the lamp, the opium needle and all the accessories. She prepared the opium ... The party remained apparently in a comatose state until about 3 o'clock on the following afternoon. (The Times, 21 December 1918)

The inquest attracted considerable attention, and the court was filled to capacity throughout the five days it took to conclude the case. Crowds queued up outside long before the day's proceedings were opened, and many well-known actors and actresses of the time were present in court. So intense was the interest aroused by the case, that the coroner had to announce after the third day of the hearing that the public would not be admitted as the court could only accommodate the large number of witnesses, their lawyers, and the sizable press contingent.

Dr Stewart testified that he had known the deceased since 1915. He described her as a drug-taker who was addicted to the smoking of opium and the sniffing of cocaine. His attempt to dissuade her from these practices had proved unsuccessful. He admitted that on a number of occasions he had supplied her with 'minute quantities' of cocaine, and given injections of morphia, allegedly for toothache. The coroner was not impressed with this latter explanation, noting that if everyone 'took hypodermic injections of morphia for toothache, we should have the country filled with morphia'. (The Times, 3 January 1919)

From the outset it was clear that some explanation would have to be found to account for the 'tragic death' of Billie Carleton, and the 'hundreds of others in the same situation, persons with good prospects ahead who end up addicted to cocaine or some other drug habit', who came from 'the smart sets of the West End', and who, in a feverish search for excitement, descend from 'fame to debauchery, and a dismal death'. (New of the World, 15 December 1918 and 5 January 1919) The situation clearly demanded scapegoats.

After the jury had found that the deceased had died accidentally from a self-administered overdose of cocaine, the coroner argued that:

> Somebody supplied her — that is certain, and it is an unlawful thing for anyone to supply anyone with cocaine. If one person supplies another, he is doing an unlawful act. If the cocaine causes death, he is guilty of manslaughter ... it is a settled principle of law in this country that if a person does an unlawful act, and by that act causes death, even if death was never intended or contemplated, he is guilty in law of constructive manslaughter. (The Times, 24 January 1919)

The scapegoat was a Raoul 'Reggie' De Veulle. He was immediately arrested after the coroner's verdict, and charged the same day with manslaughter at Bow Street Magistrates Court.

The son of a British consul, he had been an actor prior to taking up dress designing, something which he had studied in Paris. At the time of the unfolding of these events he had been engaged in the designing of theatrical costumes, including those worn by Billie Carleton. At the inquest a witness had testified that the deceased had informed her that he had obtained supplies of cocaine for her. She also stated that she had informed De Veulle that if he continued to ply Carleton with drugs 'there would be trouble'. He had promised, she said, to refuse to accede to any future requests for drugs. At his trial he admitted that he had in the past procured cocaine for her. He denied having supplied her with cocaine immediately prior to her death. The Old Bailey jury, on 5 April 1919, found him not guilty of manslaughter after a much publicised trial that lasted three days.

Immediately after his acquittal he was charged with conspiring with Mrs Ping You to procure large quantities of cocaine from unauthorised sources between 4 January and 28 November 1918. Mrs You had been found guilty on a charge of supplying prepared opium to Billie Carleton, and of preparing opium for smoking. She had been sentenced to five months imprisonment with hard labour. De Veulle pleaded guilty to the charge. Prior to pronouncing sentence, the judge informed him that 'it is perfectly clear that you well knew you were doing what was wrong. Traffic in this deadly drug is a most pernicious thing. It leads to sordid, depraved and disgusting practices. There is evidence in this case that following the practice of this habit are disease, depravity, crime, insanity, despair and death'. He was sentenced to eight months imprisonment.

All that the inquest and trials had established beyond doubt, was that Carleton, De Veulle and a handful of others, most of them actors and actresses, had indulged in opium smoking at irregular intervals, and some, like Carleton, were addicted to cocaine and other narcotics. The gulf between what could be assumed as factual and that which was reported upon in the press, was bridged by speculation and fantasy. Although it had only been established that less than a dozen people were involved in this 'drug-taking cult', reference was made to 'hundreds of others in the same situation'. According to one report, drugs were being hawked on every street corner and in every cafe in the West End of London. According to the News of the World, anybody 'who knows the ropes can buy heroin, cocaine, morphia, or any of the preparations of opium known as "chandoo" or "pop". Hashish, the drug of the Assassins, the Cannabis Indica of the pharmacopaeia, is available in cigarette form, in compressed tablet, or in the dark green treacly liquid'. (8 December 1918) The impression was created that 'cocaine parties' were a regular feature of West End night life, and that numerous young persons of both sexes 'were indulging in the vicious habits of the drug-slave, taking part in indescribable orgies, and courting the dangers so painfully exemplified by Billie Carleton's fate'. (News of the World, 5 January 1919)

Once this fantasy world of orgiastic drug-taking indulgence had been created, the gulf between fact and inference widened. Events that had previously hardly merited comment were referred to as confirming evidence. An inquest on a middle aged hop merchant revealed that he had for seventeen years been taking heroin and morphine regularly. Despite the fact that Dr. Porter Phillips of Bethlem Hospital claimed that he had considerable experience in treating addiction to narcotics, and that in his experience cases of heroin addition were rare, the News of the World reporter who attended the inquest concluded that heroin 'was growing in popularity among drug takers'. (23 February 1919) The death of an elderly patient who had been addicted to morphine for more than fifty years was described as an 'extraordinary drug case'. In fact it was probably quite a common one. The medical and pharmaceutical journals reported on such cases weekly.

To determine with any degree of precision the reasons why so much attention was devoted by the popular press to this particular series of incidents, would require a more detailed reconstruction of the times than it has been possible to present here. There were aspects of the case that made it newsworthy; at least in the eyes of editorial boards. The subject matter was novel. At the time of the Billie Carleton affair, there was no accepted lay or press paradigm relating to the non-medical consumption of drugs for purposes of pure indulgence, to which the unfolding events could be assimilated. In the process of creating one, certain strategies were relied upon in order to hold the reader's interest. An event which was atypical - the Carleton affair - had to be presented as if it were not uncommon. Hence references to 'cocaine parties' and 'hundres of others' in the same situation. The extensive coverage would have made little sense unless it could be interpreted as being representative of a sizable number of such incidents. There was also a tendency to focus on certain facets of the matter that could be relied upon to appeal to xenophobic attitudes that had been heightened during the war. The News of the World placed considerable stress on the fact that the traffic in drugs in the East End was controlled by Chinese, and suggested that in the West End it was run by Jews. (15 December 1918)

The way in which the whole affair was treated by the press, the police and the courts, would probably have been quite different but for the fact that the alleged 'victim' was an attractive young woman who was well known in certain circles. Many persons of both sexes had died as a result of accidental overdoses of narcotics long before Billie Carleton had. The Pharmaceutical Journal carried a special column in which the week's tally of accidental deaths and suicides resulting from drug overdoses was listed. When these incidents were reported in the popular and medical press, they rarely merited more than a few lines. Unlike many of these other 'victims', Carleton could be presented as a beautiful damsel in distress who had had a brilliant career in front of her, tragically curtailed by the unscrupulous activities of 'modern vampires'. Moreover, this case provided some light relief from the more serious issues of the day reported upon in the editorial columns of the Daily Mirror and the Daily Telegraph: the Peace Treaty, food prices, demobilisation, pensions for soldiers and the threatened miners stike. If the victim had been a male and the alleged perpetrator a female, the matter would probably have ended quite differently, without the outburst of 'pseudo-hysteria' that occurred. Although it was a settled principle of English law that 'if a person does an unlawful act, and by that act causes death, even if death was never intended or contemplated, he is guilty in law of constructive manslaughter', it was one that was rarely invoked in cases of death arising from overdoses of drugs. If it had been, many a pharmacist who had fallen foul of the provisions of the Pharmacy Acts would have been guilty of a similar offence. None were prosecuted or charged with this breach of the criminal law in such instances.

Once the whole matter had been blown out of proportion, a scenario created in which innocent and completely passive victims were seen as having been led to 'depravity, crime, insanity, despair and death', the only way in which the curtain could have been made to fall to the satisfaction of all concerned, was with the trial and punishment of the alleged culprit. De Veulle, being a middle-aged cocaine addict who admitted to providing others with narcotics, was a conveniently available scapegoat upon which the righteous indignation of the aroused press could be shouldered. Responsibility for this particular drug-taking cult was attributed to De Veulle in much the same way as Dr. Petro was made culpable for an increase in the number of persons addicted to heroin in England between 1965 and 1967. (cf. Scull, 1972)

The long-term impact of these trials is difficult to assess. They occurred precisely when steps were being taken to give the emergency DORA regulations more permanent form. Most of the outcry was directed at the practice of cocaine consumption, and hostility to this form of indulgence persisted. From the time that the DORA regulations were introduced, there was little doubt that some form of control would be retained over the traffic in, and consumption of these drugs after the war. The Home Office informed the Foreign Office on 6 November 1918, that is three weeks prior to the death of Billie Carleton, that 'it seems impossible that this country should go back to the unrestricted sale and use of these drugs which existed before the Defence of the Realm Regulation 40B, and suggestions for the continuance of the existing provisions have been placed before the Select Committee on Emergency Legislation'. (FO 371/3176/307-308) It seems unlikely that the press furore aroused by the Carleton affair influenced the decision of the Home Office to introduce a more permanent measure. It probably did contribute to the belief held by some officials, that such a measure would enjoy widespread public support. This would facilitate its passage through parliament, and help neutralise opposition likely to be encountered from pharmacists and their professional associations. In fact, as will be made clear later, some officials believed that support was so strong for such a measure that they could safely disregard the views of representative organisations of the medical and pharmaceutical professions.

Although there was no doubt at the beginning of 1919 that some system of controls would continue to be exercised over the manufacture, distribution and consumption of opium and cocaine, it was not yet decided how comprehensive the legislation would be. The DORA regulations applied to only some of the drugs specified in the Hague Convention. They were ad hoc measures which were amended from time to time in order to deal with eventualities which had not been anticipated when first introduced. What was still at issue, was whether the Hague Convention, and the elaborate system of controls its implementation would necessitate, would be brought into force. This depended on the outcome of negotiations over this question then being conducted at the Paris Peace Conference. Although the primary purpose of this conference was to settle issues arising out of the war, the Foreign Office had managed to ensure the inclusion of items relating to this matter on the agenda of one of the conference committees. Its reasons for doing so were related to certain difficulties which had been encountered during the war in attempting to regulate the quantities of manufactured narcotic substances exported from Britain to the Far East.

7 The Japanese menace and the Paris Peace Conference

JAPAN AND THE IMPORT CERTIFICATE SYSTEM

One of the drugs that had not been specified in DORA 40B was morphine. When Sir William Collins asked the Home Secretary whether, due to its potential for abuse, the regulation would be extended to cover it, he replied that he was not aware 'of any grounds arising out of the present emergency, for exercising those powers with respect to morphine'. (Hansard, Vol.CXV, 1917-1918, c.548) Throughout the war internal commerce in morphine continued to be regulated under relevant sections of the Pharmacy and Poisons acts. There arose, however, certain circumstances that led to a tightening of controls over external commerce in this drug.

In January 1916 Jordan wrote to the Foreign Office in connection with the spread of morphine addiction in China, particularly in Manchuria. He noted that most supplies of the drug were furnished by Japanese traders. Upon raising the subject with the Japanese Minister, he had been assured that everything possible was being done to curb their activities, due to the discredit they were bringing on the 'good name of Japan'. The North China Daily News stressed the gravity of the situation in an article published in 1915:

> Undoubtedly one of the most serious questions that requires the immediate attention of the Chinese authorities is the injection of morphia by the poorer Chinese. The evil is growing and increasing with alarming rapidity throughout Southern Manchuria. It is worse than opium-smoking for even the poorest coolie can acquire the habit of injection at a cost of as little as 3 cents, while the bad effects produced are much more rapid than those of opium. (3 September)

There were a number of factors contributing to the extensive participation of Japanese nationals in this illicit traffic. By the mid-war years Japan had increased its hegemony over China considerably. This was achieved without arousing much opposition from other powers, although they were by no means disposed to permit her to extend her suzerainty without limit. The United States acquiesced in this situation because her naval power in the Far East was no match for that of Japan:

> Somewhat belatedly, Theodore Roosevelt realised the Phillipines were an `Achilles heel' indefensible against the power of the Japanese fleet. This perception soon reflected itself in a new style of American diplomacy ... which tacitly confirmed Japan's special position in Korea and South Manchuria. Parallel with this Japanese-American rapprochement, the Russian and Japanese governments negotiated in 1907 and 1909 an entente by which they recognised each other's position in North and South Manchuria. (Crowley 1976, p.231)

In 1915 the Japanese launched a new diplomatic offensive against China, encouraged no doubt by the fact that the other powers were fully preoccupied with the European war. A series of demands, the aim of which was to increase Japanese control over large areas of China, were presented to the Peking authorities. In consequence, `China was forced to sign two treaties, conceding the transfer to Japan of German interests in Shantung and giving new privileges to Japan both in South Manchuria and the eastern part of Inner Mongolia'. (Storry 1967, p.153)

These developments were accompanied by an influx of Japanese nationals into areas under Japanese control, and an expansion of Japanese commerce. Both provided increased opportunities for her traders and officials to distribute morphine and other narcotics in China. Japanese owned drug stores were opened all over China. For the most part they specialised in distributing morphine to Chinese addicts. Getting the drugs into China was not difficult. There was a large traffic of steamers between Japan and China. The personnel of the Chinese Maritime Customs in ports which were in areas under Japanese hegemony were manned entirely by Japanese nationals. Since Japanese citizens enjoyed extra-territorial protection in China, it was impossible for the Chinese authorities to do much to curtail these illicit dealings. (Japan Weekly Chronicle, 27 January 1921)

Although the smuggling of morphia into China, and its distribution there, was udertaken largely by Japanese nationals, a large percentage of the profits from this commerce accrued to firms manufacturing the drug. Most of these were located in Britain. The British Consul-General at Shanghai, Sir E. Fraser, noted in 1916 that `the principal manufacturers of morphia and cocaine are resident in the United Kingdom, and ... the chief market is in London. It would appear from the facts which have come to my notice, that exporters are permitted a considerable lattitude in regard to ultimate destination, and that a trade ... is being allowed to grow up in China with the connivance of British firms, and to the detriment of the British name'. (FO371/2653/295) Jordan was of the opinion that the only method of effectively curbing this traffic was by imposing stringent controls on re-exports of morphine from Japan. (ibid, p.270) Fraser suggested that the matter be brought to the attention of the Board of Trade, and that steps be taken to estimate the legitimate needs of the Japanese and Far Eastern markets so that restrictions could be imposed in order to limit exports to these quantities. Max Muller contended that it was Germany which was primarily responsible for frustrating British efforts to curb the traffic in this substance, 'in order that Merck and the other great chemical manufacturers of Germany might not lose their profit in poisoning the human race on morphia and cocaine'. (ibid, p.265) There is, however, no evidence that Germany was at this time exporting large quantities of morphine to the Far East. Moreover, as he was certainly aware, the Japanese had entered the war on the side of the allies a little more than two weeks after it had begun, 'and within a matter of three months had seized German possessions and interests in Shantung'. (Storry 1967, p.152) German firms simply did not have the means of distributing morphine, even if they had desired to do so.

Despatches from British diplomats in China make it clear that British firms were the main beneficiaries on the manufacturing side of this traffic. The extent of their involvement can be gauged from the following figures, which detail the quantities exported to Japan, produced and manufactured in the United Kingdom.

Year	Quantity in Ozs
1911	68,352
1912	124,307
1913	252,110
1914	352,130
1915	204,742
1916	116,116
1917	29,204
1918	0

Source: Annual Statement's of the Trade of the United Kingdom, 1911-19

Between 1911 and the end of 1915, exports of the drug to Japan had increased more than six-fold. There is evidence, moreover, that these figures considerably under-estimate the quantities of morphia exported to Japan from the United Kingdom. They do not include morphine exported via the parcel post. Secondly, the figures given by the Board of Trade to the Foreign Office, in a letter dated 26 February 1917, reveal that there was an extremely large discrepancy between the quantities listed in the officially published returns, and amounts licensed for export. The Board reported that in 1916 licensed exports of morphia and morphia salts to Japan amounted to 1,029,616 ozs., that is 8.8 times the quantity shown in the official returns. (FO371/2914/62) Japanese imports were considerably larger even than this. The above figures do not include imports from other sources, nor morphia of British origin re-exported to Japan from other countries. There is no doubt that these imports were far in excess of Japan's annual medical requirements. The Japan Weekly Chronicle estimated these at 30,000 ozs. (27 January 1921)

The League of Nations' Supervisory Body estimated the world requirements of morphine for 1935, including quantities needed for conversion into other drugs, as being 1,236,329 ozs., which was a figure not much higher than the amount estimated to have been imported by Japan in 1916. (League of Nations Supervisory Body 1934, p.4)

The lenient attitude adopted by the Japanese authorities towards those of its nationals trading in morphia and other narcotics in China, contrasted sharply with the stringent controls imposed on the internal commerce in these drugs in Japan:

> the Japanese had recognised the evils of opium long before contact with Western civilisation, and by strictly prohibiting its entry had never permitted the opium smoking habit to gain a hold ... Later when the medicinal properties of opium and its derivatives were recognised, and their value to surgery appreciated, certain amounts of opium were imported and domestically produced. Regulations were then extended to restrict its use and retail sale, and provisions were appended to the criminal code to deal with opium offenders. (Merill 1942, pp.73-74)

In Japan, in contrast to her possessions and areas of hegemony in China, these regulations were strictly enforced.

Max Muller believed that there was little that the Foreign Office could do about this situation. It would, he argued, 'be quixotic to prevent our manufacturers from supplying the Japanese with what they can easily obtain elsewhere'. (FO371/2653/265) Nevertheless, Fraser's proposals were communicated to the Board of Trade. The Board replied cryptically that exports, except under licence, were already prohibited. It did not deem it necessary to account for the fact that large quantities of British manufactured narcotics were still being smuggled into China. (ibid, p.355)

During 1916 and 1917, a number of protests were received by the Foreign Office requesting the introduction of restrictions on the export of morphia to Japan. The United Free Church of Scotland brought the matter to the attention of J.W. Gulland, M.P., requesting that he prompt the relevant government department to introduce measures to rectify the situation. (ibid, p.300) In July 1917, the Secretary of the Presbytry of Newcastle transmitted to the Foreign Office a resolution deploring the continued exporting of morphia to Japan, and urging the govenment to 'regulate the sale and export of morphia for the sake of the victims in China as they have recently dealt with Opium at the instance of the Shipping Companies, and with Cocaine, for the sake of our soldiers'. (FO371/2914/43) The Archbishop of York pointed out that if something was not done immediately, the work achieved by the cessation of the Indo-China opium traffic would be undermined. (ibid, p.220)

Correspondence on this matter was eventually passed to the War Trade Department. It was the department responsible for issuing export licenses. At the end of 1916 it informed the Home Office that exports of morphia 'under licence could ... be restricted to such an amount as might be considered sufficient for the legitimate medicinal needs of Japan, but such action would only be taken with the concurrence of the Foreign Office'. It was noted that it had not 'hitherto been considered jutifiable to refuse licences to export to approved consignees in an allied country consignments of Morphia which are not required in this country'. (ibid, p.52) T.H. Lyon, a clerk in the Far Eastern Department, noted that there were already two 'important steps' under consideration which were likely to sour Anglo-Japanese relations: the raising of the Indian import duty on foreign cottons, and the prohibition of certain imports from Japan. If the policy advocated by the War Trade Department and Fraser was adopted, it would 'only add fuel to the fire of Japanese irritation'. (ibid) In response to a Home Office query which was received three weeks later, concerning whether a licence should be granted permitting the export of 7,500 ozs. of cocaine to Japan via Holland and France, the Foreign Office replied that they would 'deprecate a refusal of licences unless such refusal could be based on the requirements of this country'. (ibid, p.54)

Copies of the correspondence on this matter had also been sent to the Board of Trade. Despite the fact that it had objected previously to the adoption of any self-denying policies in the absence of an international agreement on this question, its officials now suggested that the licensing authorities 'should be instructed to restrict exports from the United Kingdom to Japan to the quantity which may reasonably be assumed to be required in the country for legitimate medical purposes'. (F0371/2915/62) This change of attitude was probably a product of the fact that during the war years the United Kingdom was the main source of supply of morphine, cocaine and other narcotic substances for the Far Eastern market. There was, therefore, little likelihood that any loss incurred by British firms resulting from the imposition of restrictions on exports to Japan, would be reflected in an increase in sales by other manufacturing countries. The Board was quite prepared to sacrifice the vested interests of British firms in this trade if the nationals of other countries would not thereby gain an advantage.

Lyons now made an adroit about-face, arguing that 'we might stretch a point in the interests of peace and quietness and of the Manchurian population. We shall never be left alone until something definite has been done'. (ibid) The source of disquiet originally had been a letter from the Edinburgh Anti-Opium Committee. It was suggested that the co-operation of the Japanese authorities in restricting imports of morphia to quantities necessary for medicinal needs, be sought. The committee constantly bombarded the Board of Trade with letters on the subject, as did the Anglo-Oriental Society. In the Commons, Sir William Collins asked the Foreign Secretary whether there was any truth to the rumours that morphia exported to Japan found its way to the Chinese population of Manchuria. to this he received the then standard reply that there was no information on this point. (ibid, p.70) During May to June 1917 numerous protests were lodged with the relevant departments of state. In this cause the Edinburgh committee and the AOS enlisted the support of some of their surviving auxilliaries, in an endeavour to create the impression of widspread support for a policy of restricting exports to Japan. Petitions on this subject were also received from the China Inland Mission, the Temperance Committee of the United Free Church of Scotland and from that church's Edinburgh Presbytery. (cf. F0371, Vol.2915)

In April 1917, the British Ambassador in Tokyo had been asked for his observations on accusations made by the Edinburgh Anti-Opium Committee that the Japanese authorities were diverting large quantities of morphia for sale to the Chinese in Manchuria. In his reply he noted that there were good grounds for believing in the accuracy of such accusations. He recommended that in future export licences should only be granted if 'certificates are obtained from the Japanese Home authorities or the authorities of the Kwantung leased territory showing that the morphia is for actual consumption in Japan or Dairen and vicinity for medical purposes only'. (ibid, p.122) Since he was of the opinion that the unilateral adoption of such a policy by the British government would not cause any serious outcry, the Board of Trade was authorised by the Foreign Office to make the issuing of licenses dependent upon the fulfillment of these conditions. The restrictions were also applied to exports of cocaine to Japan.

Once this change of policy had been accepted in principle, it was not long before it was extended to cover exports to other countries. One of the Foreign Office clerks pinted out that 'it would seem necessary to apply them to China ... and to any countries which may be re-exporting morphine, etc. to China, so as to avoid any appearance of differentiating against Japan'. (ibid, pp.167-168) Such steps also proved necessary because of the way in which British manufacturers, Japanese smugglers, and the Japanese authorities reacted to the imposition of restrictions on exports of these substances to Japan. The predictions repeatedly made by the German delegates to the Hague conferences, and by Board of Trade officials, that the introduction of such a scheme by a limited number of powers would simply mean that the traffic would be re-routed via countries not party to the agreement, were fully borne out. The decline in morphia exports to Japan was soon met by an increase in exports to the United States, Canada, Cochin China, Switzerland and other countries. The response of the Foreign Office, the Board of Trade and the War Trade Department, was to conclude with these countries agreements similar to the policy adopted in relation to Japan. In due course the drugs were simply routed via countries that had not as yet agreed to introduce the British import certificate system.

The way in which the system developed during the first year of its operation was described in a letter from the War Trade Department to the Board of Trade:

> Following upon the imposition of these restrictions (on exports to Japan) it came to the notice of this department that orders for morphine and other opium alkaloids were being diverted to the United States and it became evident that unless similar restrictive measures were imposed by the United States Government, the object of the British regulations would be to a great extent defeated. This matter was accordingly communicated to the Foreign Office ... and the Foreign Office communicated in due course with the British Embassy at Washington with the result that eventually an agreement was arrived at between the two countries that no consignments of opium or opium alkaloids should be allowed to proceed to the United States of America unless a request for a British export licence was specifically supported by the United States Embassy in this country. (FO371/3686/443)

Once the American route was blocked, the War Trade Department noticed a 'massive increase' in exports of morphia and its salts to Switzerland. In September 1919 these amounted to 25,160 ozs; by the end of October the figure had trebled to 76,740. Their officials concluded that these drugs were probably destined for the Far East, and suggested that it might be wise 'to communicate with the Swiss Government with a view to instituting similar guarantees in the case of Switzerland as have recently been effected in the case of France'. (F0371/3687/459) No sooner were negotiations underway with the Swiss authorities than the Imports and Exports Licencing Section of the Board of Trade noticed a sudden increase in exports of these drugs to Cuba, Denmark and Belgium. (ibid, p.558) A month later Panama, Norway, Guatemala and Holland had joined the ranks of large importers of morphia, its derivatives and preparations. The Board suggested that agreements similar to those recently concluded with the United States, France and Japan, should be agreed with these other countries. It was also stressed that:

> The question as to whether a uniform policy should not be adopted in the case of the export to all countries of Opium and its preparations, opium alkaloids and their salts and preparations and cocaine ... would seem to be growing more insistent every day. (F0371/3687/697)

In response the Foreign Office addressed a circular to all British representatives abroad, instructing them to approach the governments to which they were accredited, with a view to concluding agreements similar to those already agreed with others. In the event of a refusal on the part of a country to comply with their request, licences to export the drugs in question would be refused. (ibid, p.707) Eventually, during the nineteen-twenties, agreements on the introduction of an import certificate system were reached with all of those approached.

The system proved to be less than perfect. Some of its defects were pointed out in an article by Lennox Simpson in the Peking Leader:

> Although licences are necessary for ordinary trade export, no licences are required for despatch by parcel post from England ... And when petty Japanese officials in Dairen are empowered to issue licences, accepted by the British Government as justifying export in unlimited quantity, we begin to see what is behind this business ... The Chinese Customs figures for 1917 show that 66,000 ounces of morphia (130 million injections) were openly imported into the Kwantung Leased Territory for medical purposes only according to the Foreign Office formula, when the whole importation for the same period for legitimate use in China was only 40 ozs. That is to say that Manchuria, a country of twenty million inhabitants, obtained one thousand five hundred times as much morphia as was legitimately needed in the whole of China. (2 August 1919)

Leakages via the parcel post, and by other means, were bound to occur so long as controls were not imposed on the manufacture of morphia, its salts and preparations. Jordan had in fact suggested in August 1919 that it might be desirable to impose some form of control over production. (F0371/3687/401) This was the only way in which the matter could be effectively dealt with. Unless a complete check was kept on the amount of raw opium imported, the quantity converted into morphine and other drugs, and amounts used for internal consumption, it would not be difficult to smuggle large quantities out of the country. The large discrepancy in the prices of these articles in Britain and in China, was an incentive to evade existing restrictions. As Simpson noted:

The real secret of this nefarious trade is that the manufacture of morphia is not entirely controlled by the British Government. Although officers of the Excise are placed in every tobacco factory in England and every ounce of tobacco and every cigarette is rigidly controlled, the manufacturer of morphia can do as he pleases, the licencing system being a farce. (ibid)

Max Muller recommended that the Home Office be informed, and urged to put a stop to this 'scandal'. He noted that at the various opium conferences the British delegates had 'always maintained that the only way to prevent illicit trade in these drugs was to control the production as well as the trade. Every ounce of morphia manufactured in this country should be under control from the moment it is produced to the moment it is consumed in accordance with medical prescription or exported under licence'. (F0371/3687/398) It was a 'disgrace' that 'chemical manufacturers should continue to turn out quantities of morphia far in excess of the possible world requirements for legitimate purposes'. (ibid, p.694) In bringing these matters to the attention of the Home Office, he stressed that 'the control of production is a necessary complement of control of export if the illicit trade in morphia is to be successfully checked'. (ibid, p.451)

Adequate controls over manufacture and consumption would not have sufficed to ensure that an import certificate system, of the type introduced in Britain, would prevent the funnelling of narcotics into the illicit Far Eastern traffic. The effectiveness of such a scheme depended essentially on two factors: (a) that officials of the importing country were not directly or indirectly lending encouragement to those of their citizens who were engaged in this commerce, and (b) that the exporting countries could control the supply of raw materials necessary to produce the manufactured articles. During the periood 1917-26 neither of these conditions held with respect to Japan. There is no doubt that the assurances accompanying Japanese applications for exports of morphia and allied drugs, namely, that they would be used for medicinal and scientific purposes only, were false. Board of Trade officials were aware of this. They began to refuse export licences even when the necessary assurances were given, if they considered that the amounts involved were excessive. (e.g. F0371/3687/P179137)

Even if the amounts of raw opium exported from Britain and other manufacturing countries were drastically reduced, this would not solve the problem unless it could be ensured that Japan could not obtain supplies from other sources. One of the major weaknesses of the Hague Convention was that whilst provisions were made by it for the imposition of stringent controls on manufactured drugs, those relating to the raw materials from which they were produced were much weaker. In particular, there was no stipulation that the quantity of opium produced should be related to global or regional medicinal requirements, or even that its use should be confined to such purposes. Notwithstanding these major deficiencies, the British import certificate system was later adopted by other signatories of the convention. It became one of the corner-stones of the system of international drug control developed by the League's Advisory Committee on Traffic in Opium. (Advisory Committee on Traffic in Opium, Proces Verbal, First Session, 1921, pp.17-22) By the end of May 1926, 33 of the 57 countries which had ratified the convention had introduced the scheme.

There are a number of points worth noting about the genesis of the import certificate system. To begin with, it was introduced prior to ratification of the Treaty of Versailles and the enactment of the Dangerous Drugs Act 1920. The placing of retrictions on the export of morphia and allied drugs, was effected primarily due to complaints voiced by Jordan and other British diplomatic representatives in the Far East. Their concerns were twofold. First, that the extensive involvement of British firms in the illicit traffic in morphia, albeit by proxy, was tarnishing Britain's already poor image, as well as that of British firms. On 7 November 1919, for instance, representatives of some fifteen British Chambers of Commerce in China passed a resolution calling for the immediate putting into effect of the Hague Convention, in the interest of British prestige and commercial prosperity in the Far East. (FO371/5307/221) In addition, Jordan and others were genuinely concerned that the increase in consumption of these drugs was having undesirable effects on the welfare of the Chinese population. According to Jordan, there was 'no doubt whatever that the population of Manchuria and North China generally is being debauched by the use of a drug which enters the country in enormous quantities from abroad'. (FO371/3687/416) His advocacy of increased restrictions on exports, was probably facilitated by the cooling of British-Japanese relations consequent upon the growing stranglehold exerted by the latter over Manchuria, and the adoption by the Kwantung Government-General of what were regarded by British firms as unfair methods of economic competition. The ending of the Indo-China opium trade also enabled Jordan to adopt more convincingly a policy that was directed at curbing the consumption of opium and other drugs, now that Britain appeared to have no vested interest in their sale in China. These considerations suggest that restrictions on the export of narcotics would have continued to be imposed, regardless of whether the Hague Convention had been brought into force by the signatories of the Versailles Treaty and the Covenant of the League of Nations.

THE VERSAILLES TREATY AND THE BRINGING INTO FORCE OF THE INTERNATIONAL OPIUM CONVENTION

Between 1914 and 1918 the question of whether steps should be taken to bring the Hague Convention into force, if only by a minority of powers, was not the subject of international negotiations. In August 1918 the United States ambassador informed the Foreign Office that he had been instructed by the Department of State to ascertain whether the British govenment would now be willing to agree to the immediate putting into force of the convention. The view of the American government was that:

> There seems reason to fear that one result of the war ... will be that many sufferers will have become so accustomed to the use of opiates as to be in danger of enslavement thereby and that, unless prompt measures are taken to put into force the convention upon which the civilised Powers have agreed, a widespread use of opium derivatives will threaten the health and efficiency of their peoples. (FO371/3176/171-181, 23 August 1918)

Although the Foreign Office records contain no information that explain what prompted the State Department to advance this suggestion at this particular moment, it is probable that restrictions imposed by the British government on the exporting of morphia to the Far East had some bearing on the matter. It will be recalled that the American authorities had, in the early part of 1918, agreed to vet all requests for licences to export morphia to the United States, subsequent to representations being made on this issue by the Foreign Office. It is likely that in the course of these negotiations, the desirability of bringing the convention into force suggested itself to State Department officials.

The attitude at the Foreign Office was that it was still essential to secure the co-operation of all contracting powers prior to any further steps being taken in relation to this matter. The Home, India and Colonial Offices, and the Board of Trade, were informed that it was intended to advise the American ambassador accordingly. In their reply to the Foreign Office, the Board of Trade stressed that although they would not go so far as to insist that it was essential to secure the co-operation of all the convention's signatories to make the implementation of its provisions effective, it was imperative that the more important producing and manufacturing countries should do so, particularly Germany. (FO371/3176/244) The Colonial and India Offices concurred in the course of action suggested by the Foreign Office. Only the Home Office raised fundamental objections. In their reply they stressed that the pre-1914 situation had altered substantially as a consequence of restrictions being imposed during the war on the consumption and external commerce in the drugs covered by the convention. Their view was that 'the disadvantage of the convention being only partially operative need not now be regarded as sufficient reason for not attempting to make it operative as far as possible. If only a number of powers, e.g., the Allied powers, were to agree to put it into force, it would certainly do much to control the trade, and their action might be expected to influence the smaller states'. (ibid, pp.307-308) They proposed that the United States government be informed that if the more important Allied powers agreed to implement the convention, the British government would do likewise. The attitude of Home Office officials to this question is not difficult to understand. From 1916 onwards its officials had been responsible for enforcing the DORA regulations. They had already suggested that these provisions should be continued after the war. It must have been clear to them that the effectiveness of any drug control policies introduced in Britain would depend in some measure on whether equivalent restrictions were enforced in other countries. Having no responsibility for promoting British trade, they regarded the convention primarily as an instrument directed at extinguishing or continuing drug addiction.

Senior Foreign Office officials were of the opinion that the Home Office suggestion was impractical. Ronald Macleay, then in charge of the Far Eastern Department, took the view that immediate enforcement of the convention would prove ineffective as long as Germany, Turkey and Austria-Hungary refused to abide by its provisions. He suggested that:

It might be worthwhile to consider whether in view of recent events and the prospect of the early termination of the war it would not be better to suggest to the United States that the question of putting into force of the 1912 convention should be raised at the Peace Conference as a matter affecting the physical and moral welfare of mankind with a view to securing the general acceptance of its provisions and of the obligation of all the states represented at the Conference not only to adhere to it, but to enact immediately the necessary legislation. (ibid, pp.173-174)

In the context of the development of both international and domestic drug laws and controls, this was an extremely important turning-point. From the extended discussions that took place at the Second and Third Hague Conferences relating to the ratification and bringing into force of the convention, it was apparent that some countries with major interests in the traffic in narcotic drugs, particularly Germany and Turkey, were unwilling to do so. Since it was unlikely that it would be possible to get all interested parties to do so simultaneously, no progress had been made by way of multilateral or bilateral negotiations. At the Peace Conference, on the other hand, it might be possible to obtain the agreement of other Allied powers to compel Germany and Turkey to ratify the convention. Furthermore, as Macleay noted, the 'smaller states' might be persuaded to follow suit.

The United States Ambassador was informed that the view of the Foreign Office was that prior to any action being taken on the suggestion advanced by the State Department, a further effort should be made to secure the adhesion to the convention of all the more important producing and manufacturing countries. The question should therefore 'be raised at the Congress with a view to the adoption of a resolution binding all the belligerents to take immediate steps to enact the legislation contemplated in the Convention'. (ibid, p.340, 10 December 1918)

The proposal evoked little enthusiasm. The attitude adopted by the State Department was that the question of suppressing the illegal trade in opium and other habit-forming drugs was not one that could properly be brought before the conference, whose terms of reference included only matters arising out of the war, and related subjects. Nevertheless, the delegates of the United States would not raise objections if a resolution in the sense suggested were put before the conference. (FO608/211/p.1650) Max Muller agreed that, strictly speaking, this question did not 'grow out of the war'. He noted, however, that this applied in equal measure to other subjects on the agenda, such as the regulation of labour conditions. His view was that since many remote questions were likely to be raised, the occasion might also be found:

> to pass a resolution on a matter so nearly affecting the physical and moral welfare of the human race ... international agreements on humanitarian questions, which in order to attain their full effect must be of more or less universal application, such as measures for the suppression of the white slave traffic, drug taking, etcetera, might very properly be brought within the sphere of activities of the League of Nations. (FO371/3686/398)

Macleay, who was already in Paris by then, was informed that Curzon, who was in charge of the Foreign Office in the absence of the Secretary of State, was of the opinion that efforts be concerted with the United States delegation to ascertain the best method of bringing this question before the conference. The objective was to obtain a unanimous resolution committing all the belligerents to enact and enforce legislative measures necessary to give effect to the convention. (FO608/211/p.1650)

Unfortunately, the material contained in the Foreign office archives relating to the handling of this question at the conference is sketchy. In the context of other issues before the delegates this one was not particularly important. None of the authorities who have written about the conference, a few of whom played an important role in its deliberations, considered that it merited more than a brief mention, and usually not even that. The subject was apparently raised before only two of the conference committees. The first was a Treaty Revision Committee, which was concerned with it solely from the point of view of whether it was desirable to allow this 'inchoate' convention to come into force. (FO608/211/p.1911)

The other organ of the conference that dealt with this matter was the League of Nations Commission. Although minutes of its meetings were eventually published, these fail to make any reference to the international traffic in opium, despite the fact that the League was granted extensive powers to monitor the implementation of the Hague Convention. President Wilson, who chaired this Commission, was of the opinion that the minutes 'should be very summary indeed, recording only the action taken'. (D.H. Miller 1928, Vol.1, pp.118-119) Since no stenographic record was made of the discussions, it is unlikely that the reasons for the decisions taken by the delegates in relation to this matter will ever be known. Their recommendations were likely to be influenced, however, by the nature of the role it was envisaged that the League of Nations would play in international affairs.

This was an issue over which there were considerable differences of opinion between the leaders of the allied powers. These were partly related to the importance they placed on providing for the establishing of an international organisation in the peace settlements with the enemy powers. Whereas Wilson was of the opinion that such a step was essential to the preservation of peace in Europe, Lloyd George was less enthusiastic, considering the proposed League 'as an accessory rather than an essential'. (Temperley 1920, Vol.1, p.194) Clemenceau, who disparagingly referred to Wilson as an 'inspired prophet', a 'slave' to a 'noble ideological venture', was openly hostile to the proposal. Their differences were rooted in contrasting attitudes relating to issues of territorial security. Wilson was of the opinion that the war had been fought to do away with 'the old order', which had been based on 'the balance of power' and maintained by the 'unstable equilibrium of competitive interests'. The outbreak of war in 1914 had, in his view, demonstrated how reliable a means of maintaining the peace this was. There was now, he thought, a call for a different type of balance of power, 'not of one powerful group of nations set off against another, but a single overwhelming, powerful group of nations who shall be trustees of the world'. (Noble 1968, p.88) Clemenceau refused to be impressed. He retorted that since France was the country nearest to Germany, he would continue to place his faith in the old system of 'solid frontiers' and the 'balance of power'. (ibid)

Despite their lack of enthusiasm, Clemenceau and Lloyd George were willing to give way on this issue in return for concessions in other spheres. Wilson was, in any event, so incensed with the establishing of a League, that he was prepared to blackmail the other allied powers into agreement by threatening to sign a separate peace with Germany. Consequently, 'the allies agreed to Woodrow Wilson's proposal that a Commission to draft the constitution of the League should be set up as one of the first acts of the Paris Peace Conference and that the resulting constitution would be incorporated into the peace treaties to be concluded with the ex-enemy powers'. (Henig 1973, p.3) The significance of this decision cannot be exaggerated. It is as certain as one can be on questions of this sort, that if it had not been agreed that the Covenant of the League would be incorporated in the final peace treaty, a League of Nations would not have come into being at this time. As Temperley points out:

> To have produced unanimity on this point amongst the twenty-six States who signed the German Treaty would almost certainly have been impossible, unless the signature had been made the only way to enjoy the benefits of the peace. So many vested interests were challenged by the League, and so many new forces had been liberated in Europe, which were antagonistic to it, that unless the League had been made part of the peace it might have been postponed for a generation. (1920, Vol.1, p.276)

Although Wilson had secured the agreement of the allies to incorporate the constitution of the League in the peace treaties, the functions it would be expected to perform had yet to be determined. In all the schemes that were drafted prior to the armistice, the proposed organisation was granted no jurisdiction over anything other than the pacific settlement of international disputes. The only plan that envisaged entrusting the League with much wider powers was drawn up by the South African Defence Minister, General Jan Smuts. From the perspective of the present study his most important contribution was to advocate granting it extensive powers to tackle issues of international concern which were not directly related to the causes or settlement of international conflicts. In his view it was essential to move away from this narrow conception of the League's functions:

> to view it not only as a possible means of preventing future wars, but more as a great organ of the new international system which will be erected on the ruins of this war ... It must become part and parcel of the common international life of states, it must be an ever visible living working organ of the policy of civilisation. It must function so strongly in the ordinary peaceful intercourse of states that it becomes irresistable in their disputes; its peace activity must be the foundation and guarantee of its war power. (D.H. Miller 1928, Vol.2, pp.24-25)

Underlying his approach was the conviction that since war and peace were resultants of many complex forces, these would have to be dealt with by the League if peace was to be effectively maintained. Although his plan was never adopted officially by the British government, its influence on British delegates to the League Commission, and on Wilson, was apparent.

Two schemes formed the basis of subsequent discussions in the League Commission. One of these was drawn up by the British delegation, which was headed by Lord Robert Cecil, and forwarded to Wilson on 19 January 1919. Amongst other things it was proposed that the contracting parties 'appoint commissions to study and report to the League on economic, sanitary, and other similar problems of international concern, and they authorise the League to recommend such action as these reports may show to be necessary'. (ibid, pp.106-111) It was also suggested that certain conventions be annexed to the Covenant. These included those dealing with the arms and liquor traffics, and others concerned with the 'tutelage of backward races', as well as those dealing with 'standard international activities of a more scientific or technical character', such as health. In each case international bodies would be established to carry out the terms of each convention, whether Commission of Enquiry or Administrative or semi-Administrative Commissions. Although not specifically mentioned in this draft proposal, the terms of reference of the International Opium Convention were such that it could easily be classed alongside these other conventions.

At a conference held on 31 January attended, amongst others, by Wilson, Cecil and Smuts, it was decided that David Hunter Miller, a technical advisor to the American Peace Commission, would confer with Cecil Hurst, legal advisor to the British Peace Commission, in an attempt to produce an agreed scheme which could then be submitted to the League of Nations Commission. The scheme worked out between the two, known as the Hurst-Miller Draft, was the document that formed the basis of subsequent discussions in the commission. There was no reference in this draft to the appointment of commissions to deal with economic, sanitary or health questions, or other issues of international concern. There was also no clause allowing for the annexing to the covenant of any of the international conventions specified in the earlier British draft. (D.H. Miller 1928, Vol.2, pp.231-237)

In one of the sessions of the Drafting Committee - a sub-committee of the League Commission - Cecil again raised the issue of including in the draft covenant then under consideration, provisions for the establishment of international commissions. He proposed that subsection 10 of the preamble stipulate that the contracting parties agree to:

> include in the organisation of the League machinery for the investigation, administration or settlement of any matters of common concern to the life, health or interests of their people which may be entrusted to the care of the League by the treaties of peace or by any future international agreement. (ibid, Vol.1, pp.217-218)

He also noted that there were a number of matters, such as 'the international control of opium, morphia and other dangerous drugs which the competent British officials are anxious to bring within the scope of the League'. (ibid, Vol.2, p.315) The suggested changes to the preamble would have altered it substantially. Having been briefed by Miller on their content, Wilson instructed him to convey his opposition to their inclusion to the Drafting Committee, with the result that most were omitted from the draft covenant presented to the full conference on 14 February 1919.

On the previous day the Foreign Office had received a letter from the United States ambassador in which he pointed out that whilst his government was in sympathy with the suppression of the illegal trade in opium, 'it nevertheless hesitates to agree in advance to whether this is a matter which may be incorporated in the Peace Treaty until such time as the subject is actually brought to the consideration of the Conference'. (FO608/211/p.3038) Two weeks prior to the receipt of this communication, James Shotwell, a technical advisor to the American delegation, had discussed this question with Dr. Alfred Sze, the Chinese ambassador to Great Britain who was a member of his country's delegation to the conference. In his diary entry for 3 February Shotwell noted that he had 'arranged with Dr Sze the procedure for handling the question of the opium trade at the Conference'. (Shotwell 1937, p.163)

The lack of co-ordination of policies between State Department officials in Washington and the United States delegation in Paris, was probably responsible for the inconsistency in the American approach to the handling of this question. On 19 March, Arthur Balfour, the British Foreign Secretary, received a letter from the American Secretary of State, Lansing, who was then in Paris, the contents of which amounted to a reversal of earlier American policy on this issue. After recounting the historical circumstances that gave rise to the Hague Convention, he noted that since 'so many powers are represented in Paris it appears to me possible and desirable that this project should be brought to completion'. (FO608/211/p.4861) He requested that Balfour inform him of his views on the best way to accomplish this objective. The fact that American delegates on the League Commission had five weeks earlier rejected proposals to include a clause in the draft covenant that would have secured this aim, after Shotwell had already agreed with Sze to take up the matter, was a product of the lack of co-ordination between American delegates representing the United States on the numerous committees and commissions set up by the conference:

> The work of American representative on different commissions was not co-ordinated as the conference progressed. No effort was made to keep anyone informed of the steady progress of events. Each specialist was supposed to work on his tasks without regard to what his colleagues were doing in other fields. It was even regarded as somwhat illegitimate ... for any of the so-called technical experts to inquire about anything not in their own fields. (Shotwell 1937, p.45)

From the beginning of March, Shotwell and Miller began to work together on Chinese questions. It was probably this development which was responsible for the changed attitude expressed in Lansing's letter to Balfour. One of the consequences was that American representatives on the League Commission withdrew their opposition to Cecil's earlier proposals relating to the opium trade. At the thirteenth meeting of the Commission, on 25 March, Cecil proposed that one of the articles of the draft covenant then under consideration should provide, _inter alia_, that members of the League would entrust it 'with the general supervision over the execution of such agreements as shall have been jointly come to with regard to the traffic in opium and other dangerous drugs'. (D.H. Miller 1928, Vol.1, p.339) This provision features as subsection (c) of Article XXIII of the Covenant of the League of Nations, the only addition to the final text being the insertion of the words 'traffic in women and children' prior to 'traffic in opium', etc.

Although it had thereby been agreed that the League would assume responsibility for monitoring the traffic in opium, the problem of ensuring that the more important producing and manufacturing countries would ratify the Hague Convention, and later bring it into force, remained to be resolved. Lansing's letter to Balfour addressed itself to this facet of the problem. In his reply Balfour pointed out that he was:

> fully in accord with the views expressed in your letter and I have already caused a Memorandum to be prepared for submission to the conference ... Appended to this ... is a resolution proposed by the

British delegation to the effect that the Supreme Allied Council is of the opinion that in the Preliminary Treaty of Peace with Germany an article should be inserted imposing upon her the obligation to ratify the Opium Convention .... and to enact the legislation necessary to enforce it. In the corresponding treaties with Austria-Hungary and Turkey articles should be inserted imposing upon them the obligation to sign and ratify the Treaty and to enact the legislation necessary for enforcing it. (FO608/211/p.4861, March 26 1919)

At this stage an element of competition between the delegations in relation to this issue was evident. After some members of the American delegation had acknowledged that it was desirable to insert an article in the Treaty which would ensure the implementation of the convention, they apparently considered that it would be advantageous to capitalise on the 'kudos' that would attach to the delegation that submitted the proposal to the conference. Undoubtedly this was a factor which was also taken cognisance of by some members of the British delegation. In February Cecil Harmsworth had informed Phillip Kerr, Lloyd George's private secretary, that such a resolution was likely to be tabled by one power or another. He suggested that the British delegation pre-empt the situation 'if only for the reason that we ought to have the credit of taking a step which would be warmly welcomed by influential bodies of opinion in all countries. If we do not do it, the Americans probably will, and get all the credit'. (FO371/3686/448-9) This was probably one of the considerations that prompted Lansing to suggest to Balfour that instead of the United States supporting the British resolution:

you permit the American Delegation to join with the British in proposing the Resolution. I feel sure that you will recognise the suggestion as a very natural one in view of the fact that the American Government has taken the lead in proposing the various conferences that have hitherto been held to deal with this question. (FO608/211/p.6799, 8 April 1919)

Macleay was not particularly enamoured with this suggestion. He considered that it was interesting that having 'thrown cold water' over the proposal when it was first advanced, they now rushed to embrace it with such enthusiasm. He consoled himself with the thought that 'as we have got in first with our memorandum we shall not I hope lose the kudos of having been the originators of the idea of bringing the matter up at the Peace Conference'. (FO371/3686/609)

In his letter to Balfour, Lansing also proposed that the phraseology of the proposed resolution should be such as to bind all signatories of the treaty, not merely ex-enemy powers, as in addition to these there were several others whom as yet had neither signed nor ratified the convention. In acceding to the request that the resolution should be jointly submitted, Balfour informed Lansing that the desirability of proceeding in this way had not escaped him:

I came to the conclusion that the best means of securing this objection would be by insertion in the Final Act of the Congress of a general clause binding all those of the High Contracting Parties, who either had not signed or, having signed, had not yet ratified, the Opium Convention, to proceed at once to signature or ratification or both, as the case might be, and, as soon as their ratifications have been deposited, to sign the Special Protocol opened at the Hague in 1914 for signature by those Powers who, having ratified the Convention, were desirous of putting it into force. (FO371/3686/648-649, 11 April 1919)

This is the last communication in the Foreign Office files dealing with the handling of this question at the conference. An article in the above sense was jointly proposed by the British and American delegations, and having been approved by the conference in plenary session, features as No.295 in the final treaty of peace with Germany. A similar clause was incorporated in the treaties concluded with other ex-enemy powers.

It is unnecessary to dwell further on the importance of these provisions. Without the insertion of such a clause the Hague Convention might never have been implemented. The main reason that it had not been brought into force earlier was the refusal of Germany and Turkey to ratify or sign it respectively. Since both countries happened to have been on the losing side in the war, those powers who were desirous of securing its implementation availed themselves of the opportunity of securing an imposed solution. This was an option that was not likely to recur soon. The enemy powers had no alternative but to acquiesce. Although nominally the Paris meeting was a peace conference, in practice it was an assembling of the allied powers whose aims were, as Shotwell, in reversing Clausewitz's dictum has noted, 'the continuation or summation of war' by diplomatic means. The terms of the treaty, as is well known, were dictated, not negotiated.

The way in which the drafting of the preliminary treaty was undertaken, the complexity of the multitudinous issues involved, and certain domestic constraints, made this inevitable. (cf. Lloyd George 1938(a), Vol.1, p.151) Since there were many issues to resolve and a large number of participants, it became necessary to delegate much of the work to specialist committees and commissions. In Shotwell's opinion, these organisational constraints were hardly less decisive in determining the content of the treaty, than the diplomatic strategies adopted by the more influential leaders of the allied powers. It led to a lack of articulation between different organs of the conference, and made it virtually inevitable that when the work of the separate bodies was pieced together in one document, this would be presented to the Germans and other ex-enemy powers as a dictat rather than a text that would form the basis for subsequent negotiations. The preparation 'of a detailed provisional text created a situation which could not easily be changed and a text which could not readily be done over again'. (Shotwell 1937, pp.38-39)

This method of drawing up the treaty facilitated the inclusion in the final text of clauses relating to matters which by no stretch of the imagination could be considered as arising out of the war, or, for that matter, being essential to the maintenance of the peace. Such were those relating to the traffics in opium, liquor, and women and children. Nonetheless, the achieving of near-universal adherence to the International Opium Convention of 1912, and the establishment of administrative machinery to ensure the enforcement of its provisions, was no less consequential because it had been brought about by circumstances unrelated to the conditions that had originally prompted the securing of a concerted international approach to this problem.

8 Doctors in ascendancy: the Dangerous Drugs Act and the regulations

THE DANGEROUS DRUGS ACT 1920

The Treaty of Versailles was signed by the German delegation to the Peace Conference on 28 June 1919. Under the terms of Article 295, the contracting powers were obliged to introduce such legislation as might be necessary to bring the International Opium Convention into force not later than twelve months after its signing. In May 1920, the Home Secretary introduced the Dangerous Drugs Bill in the Commons. It was designed to regulate the exportation, importation, manufacture, sale and use of opium and other dangerous drugs. Although the official line taken by the Home Office was that its enactment was necessary in order to comply with international treaties recently entered into by the government, the fact that the statutory regulations later issued under its provisions went beyond what a literal interpretation of the Hague Convention required, indicates that this explanation was primarily directed at deflecting opposition against legislation which was deemed necessary on additional grounds. I have noted earlier that Home Office officials had taken steps to ensure that DORA regulations would continue in force until such time as a more permanent measure could be placed on the statute books, and that this step was taken prior to a decision having been made to raise this question at the Paris conference. The Home Office verdict on the DORA regulations was that although the system of control had been largely successful, the traffic had not been completely eradicated, 'as the disclosures in the "Billie Carleton" case and other cases have shown'. (HO45/Box 10969/File 399514/D.2) Despite the fact that with the conclusion of De Veulle's second trial press coverage of the illicit traffic declined markedly, officials were of the opinion that a more permanent measure to regulate the use of narcotics was necessary to prevent resurgence of the problem.

The provisions of the Dangerous Drugs Bill were, for the most part, similar to those allowed for by the Hague Convention. Under the terms of Part 1, relating to raw opium, licences would henceforth have to be obtained by importers and exporters. The Secretary of State was empowered to attach conditions prohibiting exports to countries which banned or restricted its import. Under the terms of Section 3, powers were granted to subsequently introduce regulations directed at controlling its production, sale and distribution. This part of the bill closely parallels and fulfills the requirements of Chapter 1 of the convention.

Part II relates to prepared opium. In substance it is nearly identical to section 7 of DORA regulation 40(B), as amended in October 1917. (cf. supra, p.97) This stipulated that it would be unlawful to import or export opium prepared for smoking, to manufacture, sell, deal in or possess it, to permit premises to be used for its preparation, smoking or sale, to be concerned with the management of premises used for such purposes, to possess opium smoking utensils, or to smoke it. The provisions of this part of the bill, like the equivalent DORA regulations, went beyond what was required in order to fulfil the requirements of Chapter II of the Hague Convention.

Article 6 merely required that the contracting powers take steps to secure the 'gradual and efficacious suppression' of the manufacture, the internal traffic in and use of this substance, and then only insofar as the different conditions peculiar to each nation shall allow'. Opium smoking, however, was a practice that had few advocates in Britain. As it was indulged in primarily by persons of Chinese extraction, measures directed at its extinction were unlikely to arouse much opposition.

Part III of the bill related to controls to be imposed on the manufacture, sale, distribution and use of opiates and cocaine, and preparations containing these substances. It did not actually specify precisely what types of controls would be exercised. As in the case of raw opium, the Secretary of State was simply empowered to make regulations in respect of these matters in relation to morphine, cocaine, ecgonine and diamorphine, and their respective salts. The same applies in respect of medicinal opium, and any preparation, admixture, extract, or other substances containing not less than one-fifth percent of morphine or one-tenth percent of cocaine, ecgonine or diamorphine. These substances included all those mentioned in Article 14 of the Hague Convention.

Part III of the bill also empowered the authorities to extend any regulations that might be made, not only to 'every new derivative of morphine, cocaine or their respective salts or to any other alkaloid of opium' which might prove to give rise to 'similar abuse and result in the same injurious effects', but also to 'any other drug of whatever kind', which it appears 'is or is likely to be productive, if improperly used, of ill effects substantially of the same character or nature as or analogous to those produced by morphine or cocaine'. This clearly went beyond what was required under the terms of the Hague Convention. The extent to which this part of the bill would make inroads into the profitable trade of pharmacists in proprietary preparations containing narcotics would depend upon the content of the regulations which were to be published later. The bill's provisions indicated that these would be considerably more restrictive of the trade in and use of these substances than had been the DORA regulations. It will be recalled that under their provisions no controls were introduced during the war on the internal commerce in morphine and 'patent medicines' containing opiates. They continued to be regulated under provisions of the Pharmacy and Poisons Acts.

Despite its lack of specificality there were still some aspects of the bill which the Pharmaceutical Society found objectionable. Its Secretary, Sir W. Glyn Jones, noted that it gave the Home Secretary virtually unlimited powers to modify many of the provisions of the Pharmacy Acts. This interpretation was essentially correct as far as the sale of poisons was concerned. Under the terms of section 8(2), he was empowered to make regulations with respect to any drug liable to abuses similar to those associated with the opiates and cocaine. Moreover, it was technically possible under the terms of section 7, which authorised the issue of regulations to control the manufacture, sale, possession and distribution of these drugs, to override section I of the Pharmacy Act 1868. This restricted the sale of poisons to persons registered in accordance with the provisions of the act. Consequently, this could enable the Secretary of State to authorise the sale of these drugs by persons not authorised by the Pharmaceutical Society to deal in these substances. At this stage the council of the society was primarily concerned to ensure that, whatever the substance of the regulations which would be published subsequently, the privileges of registered chemists and druggists in relation to the compounding and dispensing of poisons would be maintained. In a letter to the Home Office, Glyn Jones noted that the view of the council was that the bill required amendment in three respects:

(1) That the restrictions imposed by this Act, or any regulations made under it, shall be in addition to, and not in substitution for, the provisions of the Pharmacy Act and Poisons and Pharmacy Act. (2) The right of a Pharmacist or Corporate Body legally entitled to keep open shop for the sale of Poisons to be authorised to dispense and retail the substances under the Act, and that the power to remove the authorisation of a pharmacist for any breach of the Regulations should be subject to the right of appeal to the Courts. (3) That the Pharmaceutical Council shall be consulted before any Regulations are made under the Act. (HO45/Box 20969/ File 399514-6a)

Home Office officials were prepared to countenance amendments to meet objections raised in (1) and the first part of (2), and the bill was altered accordingly. Subsection (3) of section 7 confirmed that the keeping of an open shop for retailing, compounding or dispensing of any poison, would continue to be confined to persons who were so authorised under the terms of the Pharmacy and Poisons Acts.

They were not prepared to give way on the question of granting a right of appeal to the courts. One Home Office official noted that such a right did not exist under the Pharmacy Act 1868. Under section 26 the Privy Council was empowered to strike a man off the register if he was convicted of an offence under the Act. Moreover, under the terms of subsection (10) of DORA regulation 40B, similar powers were granted to the Secretary of State. The society did not, therefore, have any precedent which they could refer to as justifying the granting of such a right. The main opposition to conceding this point came from officials of the Ministry of Health.   They argued that acceptance of the proposed amendment would create certain difficulties, since no such provision was allowed for in the National Health Insurance Act, 1911.   Section 15(5b) granted Health Commissioners powers to remove a chemist from the list if they were satisfied that his continuance thereon would be prejudicial to the medical services of the insured.   A similar provision applied to medical practitioners, 15(2b).   During the Committee stage of the National Health Insurance Bill, 1920, a 'desperate attempt was made on the part of the medical practitioners to insert a new clause providing for the right of appeal to the High Court against the Minister's decision'.   (ibid, D.6a)   This was successfully resisted.   Dr. Smith-Whitaker, a Senior Medical Officer at the Ministry, stressed in a letter to Delevingne, the Permanent Under-Secretary at the Home Office, that it was essential to oppose the insertion of a similar amendment in the Dangerous Drugs Act.   'If you now weaken' he wrote 'we shall undoubtedly have fresh trouble with the doctors, and no doubt then also with the chemists, who have so far not taken the point against us under the Insurance Act, but will no doubt be very glad to do so if they see the opportunity'.   (MH58(51)/File 95006/1/27)   After receiving further representations the Home Office agreed to incorporate a minor amendment. This committed the Secretary of State to consult the Council of the Pharmaceutical Society when it was intended to withdraw a chemist's authorisation to dispense the drugs in question, subsequent to his having been convicted of an offence under the act.

The only other important amendments were made at the behest of the Commissioner of the Metropolitan Police.   According to a letter written by Delevingne to W.J.U. Woolcock, M.P., a former Secretary of the Pharmaceutical Society who was acting as their parliamentary lobbyist, they were 'wanted for the purpose of dealing with the cocaine vendor and the opium smuggler and persons of that class'.   (HO45/Box 10609/File 399514-11b.)   The most important of these concerned the severity of penalties to be imposed for transgressions against the acts provisions. Under section 13(2) of the original bill, anyone guilty of an offence was liable on summary conviction to a fine not exceeding 200, or to imprisonment, with or without hard labour, for a term not exceeding six months.   This was altered at the committee stage so that an offender could be both fined and imprisoned.   In addition, it was provided that in the case of a second or subsequent conviction, the fine could be raised to 500, and the term of imprisonment increased to two years.   In the context of the sentencing powers granted to courts of summary juris-diction in other matters, the penalties allowed for under this act were draconian.   One Home Office official noted that 'for no other offence can they impose more than 6 months imprisonment - and in only three cases can they fine £100 - continuing offences excepted.   (HO45/Box 11252/File 432253-6)

Once the Home Office and Pharmaceutical Society had ironed out their differences, the bill had an easy passage through parliament.   In fact, it was so non-controversial that the problem was not that of overcoming opposition, but of raising the interest of a sufficient number of members to get the measure passed: 'After four postponements because of failure to get a quorum, Standing Committee C was constituted ... and disposed of the Dangerous Drugs Bill, amendments and all, in twenty minutes. (Pharamaceutical Journal, 31 July 1920, p.133)

A number of factors account for the lack of opposition.   First, those most likely to be affected by its provisions either agreed with its general aims or obtained satisfactory concessions. The medical profession was generally in favour of any measure that would restrict the availability of opiates and other poisons to the general public. Doctors had for many years inveighed against the laxity of controls governing their sale. Pharmacists, on the other hand, were forced to recognise that there was no possibility of returning to the pre-war situation. Since similar controls had been in force for some four years, they had either to argue that consumption of these substances, and easy access to supplies by the general public was desirable, or concentrate their efforts on ensuring that the controls that were introduced on a more permanent basis would encroach as little as possible on their interests in the trade. The former option was never really available. There were few, if any, who maintained that addiction to narcotics was something to be encouraged. The council of the Pharmaceutical Society therefore directed its efforts at minimizing the impact of the proposed measures on members of the profession.

Acquiescence was also facilitated by virtue of the fact that the Home Office could argue that the bill's provisions were dictated by stipulations of the Hague Convention. Thus, the Law Committee of the Parmaceutical Society of Ireland concluded that the bill arose out of certain international obligations, and that there was therefore little that could be done about the matter. (Pharmaceutical Journal, 1920, p.601) It was, in any event, exceedingly difficult to find anything tangible in the bill to which objections could be raised. With the exception of that part which dealt with prepared opium, no specific controls were spelt out in the bill itself. Precisely what impact the act would have on members of the medical and pharmaceutical professions, would only become known once the regulations were published. If these had been incorporated in the bill itself, it is certain that the Home Office would have encountered considerable difficulty in getting it passed.

THE BATTLE OVER THE REGULATIONS

The original Dangerous Drugs Regulations were published on 7 January 1921. They had been drawn up by the Home Office in consultation with the Ministry of Health. Whilst the observations of various interested bodies had been called for, including those of the General Medical Council and the Pharmaceutical Society, no deputations had been received, and no discussions took place between officials and representatives of these organisations. The regulations that aroused most opposition were those which imposed controls over the dispensing, prescribing and sale of morphine, cocaine, their salts, preparations, etc., that is, those made under Section 7 of the act. Pharmacists and doctors objected to the detailed records that it would henceforth be necessary to keep in connection with each transaction in these drugs. For instance, regulation 9 stipulated, inter alia, that every person who supplied any of these drugs should comply with the following provisions:

(a) He shall enter or cause to be entered in a book kept for the purpose all supplies of the drug purchased or otherwise obtained by him and all dealings in the drug effected by him (including sale to persons outside the United Kingdom) in the form and containing the particulars shown in the Schedule to these Regulations.

(b) Separate books shall be kept for (i) cocaine and ecgonine and substances containing them, (ii) morphine and substances containing it, (iii) diamorphine and substances containing it, (iv) medicinal opium ... (c) Where he carries on a business at more than one set of premises he shall keep a separate book or books in respect of each set of premises. (Pharmaceutical Journal, 1921, p.34)

Pharmacists took particular exception to regulation No.4. This provided that:

Except when the drugs are lawfully dispensed in pursuance of a prescription given by a duly qualified medical practitioner in accordance with the conditions hereinafter specified, no person shall supply or procure, or offer to supply or procure, the drugs to or for any person in the United Kingdom who is not licensed or otherwise authorised to be in possession of the drug, nor to any person so licensed or authorised, except in accordance with the terms and conditions of such licence or authority. (ibid)

Regulations 5 and 6 listed the requirements to be observed by medical practitioners when writing out prescriptions. In future they would have to date them, and mark them with the words 'not to be repeated', except in instances of prescriptions issued for National Health Insurance purposes on the forms provided by the Insurance Committee. Regulation 7 stipulated that no-one was to be in possession of these drugs unless:

(a) He is licensed to export or import the drug, or (b) He is licensed or otherwise authorised to manufacture or supply the drug, or (c) He is otherwise licensed by the Secretary of State or authorised by these Regulations or by any authority granted by the Secretary of State to be in possession of the drug, or (d) He proves that the drugs were supplied on and in accordance with such a prescription as aforesaid. (ibid)

Although both pharmacists and medical practitioners raised strong objections to the extra clerical work that would be entailed by these regulations, only in the case of doctors would this constitute a new departure. Persons authorised to keep open shop for the retail of poisons were already required to enter all transactions in such substances in a special book or register. Many in fact failed to comply with these requirements, and since neither the representatives of the Pharmaceutical Society nor the local and national authorities had powers entitling them to enter premises or inspect registers, or take samples, there had never been any means of ensuring that they were complied with. Subsection (g) of Regulation 9 now provided that any person supplying these drugs:

shall furnish to the Secretary of State or to any person authorised by any order of the Secretary of State for the purpose all information in regard to any purchases by him of the drugs, all stocks held by him of the drugs, and all transactions effected by him in the drugs as may be required by the Secretary of State for the purpose of seeing that the provisions of the Act are observed. (ibid)

The objections of chemists, druggists and pharmacists to these regulations most probably were not prompted by any extra clerical work their implementation would entail. Their primary concern was with the large number of proprietary preparations containing the drugs listed in Part III of the Dangerous Drugs Act whose sale had not previously been the object of any form of control. These would now only be available on medical prescription. The Pharmaceutical Journal listed 84 which would now come under the terms of the Act and Regulations. The extension of the Regulations over the commerce in these substances would have important financial repercussions on the retail trade in these remedies. They were extremely popular concoctions, and the financial returns of pharmacists from this trade were large. Moreover, as they were only to be made available on medical prescription, a significant proportion of this trade might be transferred from pharmacists to those medical practitioners who dispensed their own drugs.

It is impossible to determine with any degree of exactitude the amounts of opium and opium-based preparations that were actually consumed by the British population at any time prior to 1921. Until 1909 no government department or other body attempted to establish precisely how much opium or cocaine was imported. Data appertaining to the quantities of morphia manuactured in the United Kingdom only became available after the coming into force of the Dangerous Drugs Act. On the basis of reports published in the medical and pharmaceutical journals, the number of deaths attributed to poisoning from opium and other narcotic substances in the annual returns of the Registrar-General, and statements given in evidence before a number of parliamentary Select Committees, Lomax concluded that during the nineteenth century opiates were probably more extensively consumed in England than in any other European country:

> They were taken with, or without medical authorisation for major, minor, or even imaginary ailments, and sometimes exclusively for their euphoric effects. They were as readily available as aspirin today and just as cheap. For one penny a man could purchase a pint of beer and, for the same sum, a quarter of an ounce of laudanum, containing about ten grains of opium. (1973, p.167)

The reasons for consumption were varied. In all probability only an extremely small minority used them for purposes of `mere indulgence', or in order to experience `euphoric effects'. More frequently they were used as therapeutic agents, tranquillizers and prophylactics.

The Fenlanders of Lincolnshire, Cambridgeshire and Norfolk employed opium as a malarial antiperiodic in much the same way as it was used on the Indian subcontinent. In 1864 a writer noted in the British Medical Journal that there could be no denying the validity of statements made regularly by surgeons working in the marsh districts, that `there was not a labourer's house in which there was not a bottle of opiate to be seen and not a child who did not get it in some form. Immense quantities of opium are sent to those districts and the retail druggists often dispense as much as 200 pounds a year'. (pp.394-395)

Throughout the nineteenth century proprietary medicines containing opium were extensively used by mothers and nurses to sedate young infants. Appropriately advertised as `quieteners' or `soothing syrups', they were primarily used by mothers whose economic circumstances necessitated their leaving their younger children in the care of baby-minders whilst they went out to work. These minders were often extremely reluctant to accept into their care troublesome children and since the rates they charged at times varied with the docility of the infant, concoctions containing narcotics were used to pacify the unruly. (Engels 1969, p.135) Poverty was undoubtedly the most important factor underlying this practice. Lack of adequate food, the necessity for mothers of young children to seek employment outside the home, lack of adequate medical facilities and an inability to pay for those available, ignorance of the addictive properties of these concoctions, all contributed to making these preparations appear to be functional cure-alls. They suppressed appetite and pain, and made the task of caring for young children easier for all concerned. Few mothers could have known what dosage it was safe to administer. On occasion two concoctions containing opium were mixed together, or alcohol and opium were administered at the same time. There were, not surprisingly, regular reports in the medical and pharmaceutical press of infants who had died from overdoses of these substances. An instance reported in The Lancet in 1859 was probably not uncommon. In this case a mother had bought a penny-worth of opium from a druggist, mixed it with Spannish-Juice, a concoction containing alcohol and juniper berries. She then gave this admixture to her three children who were suffering from colds, with the result that the eldest died the next morning. (Vol.1, p.74)

This practice was by no means confined to the abodes of the poor. Domestic servants and nurses would frequently administer these preparations to their young charges to lessen their burden of work. The Edinburgh High Court of Justiciary sentenced a domestic servant in 1857 to eighteen months imprisonment after she pleaded guilty to culpable homicide, inasmuch as she had administered ten drops of laudanum to the infant son of her employer in order to induce sleep. (The Lancet, 1857, Vol.II, p.510) Those charged with the care of the young were not the only ones to invoke the assistance of the sleep inducing properties of opium in an attempt to ease their work load. In 1867 The Lancet reported that 'Three pounds weight of opium are ... among the "weekly requirements" of the dispenser at St. Pancras Workhouse ... for administration in the form of pills to get the "poor old people" to sleep'. (Vol.II, p.24)

Although the deaths of young infants from opium poisoning attracted a considerable amount of publicity at various times in the nineteenth century, the most prevalent use of opium was not for quietening children, but as a therapeutic agent. Its popularity stemmed from its analgesic properties, and is not difficult to comprehend given the lack of awareness amongst most consumers of its addictive properties, and the underdeveloped state of chemotheraphy:

> When we realise that the chief end of medicine up to the beginning of the last century, was to relieve pain, that therapeutic agents were directed at symptoms rather than cause, it is not difficult to understand the wide popularity of a drug which either singly or combined so eminently was suited to the needs of so many medical situations ... in one form or another it was unquestionably the chief therapeutic agent for over two thousand years. (Terry and Pellens, 1928, p.58)

By the end of the seventeenth century it was widely used in England amongst varied strata of the population. Particularly popular was the use of laudanum. Frequently the drug was initially taken to relieve pain attendant upon some illness. Clive of India started taking it to relieve a bowel infection, William Wilberforce to alleviate a digestive illness. Once the consumer had become addicted, it was self-administered over long periods of time. Wilberforce took it continually for forty-five years.

Criticism of the practice was unlikely so long as members of the medical profession were prescribing it for all and sundry, and proclaiming it as a cure for virtually every known ailment. In 1859 a Dr. Sibson claimed to have cured rheumatism by administering large doses of opium over varying periods of time to a number of his patients. (British Medical Journal, p.645) Dr. Cormer recommended its use as a cure for epilepsy. (The Lancet, 1859, Vol.1, p.75) Others maintained that it was efficacious in the treatment of pericarditis, pleurisy, diabetes and neuralgia. Dr. James Russell's enthusiasm for its use in the cure of mental disorders was boundless. In a clinical lecture on Opium: Its Use And Abuse, he claimed that its administration was indispensable for the treatment of mental disorders involving agitated states, depressions, lack of capacity to sleep, hallucinations and 'swings of mood'. He also maintained that it was suitable for the treatment of chronic alcoholism. The alcoholic displayed the same symptoms as the mental patient: lack of adequate nutrition, inability to sleep, nervous agitation, states of elation and depression, and hallucinatory tendencies. (British Medical Journal, 1860, Vol.I, pp.314-315) Most of these symptoms, of course, were likely to be exacerbated by the administration of opiates.

Most consumers of opiates who were taking them primarily for medical reasons, did not bother to consult a physician. They preferred to rely on information gleaned from friends and neighbours, the recommendations of the local druggist, or adverts proclaiming the virtues of patent medicines which appeared regularly in the popular press. The poor, as Engels noted, simply could not afford the services of doctors throughout most of the nineteenth century. (1969, p.134) Popular concoctions such as Darby's Carminative, Mother Winslow's Soothing Syrup, McMunn's Elixir, Mother Bailey's Quietening Syrup, Batley's Sedative Solution and Collis Brown, all contained opium and were downed in vast quantities.

The indiscriminate prescribing habits of drug vendors, and some doctors, was the subject of frequent criticism in the leading medical journals, particularly after 1880, by which time senior members of the profession had become cognisant of the addicting properties of the many preparations containing opiates on the market. In 1857 The Lancet noted that a very large proportion of the 15,000 drug vendors in England were in the habit of prescribing and administering medicines which often contained poisonous substances. In Manchester some druggists were reputably selling between 12 and 15 gallons of laudanum preparations weekly. Since they 'knew nothing' of the diseases for which they pretended to provide remedies, they were simply endangering the lives of the 'ignorant poor'. (Vol.II, pp.608-609) According to Hayter, the greatest demand 'was in the cotton-spinning districts of Lancashire, and there, as De Quincey was told by a local chemist, on a Saturday afternoon the counters of the druggists were strewn with pills of one, two or three grains, in preparation for the known demand of the evening ... Laudanum was cheaper than beer or gin, cheap enough for even the lowest paid worker'. (Quoted in Hayter, 1971, p.33)

There were literally hundreds of propriatary remedies on the market. Their contents were frequently unknown to druggist and doctor alike. The British Medical Association, in an attempt to expose the fraudulent claims of medicine vendors, subjected hundreds to laboratory analysis. Most were found to contain a mixture of therapeutically useless substances. The most common field of exploitation related to diseases which were widely prevalent and sufficiently grave to cause serious suffering and incapacity, 'inasmuch as such disorders lend themselves to sensational descriptions of the dire consequences which will follow if the one and only real and certain cure is not purchased'. (British Medical Association, 1909, vii) The authors of the report attributed the popularity of these remedies to the secrecy of their ingredients:

> To begin with, there is for the average man or woman a certain fascination in secrecy. The quack takes advantage of this foible of human nature to impress his customers. But the secrecy has other uses in his trade; it enables him to make use of cheap new or old fashioned drugs, and to proclaim that his product possesses virtues beyond the ken of the mere doctor; his herbs have been culled in some remote prairie in America or among the mountains of Central Africa, the secret of their virtues having been confided to him by some venerable chief; or again he would have us believe that his drug has been discovered by chemical research of alchemical profundity, and is produced by processes so costly and elaborate that it can only be sold at a very high price. (ibid, p.v)

Very few of the hundreds of remedies analysed actually contained opiates or cocaine, although some of the more popular cough remedies did. A few carried warnings that morphine was included amongst their ingredients, although the exact quantity was not specified. The advertisements for some others, such as Beecham's Cough Pills, declared that they contained no opiates despite the fact that laboratory analysis revealed that they did. (British Medical Association, 1909 and 1912)

If poverty, ignorance and lack of adequate medical facilities account for the bulk of the demand for opium-based preparations in nineteenth and early twentieth century Britain, the suppliers' prospects of lucrative pecuniary rewards, for very little capital outlay or ingenuity, were enhanced by the near complete absence of restraints on the internal commerce in these substances. In contrast with other European countries, such as France and Germany, pharamacists, manufacturers and quacks enjoyed almost complete freedom to narcotise the population. A barrister, in commenting upon the statutory regulation of the sale of poisons in Britain, noted that the law permitted anyone:

> to manufacture and put up for sale medicines for human use, and to label them with such fantastic virtues as a vivid imagination may suggest, provided only that if in the exuberance of his verbosity the proprietor claims ... that his preparation will cure disease or that he and he alone knows the secret of its composition, he is taxed to the extent of 12 1/2 per cent. of the value he puts upon his remedy, with the compensating advantage of receiving an official acknowledgement which to the illiterate seems to lend authority to audacity. For the retailing of stamped poisons a licence is required, but seeing that such can be obtained for 5s per annum, there is practically no restraint on the vending of them.

(The Lancet, 1911, Vol.II, p.933)

Although it is impossible to determine with precision the quantities of opium that were being consumed during the first decade and a half of the twentieth century, in either pure form or as ingredients in proprietary medicines, the massive imports of raw opium, the absence of effective restrictions on their sale in the United Kingdom, and the frequent reports in the press and in medical and pharmaceutical journals of deaths from accidental overdoses of preparations containing it, suggest that its use was considerable. It is primarily in this context that the opposition of pharmacists and their professional associations to the Regulations must be understood.

Opposition to the regulations amongst lower echelon members of the pharmaceutical and medical professions grew rapidly during the first six weeks subsequent to their publication. It soon became apparent that there were considerable differences of opinion between them and their representatives on the executive bodies of their professional organisations. The latter had, as the Home Secretary pointed out, raised few objections to the draft proposals which had been submitted to them for comment. (Hansard, 1921, Vol.138, c.1162) The British Medical Association was inundated with protests. The Executive of its Portsmouth Division informed the council of the association that the regulations would be impossible to carry out, and that their application would mean 'either that the practitioner will be bound to ignore them, or his patients will be deprived of valuable and anodyne drugs, and thereby their sufferings will go unalleviated'. (The Lancet, 1921, p.350) The Camberwell Division, having discussed the regulations insofar as they effected medical men, concluded that 'they are so impracticable that we must decline to carry them out'. (ibid, p.408) Similar resolutions were passed by other divisions up and down the country, and members of parliament were petitioned to secure satisfactory amendments.

The pharamacists also lost little time in making known their objections. On 19 January, the North British Branch of the Pharmaceutical Society passed a resolution demanding that the matter be reconsidered by the Home Office in consultation with the society. In their view:

> these Draft Regulations are an intolerable interference with the reasonable liberties of the people and involve needless and harassing details leading to unjustifiable expenditure ... they erroneously put emphasis on mere mechanical restrictions and records and medical prescriptions, totally ignoring the fact that the only real protection for the community in the handling and distribution of potent drugs is the training and experience and knowledge and sense of responsibility of the duly qualified pharmacist or dispensing chemist. (Pharmaceutical Journal, 1921, p.74)

This latter argument was much favoured, and regularly employed, whenever steps were afoot to tighten controls over the sale of poisons.

The British Dental Association, the Royal College of Surgeons, the Royal College of Veterinary Surgeons, and farmers' associations, entered the fray once their members gave vent to their misgivings. One livestock breeder complained in a letter to the Pharmaceutical Journal, that farmers:

> use preparations containing morphine very extensively as animal
> medicines. Under the new conditions the farmer may not purchase
> them from the chemist. The veterinary surgeon may `supply' but as
> the farmer cannot be `in possession of', except by the prescription
> of `a duly qualified medical practitioner', it follows that the
> supply by a vet is limited to what he personally administers.
> (1921, p.60)

Since veterinary surgeons frequently resided far away from their
clients, the implementation of these regulations would, in his view,
cause considerable difficulties, and probably loss of livestock, to many
farmers. All in all, thirty-one professional bodies raised objections
to one or more points in the original Regulations, including, in
addition to those already named, the Association of Unregistered
Practitioners, The Drug Club - an association of wholesale druggists -
and the Association of Animal Castrators. (The Lancet, 1921, p.1193)

The Pharmaceutical Society was the body primarily responsible for
galvanizing these disparate organisations for an all-out assault on the
Home Office. An editorial in its journal stressed that it was the
business `of every Local Association ... to back up the action taken by
the Society for reasonable amendment of the Draft Regulations, and this
can best be done by the Association making direct representations to the
Home Office and at the same time notifying the Secretary of the Society
that they have done so'. (Pharmaceutical Journal, 1921, p.48) The Home
Office was not the only government department exposed to the ire of many
disgruntled professionals. The Ministry of Health was the recipient of
many angry protests from panel committees all over the country. Early
in February the council of the Pharmaceutical Society decided to seek
support of other professional bodies in its crusade, `so that a joint
representation may be made to the Government for the withdrawal of the
present Draft, and the appointment of a committee to co-operate with the
Home Office in the framing of a new Draft'. (ibid, p.88)

By this time the press had taken note of the rising volume of
discontent. Durward Macleod took a jaundiced view of the way in which
the Home Office had handled the whole affair:

> Would you believe it? Every man, woman and child in this country
> today is either a dope fiend or heading that way. You may smile and
> say the idea is ridiculous. In that case, I simply refer you to the
> intellectual giants of the Home Office ... they have applied
> themselves to the congenial task of framing a brand new set of
> barbed-wire entanglements, not only around these nasty poisons in
> their most virulent forms, but around a plethora of harmless
> remedies in daily use ... These entanglements have been presented
> to the dazed and dumbfounded members of the medical profession and
> the pharmacists under the high-sounding, ominous, penal servitude
> sort of title of `The Dangerous Drugs Act' ... Well, we have had to
> stand for a lot of official buffoonery during the past few years,
> but this latest stunt, you will agree, is just about the limit ...
> Not a soul outside the Home Office wants them. (The Sunday Post,
> Glasgow, 6 February 1921)

The Times was no less critical. In a leading article it noted that the regulations could only have been framed by people who either did not know, or deliberately chose to disregard, the conditions surrounding the supply of dangerous drugs. The only conclusion that could be drawn from the handling of this matter, was that it was 'another typical illustration of the manner in which the present Administration seeks to do good by force. The weakness of this manner - as will be discovered - is its reckless disregard of instructed opinion and its reliance on public stupidity and indifference'. (10 February 1921)

In the Commons, Home Office politicians were coming under increasing pressure as well. On 17 February numerous questions were raised concerning this issue. Mr. Johnstone wanted to know whether the Home Secretary was aware that the regulations 'are causing dissatisfaction and alarm to registered pharmacists and dispensing chemists'. Mr. Tevelyan Thompson noted that the regulations 'are considered unworkable in their present form by those who will have to carry them out'. Lieut-Colonel W. Guiness expressed the view that they were 'unnecessarily irksome, totally impracticable, and likely to encourage the desire for dangerous drugs by notifying patients by means of a label whenever medicines containing morphine and other narcotics were being dispensed to them'. (Hansard, 1921, Vol.138, pp.251-256) The Under-Secretary of State for the Home Office, Sir John Baird, replied that whilst he was aware that the regulations were unpopular, and emphasised that his department would consider the objections that had been raised, stressed that they were drafted in accordance with the requirements of the Hague Convention and the Versailles Treaty. This, as I noted earlier, was not the case. The controls it was proposed to exercise went beyond what a literal interpretation of the convention required. Since clause (c) of Article 10, for instance, stipulated that as far as the keeping of records was concerned, this 'shall not apply necessarily to medical prescriptions and to sales made by duly authorised pharmacists', it could be maintained that the existing restrictions under the Pharmacy and Poisons Act met the specified requirements laid down by the convention. The fact that this and similar points were not made by those opposed to the Regulations at the time, suggests that few had bothered to read that document.

On 10 February, a memorial signed by the representatives of eighteen professional associations was presented to the Home Office. It requested that a joint deputation be received to discuss a redrafting of the regulations, and that a committee be set up to this end. The Permanent Secretary reported that:

the appointment of such a committee is not necessary, would cause much delay, and would not be likely to lead to any useful result. The interests of the matter dealt with by the Regulations are diverse ... the Secretary of State cannot agree that a solution of the difficulties caused by a conflict of interests is likely to be found by a joint committee, nor could he allow the Regulations ... be the subject of bargaining between conflicting interests. (Pharmaceutical Journal, 1921, p.172. Letter dated 25 February)

Home Office officials were probably correct in concluding that the various bodies which signed the memorial were only momentarily united by their hostility to the regulations. They therefore endeavoured to deal with each interest group separately, playing one off against the other, since a united onslaught by an impressive number of influential professional associations could only result in their having to eventually make substantial concessions. The separate organisations kept up the pressure. On 9 March, a meeting attended by more than one hundred and fifty members of parliament was briefed by their representatives on their objections to the existing draft. Woolcock was by then in a position to inform them that he had been advised that the Home Secretary would consent to the appointment of a small committee, composed of members of the House with medical expertise, and Home Office officials. This body would consider and advise on the ways in which the regulations could be re-drafted. The Times noted, with obvious satisfaction, that 'As everyone who knows anything about the subject expected, the Home Office has been forced to abandon its absurd attitude on the Dangerous Drugs Regulations. This is a signal victory over bureaucracy and its favourite method of legislation - by Orders in Council'. (14 March 1921)

The committee made few concessions, particularly to the pharmacists who had orchestrated the opposition. It rejected the argument that the provisions of the Pharmacy and Poisons Act were already sufficiently stringent to prevent the spread of addiction:

> It appears to us that the only legitimate use which members of the general public can have for these drugs is a medical one, and as a general rule, only a qualified medical practitioner can say whether they ought to be used in any particular case or not ... we have no hesitation in expressing the opinion that in view of the dangerous properties which these drugs possess, they should not be issued to members of the public except under medical direction ... That is the view which is strongly held by the British Medical Association itself. (Committee on the Draft Regulations, British Parliamentary Papers, 1921, Vol.X, p.22)

The committee was prepared, on the other hand, to recommend that certain preparations in common use, and which were unlikely to prove addictive, be exempted from this requirement. Seventeen were listed in Schedule II to the revised regulations, known as the Principal Regulations, which were published in May 1921. Other concessions were made concerning the keeping of records by doctors.

On the whole, the concessions wrung from the Home Office were few, and not particularly important in the context of the outcry that had been raised. Nevertheless, the sanctioning of the Home Office proposals by an official committee which included members of the medical profession, and at least considered the objections raised by various interested parties, satisfied both the doctors and the pharmacists. Few objections were raised to the revised regulations. Although the organised agitation had achieved little more than a clarification of the meaning of the original regulations, the conflict, and its mode of resolution, had some important long-term repercussions. The professional organisations had given an impressive demonstration of their influence, both inside and outside parliament. When subsequently additional regulation were under consideration, Home Office officials were somewhat more careful to ensure that adequate consultation with relevant interest groups preceded their publication. They also displayed a certain reluctance to proceed with policies which they had reason to believe did not enjoy widespread support amongst members of the medical profession. This was illustrated in the way in which Home Office and Ministry of

Health officials tackled the question of whether the Dangerous Drugs Regulations should be extended to cover the barbitone group of drugs, particularly veronal. It had frequently been used as a means of committing suicide. The proposal was under consideration for three years between 1923 and 1926. During this time extensive consultations with medical experts, toxicologists and the relevant professional associations took place. In addition, the Ministry conducted a survey of 291 medical practitioners. Its aim was to determine whether they considered that more stringent controls should be placed on the availability of these substances. Despite the fact that more than fifty per cent of those consulted were in favour of extending the regulations to cover them, Delevingne was of the opinion that 'there would clearly be some commotion if we persisted with the proposals' under the Dangerous Drugs Act. He suggested that the question be left to stand over until the publication of the report of the Committee on the Poisons and Pharmacy Acts, which he expected to be ready in early 1927, but which was in fact not published until 1930. (HO45/Box 15597/File 354321-55) Both doctors and pharmacists could count on the support of their professional colleagues who were members of the House of Commons when it became necessary to convince officials of the inadvisability of pursuing particular policies. When the Home Office published an Order in Council in 1922, the effect of which was to prohibit medical practitioners from prescribing dangerous drugs for their own personal use, a deputation of medical M.P.'s eventually met and persuaded the Home Secretary to announce that the regulation in question would be revoked. (HO45/Box 13351/File 423410-21)

The ability of representative organisations of the medical and pharmaceutical professions to bring considerable pressure to bear on government officials responsible for formulating drug control policies, had a profound effect on shaping official policy towards the question of drug addiction. When eventually the issue of what to do about persons addicted to narcotics arose, and required some form of authoritative answer, it was to medical and pharmacological experts that the matter was referred. This would not have been important had the views of Home Office officials and the 'experts' been identical on this issue. In fact they were radically different. Whereas the former expressed a preference for denying addicts supplies of those drugs to which they were addicted - a policy which was then being enforced in the United States - the latter favoured such access under certain conditions. It was the latter policy which was officially endorsed in 1926, following upon recommendations made to this effect by the Departmental Committee on Morphine and Heroin Addiction. One of the reasons why this particular policy was adopted, was that at the particular moment in time when Home Office officials became cognisant of the fact that the prescribing habits of some physicians appeared to conflict with the provisions of the Dangerous Drugs Acts and the Regulations, no one, other than members of the medical and pharmacological professions, appears to have been particularly concerned with the question of addicts or addiction. Since they had to take their views into consideration, because any decision taken would require their cooperation, they were in a strategically decisive political position to influence the outcome on this question.

The only other possible source of support that officials could reasonably hope to draw upon to counter-balance the weight of medical opinion in connection with drug control policies, was the press. Press coverage of cocaine and morphine consumption had played an important part in moving government officials to introduce regulations under the Defense of the Realm Act, during the war, and had neutralised to some extent possible opposition to the Dangerous Drugs Act in 1920. (cf.Stein, 1978) The press also played a decisive role in the circumstances that led to the passing of the Dangerous Drugs and Poisons (Amendment) Act of 1923. What was significant about the reports that appeared in the press throughout the period 1915-1926, was that there was never in them any discussion about the problem of addiction to these drugs. With monotonous regularity drug consumers were simply portrayed as involuntary victims of those trafficking in these substances. Since only members of the medical and pharmacological professions appeared to have had any clearly defined views on the problem of addiction, in contrast to that of the traffic, officials of the Home Office had no alternative but to acquiesce in their views given the influence they could bring to bear in the political and adminstrative arenas.

9 Theories of addiction

Despite the fact that the Hague Convention, the DORA regulations, and the Dangerous Drugs Acts 1920 and 1923 were aimed at curbing addiction to dangerous drugs, British officials who were involved in the negotiations preceding their enactment rarely directed attention to the question of whether anything should be done in respect of persons addicted to the substances whose availability was being controlled. On few occasions was this matter raised in official communications during the years 1906-22. There were a number of reasons for this. Until 1915-16 few officials, if any, were cognisant of the existence of a drug-abuse problem in Great Britain. The Shanghai and Hague conferences were directed primarily at evolving policies for curbing the spread of addiction in the Far East. European states were involved in these negotiations only because they were the main producers or suppliers of raw opium, prepared opium, or manufactured narcotics, or were in a position to influence policies adopted by the Chinese to tackle their own addiction problem. When, in 1916, it became apparent that narcotic drugs were being consumed in large quantities in Britain, and it was suspected that in London there was a thriving traffic in morphine, opium and cocaine, regulations relating to some of these drugs were introduced. These were directed at reducing the supply of these drugs. This was partly because addicts were viewed as unwillinng victims of unscrupulous dealers or 'dope pushers'. It was always taken as axiomatic, both by officials and the press, that no 'sane' person would intentionally become addicted to narcotics. It was generally accepted that individuals developed a reliance on these substances, either because they had unwittingly become dependent upon them as a consequence of repeated consumption of proprietary medicines in which they were included as ingredients, or because they had fallen prey to the wiles of dope peddlars.

After it had been decided to implement policies that would curb the spread of addiction, there were two basic approaches which could have been pursued. Either an attempt could be made to restrict the quantities of narcotics that were being produced and imported to amounts needed for 'medicinal and legitimate' purposes, thereby ensuring that none would be available for non-medical consumption; or, an attempt could be made to reduce demand by preventing people from become addicted in the first place, and by curing those that had already done so. In practice, to extinguish addiction both would have to be pursued simultaneously. Given the nature of addiction to narcotics and other substances, a reduction in the number of addicts was unlikely to be achieved if no obstacles were placed in the way of their obtaining supplies. Although a policy directed at restricting the quantities of drugs imported or produced might curb habituation to particular drugs, it would only curb addiction if the authorities could identify in advance all potentially addictive substances, and regulate the quantities coming on to the open market. These are pre-conditions that it is virtually impossible to fulfill, since the number of such substances is potentially infinite.

British drug policies during the years 1916–26 were primarily directed at tackling the problem by restricting the quantities of dangerous drugs available for non-medical use. The underlying assumption appears to have been that if the use of these substances could be confined to legitimate medical purposes, then drug abuse would necessarily be reduced or eradicated. Hence little attention was paid by officials to the question of whether some programme for treating those already addicted should be devised and implemented. Their view seems to have been that if addicts could not obtain supplies from illicit sources, the problem would solve itself. This was the policy that was implicit in the provisions of the International Opium Convention. Since its primary aim was to prevent the future spread of addiction it made no provision for dealing with those already addicted. Throughout the inter-war period the Advisory Committee on Traffic in Opium adopted a similar strategy. Its activities were directed solely at devising and implementing policies that would ensure that no drugs, over and above those quantities required for 'medical and legitimate' purposes, would be available for consumption. Their minutes indicate that during he years 1921–27 no discussions on the treatment of drug addiction took place. (League of Nations, Advisory Committee on Traffic in Opium, Minutes, 1921–1927). It is not surprising, therefore, that the Home Office lacked any policy on the treatment of narcotic addiction.

The problem was first brought to their attention by the police. In November 1922, the Home Office informed the Ministry of Health that:

A number of cases have come to light in which medical practitioners have obtained large quantities of drugs for their own use or have prescribed large quantities of the drugs for the use of their patients. The defence is generally set up in such cases that the doctor himself or his patient, as the case may be, had become a victim of the drug habit, and that the doctor was attempting to break it off by a treatment of gradually diminishing doses. Though this defence in many cases is clearly only a pretext, it is very difficult ... to secure the conviction of the practitioner on a charge that he is obtaining or assisting the patient to obtain the drugs for purposes other than legitimate

In their evidence to the Committee on Morphine and Heroin Addiction, they listed twenty-five such cases. Difficulties of securing convictions arose because Regulation 11, in pursuance of Section 7 of the Dangerous Drugs Act, stipulated that: 'Any duly qualified medical practitioner ... is hereby authorised so far as is necessary for the practice of his profession ... to be in possession and supply the drugs'. (British Parliamentary Papers 1921, Vol.X, p.242. Emphasis added) In the final analysis, whether this covered the prescribing of dangerous drugs to addicts, and under what conditions, depended upon the construction the courts placed on the words 'so far as is necessary for the practice of his profession'. Initially, the Home Office took the view that such cases were not covered by the regulations. Proceedings were therefore initiated against one doctor who was prescribing these drugs for himself. The stipendiary magistrate acquitted him, having accepted his explanation that he was curing himself by the method of gradual withdrawal. (HO45/ox 13351/File 423410-9)

In a letter to the Ministry of Health on the subject, the Home Office stressed that it 'was certainly not the intention when the Act and Regulations were passed to allow the drugs to be supplied to drug takers for the satisfaction of the craving which possesses them, and it is only in cases where there is something more than this that the prescription of the drugs by a doctor was meant to be authorised'. (MH58/275/File 95006/3/3) Since Home Office officials took this view, and had sought legal advice on the matter, it is reasonable to assume that they had been informed that the wording of the Regulations were such that the courts would fail to convict medical practitioners who prescribed narcotics for themselves or their patients. They therefore referred the question to the Ministry of Health, requesting their views as to the powers and duties of medical practitioners in such cases.

At the Ministry of Health, Dr E.W. Adams conducted an enquiry into the matter, the results of which he embodied in a memorandum on the Treatment of Addiction, which was later passed on to the Home Office. His interpretation of the intent underlying the drafting of the Dangerous Drugs Act and the Regulations was similar to theirs. Their aim was to suppress illicit dealings in the drugs of which they took cognisance, whilst placing no obstacle in the way of their use in the treatment, relief and cure of disease. In his view:

the mere satisfying of the craving of a drug addict without further object, whether this is attained by the provision of the drugs by the addict himself or through an intermediary, comes under the head of illicit dealing. That the intermediary is the habitue's own doctor makes no difference. If it did ... then the Act could only be regarded as a measure designed to enable the addict to obtain his drugs legally and easily which is absurd. (ibid)

At the same time, Adams considered that under certain conditions it would be legitimate for doctors to prescribe these drugs to addicts. He noted that medical opinion was unanimous in regarding drug addiction as a disease, a 'pathological state' that required urgent treatment and relief. Since it was widely accepted that in its treatment it was necessary to reduce dependence gradually, he concluded that it was just as legitimate for doctors to employ these drugs in the treatment of addiction as it was for them to prescribe them for the relief of any other disease. The duties of the physician, he argued:

> are concerned with treatment, cure and relief of disease and his actions must be governed by these considerations. He is not a purveyor of drugs, and must obey, in letter and spirit the law of the land. When therefore a drug addict comes to him, it is his duty to act on the assumption that the addict comes to him for treatment, and he must make it clear to the addict that he accepts him on that basis ... if the habitue desires treatment as a sick person for the relief of his pathological condition, the physician must be allowed to use his discretion in the matter of the dose of the drug to be employed, the length of time it is to be given, and other details. (ibid)

Although of the opinion that doctors should under these circumstances be allowed to prescribe narcotics to addicts, it is clear that he did not envisage that they would be kept on a permanent maintenance regime. Narcotics would only be administered as part and parcel of a programme directed to a gradual weaning of the addict from his dependence. His recommendations were based on an appraisal of the available literature on the subject, particularly American. From his review he concluded that the cure of addiction by abruptly ceasing the administration of narcotics was only advocated in those cases in which the addict could be properly cared for in an institution: 'Sudden withdrawal means institutional treatment. I have not come across any reasonable U.S.A. authority who maintains that such a method is practicable when applied to the treatment of an addict by his private doctor'. (ibid) Moreover, opinion was divided as to its suitability in medical institutions. He noted that there was a distinct cleavage between official and non-official American medical opinion. Medical officers employed by state and federal authorities tended to favour the method of sudden withdrawal, whereas practitioners in private practice preferred a treatment regime based on the diminishing doses method.

Adams stressed that there were important differences between the American and British situations as far as the provision made for institutional treatment were concerned. These would have to be borne in mind when devising a programme for the treatment of addiction, since they placed constraints on the choice of methods that could be resorted to. The institutional reservoir in the United States was 'immense' contrasted with the dearth of such facilities in Britain:

> Many thousands of cases of drug addiction appear to be treated there in Hospitals and Institutions and considerable bed space for this class of case is available. Here, however, no general hospital, I think, takes cases or would take cases of drug addiction qua addiction; there are few private Institutions which deal with the treatment of the narcotic diseases; and these are only available for people of ample or at least moderate means. Therefore even could it be shown that the method of abrupt withdrawal were the best, or even the only proper treatment for drug addiction, yet this method, depending as it does upon Institutional space, would be ruled out so far as we are concerned. And that it is the best method is far from proved. (ibid)

Delevingne was satisfied that the arguments advanced by Adams provided an adequate rationale for treating narcotic addiction by the method of diminishing doses. Nevertheless, he considered it desirable to obtain an authoritative statement, either from the Ministry of Health or the Royal College of Physicians, which could be published and used in the course of departmental contacts with doctors, as well as by the courts. This was necessary in order to make it clear that 'regular prescriptions of the drugs on the ground that without them the patient will suffer or even collapse, without any attempt to treat the patient for the purpose of breaking off the habit, is not legitimate, and cannot be regarded as medical practice'. (ibid) He felt that guidelines should be drawn up for doctors which would lay down general principles for effecting the cure of addicts by the method of gradual withdrawal. In March 1923, the Secretary of the British Medical Association had informed him that they were receiving enquiries from practitioners as to what they should do in such cases. Delevingne suggested to Dr. Macleary of the Ministry of Health that in these circumstances 'an authoritative announcement by a responsible body ... would be welcomed by the profession'. (ibid) It is clear that Delevingne was primarily concerned to place strict limits on the prescribing habits of doctors. He was not particularly concerned about the need to establish a treatment programme to cure addiction. He had a number of meetings with Macleary in which this subject was discussed, and hoped that 'the sudden withdrawal of the drug ... might become the recognised treatment of drug addiction in this country'. (ibid, Memo from Macleary to Smith-Whittaker, 13 March 1923) Macleary felt that it would be extremely difficult to lay down precise guidelines which could be used in order to delineate legitimate from illegitimate withdrawal therapies.

After further consultations between Delevingne and officials of the Ministry of Health it was decided the matter could best be resolved by referral to a committee, whose members would be drawn from the ranks of the medical and allied professions, and which would be appointed by the Ministry of Health. It was agreed that it would be asked to consider and advise:

> as to the circumstances, if any, in which the administration of morphine to persons suffering from morphine addiction may be regarded as medically advisable, and as to the precautions which it is desirable that medical practitioners so prescribing morphine should adopt for the avoidance of abuse, and to suggest any administrative measures that seem expedient to securing the observance of such precautions. (ibid, Smith-Whitaker to Delevingne, 14 May 1924)

Whilst concurring in the proposed terms of reference, Delevingne suggested that they be widened to include preparations containing morphine, and heroin as well. This was agreed. Later, at the committee's behest, the terms were further added to, in order to enable it to consider:

> whether it is expedient that any or all preparations which contain morphine or heroin of a percentage lower than that specified in the Dangerous Drugs Acts should be brought within the provisions of the Acts and Regulations and, if so, under what conditions. (ibid, Minute dated 2 February 1925)

This was proposed because a number of cases had been brought to their attention, of patients who had become addicted to preparations containing narcotics whose sale and use were not subject to the provisions of the Dangerous Drugs Acts or the Regulations.

The terms of reference required the committee to enquire first into the circumstances, if any, in which the administration of these drugs to those addicted to their use was medically advisable. This left open the question of whether addiction to these substances was a medical, or some other sort of problem. If the latter was the case, then non-medical intervention and programmes might be justified. However, as the matter was referred to a committee composed entirely of medical and pharmacological experts, it was inevitable that they would approach this issue from a medico-therapeutic perspective. The referral of this question to such a committee virtually amounted to official recognition of the fact that drug addiction was, first and foremost, a 'medical problem'. At the very least it implied that it was up to members of the profession to establish what type of problem it was. In fact, the committee did not devote much time to consideration of this question. The questionnaire used to elicit information from witnesses appearing before it, included none relating to the determination of whether narcotic addiction was a 'disease'. In the final report it was simply noted that:

> there was general agreement that in most well-established cases the condition must be regarded as a manifestation of disease and not as a mere form of vicious indulgence ... the drug is taken in such cases not for the purposes of obtaining positive pleasure, but in order to relieve a morbid and overpowering craving. (Departmental Committee on Morphine and Heroin Addiction, p.11. Hereafter referred to as Addiction Report)

MEDICAL VIEWS ON DRUG ADDICTION

By 1924, when the committee first met, it had long since been accepted as axiomatic by all leading medical and pharmacological experts on drug addiction, that the phenomenon was a 'disease'. It was, however, no ordinary disease. In order to establish what type of infirmity doctors considered it to be, it is useful to employ the distinctions drawn between alternative medical approaches to the conceptualising of diseases advanced by Sir Henry Cohen, a former President of the Royal Society of Medicine. He argues that throughout the course of the development of medicine, physicians have employed the concept of disease in one of two ways:

> These are (i) diseases as a distinct entity; when a healthy man A falls ill he becomes A plus B, where B is a 'disease'. This view maintained that there are innumerable Bs, each with individual and recognisable characters. And (ii) disease as a deviation from the normal; a healthy man A, through the influence of any number of factors (X_1, X_2, X_3 ... X_n) - physical or mental - is changed and suffers; he is diseased (A). (1955, pp.155-156)

As a rule most medical textbooks are still dominated by that approach which regards disease as a 'clinical entity', wherein the symptoms typically associated with such phenomena as typhoid fever, diptheria, jaundice, etc., are listed and described. This applied, at least,

144

during the period currently under consideration, that is 1870-1930, to etiological explanations of physiological and anatomical pathogenicity. On the other hand, the conceptualising of disease as a deviation from the normal, was employed most extensively by those working in the field of psychological medicine.

Causal explanations of addiction, to whatever substance, posed certain problems, since the presenting symptoms and characteristics of patients appeared to require the simultaneous invocation of both these conceptions. It was widely recognised that addiction was generated by both physical and psychological variables. There was virtually unanimous agreement that the repeated self-administration of certain substances, such as alcohol, opiate-narcotics and, to a lesser extent, cocaine, brought about certain anatomical and psychological changes in the structure of the human organism. These changes manifested themselves in the appearance of a clearly recognisable set of symptoms if consumption of the drugs was discontinued. Edward Levinstein, an eminent German expert on narcotic addiction who was one of the first to investigate systematically this aspect of habituation, concluded that every person, 'whether of a strong or weak constitution, has a tendency towards a morbid craving for morphia, if from any disease he has become accustomed to injections of morphia, providing these injections were under his control'. (1878, p.7) He was virtually unique amongst experts on addiction at the time in that his conclusions were based on findings arising out of experiments conducted on animals and patients. These indicated that physical dependence upon morphine could be established in both following the repeated self-administration of the drug. Up until the late nineteen-twenties his conclusions were rarely challenged. The large number of narcotic addiction cases which appeared to be iatrogenic in origin lent credence to his hypothesis. Most physicians and pharmacologists who laid claim to expertise in this field were agreed that a significant proportion of all those addicted to these drugs had contracted the habit as a result of taking drugs for the relief of pain, or the treatment of disease. (e.g. Dixon 1925, pp.108-109) By the nineteen-twenties there was universal agreement amongst British experts that there was a physical basis to addiction, that repeated administration of these drugs produced changes in the structure and/or fuction of the human organism, and that, consequently, the alleviation of this condition fell within the orbit of medical therapeutics.

Physicians were aware, however, that there was another side to addiction. Physiological dependence on its own could not account for certain organic, etiological and therapeutic phenomena associated with this syndrome. First, narcotic addiction varied in one important respect from chronic alcoholism, alongside which it was most frequently classified. Dr. Norman Kerr, a leading expert on addiction, and founder of the Society for the Study and Cure of Inebriety (SSCI), noted in one of the more important medical texts of the time, that:

> Morphinism and opiumism present characteristics somewhat different from alcoholism, though morphine, opium and alcohol have the common property of establishing a hold on the organism, especially on the nervous system ... The pathology of opium presents differences from that of alcohol. In chronic alcoholism the post-mortem appearances are significant of profound and widespread pathological inflammatory changes, of structure-destruction, tissue degradation, and

connective-tissue proliferation. In chronic opiumism usually the textural destruction and tissue inflammatory degenerations are practically absent, while the disproportionate fibrous-tissue redundancy is comparatively slight. (In Steadman (ed) 1895, Vol.III, pp.70-72. Emphasis in original.)

Secondly, the fact that addiction was largely self-induced, excepting those cases arising from the prescribing practices of physicians, appeared to differentiate it from medical phenomena which were caused by external agents, such as polio mellitus, or those of idiopathic origin that were physical rather than psychological, such as diabetes mellitus. This was a point that was frequently expressed by Sir William Collins, who noted in one instance, that:

When we are dealing with agencies which abrogate consciousness and subordinate conscience to appetite, we are outside the range of histology, of physiological physics, or even of bio-chemistry ... It is all very well to assert ... that inebriety is a disease. A disease it may be called, but a disease of the will ... and assuredly a disease in which the individual possessed has in many instances a most essential co-operative influence in his own worsenment or betterment. (1916, pp.41-42. Emphasis in original.)

Finally, despite the ease with which it was possible to eliminate the patient's physiological dependence upon narcotics, many physicians considered that their long-term prognosis was poor. Dr. Harry Campbell, one time president of the SSCI, and editor of the Medical Press and Circular, distinguished between three categories of addict; those belonging to the 'distinctly degenerate class', who although they might be weaned temporarily were almost certain to relapse; addicts of many years standing in whose case it was, for medical reasons, unwise to withdraw the drug completely; and those whose addiction was of recent origin and who belonged to the 'stable type'. Only with respect to the latter did he consider that there was any hope of a permament cure. (1923, p.153) Since most experts took the view that addicts of the 'stable type' were few and far between, if they existed at all, most inclined towards acceptance of the position advanced by Levinstein, namely, that whilst 'the prognosis is favourable with regard to abstinence' it was 'dubious with respect to the relapses'. (op. cit., p.109)

There were, therefore, a number of known phenomena associated with addiction to narcotics which indicated that it was not simply a 'pathological entity like malaria or syphilis, and curable by agents like quinine, atoxyl or mercury, acting on a materies morbi'. Instead, it appeared to be a 'general pathological disturbance caused by the withdrawal of an accustomed stimulant which effects all functions of the body', including the functioning of the mind. (Jennings 1909(a), p.29) The recognition of the part played in its etiology by psychological variables, particularly in relation to the onset of the disease, and the relapse of patients who had been relieved of the physical concomitants of narcotic withdrawal, had the effect of directing attention of physicians away from the purely physiological facets of the syndrome. By the nineteen-twenties this aspect of the disease featured as a relatively unimportant variable in most causal explanations of narcotic addiction. This shift in emphasis can be gauged from changes in both the titles and contents of the writings of Oscar Jennings, one of the most prominent and frequently quoted experts on the subject. In 1890 he wrote a short book under the title On the Cure of the Morphia Habit Without Suffering. This was expanded and published in a second edition in 1901. He argued there that:

> The most important factors of the craving ... being heart depression, hyperacidity, and nervous irritability, the relief of either of these conditions may be sufficient help to enable a patient who might otherwise be unsuccessful, to get well; but there will be a much better chance of recovery without suffering by the application simultaneously of the means that remedy each of these conditions, and so prevent or alleviate the craving in all its factors. (p.5)

He recommended the administration of heart tonics to relieve heart depression or sluggishness, bicarbonate of soda to relieve hyperacidity of the stomach and the organism generally, and hot-air baths to reduce the 'moderate restlessness which occurs when patients are properly treated', on the grounds that the 'subsequent massage and cold douche form the most perfect sedative that a morphia patient can be allowed'. (ibid, p.73) Although in his earlier work he did stress that 'the best safeguard against relapse is really re-education of the will effected by gradual progresion', he did not devote much space to dealing with this facet of therapy. He implied that gradual withdrawal of the drug would help to achieve this.

By 1909 the title had been changed to The Morphia Habit and its Voluntary Renunciation. Although in it he covered much the same ground as in his earlier works, he now stressed that he was:

> more than ever convinced that the morphia habit, which is a psychosomatic affection, and in which the mental and physical troubles are interdependent, conditioned the one by the other, the success of therapeutic measures, properly so called, depends on the mentality of the patient, and reciprocally. (1909(a), p.2)

To emphasise the importance of the psychological side of addiction, he published in the same year a small pamphlet entitled The Re-Education of Self Control in the Treatment of the Morphia Habit. (1909(b)) Therein he concentrated solely on discussing this aspect of the question.

There were others who had from the outset paid greater attention to the psychological concomitants of the addiction syndrome. Amongst them Kerr was probably the most prominent and influential. The differences between Kerr's approach, and that of Levinstein are traceable in part to the fact that the mentalists and physicalists approached the problem from different points of origin, and employed radically different conceptual frameworks in attempting to account for the phenomenon. Jennings and Levinstein, although fully alive to the fact that the physical accompaniments of morphine addiction bore a certain surface resemblance to those associated with acute or chronic intoxications that attended consumption of other substances, such as alcohol, lead and arsenic, tended to regard the morphine-addiction syndrome as a distict clinical entity. Accordingly, they tended to emmphasise the differences between it and other forms of intoxication, rather than stress their similarities. Levinstein noted that on the basis of the state of excitement caused by the administration of morphia, 'we might easily be induced to classify the morrbid carving for (it) among the mental diseases following intoxication, such as chronic intoxication with alcohol, lead, arsenic and oxcide of carbon'. He stresed, however, that 'the latter are caused by changes functional derangements; furthermore, mental disorders due to intoxication with (the latter) last for months and years at a time; those from morphia disapearing again in a few hours'. (1878, p.7) Recognition of differences between morphia and other types of craving, is what led Jennings to apply special therapeutic techniques evolved specifically for its alleviation. In his view a therapeutically efficacious withdrawal regime had to be based on awareness of those physiological phenomena which were morphia-specific. As both Levinstein and Jennings regarded morphia addiction as having a natural history of its own, in the sense that its onset followed a regular course and the symptoms that appeared following withdrawal of the drug formed a medically specific and recognisable syndrome, they had no difficulty in classifying it as a disease. The theory of disease which they employed in arriving at this conclusion was that which views diseases as distinct clinical entities. In this they differed from Kerr, and many other experts.

Kerr approached the question from the perspective of the temperance reformer. The son of a merchant, he graduated from the University of Glasgow M.D. and C.M. in 1861. Whilst a student he developed an intense interest in the problem of alcohol addiction, and was instrumental in establishing there a total abstinence society. For the rest of his life he devoted most of his energies to the cause of temperance reform and the study and cure of inebriety. Since he was a 'ready speaker', his services on the platform 'were in constant requisition in all parts of the country'. (Winskill 1892, Vol.4, p.4) More of a medical politician and polemicist than a scientific investigator, much of his time was taken up with attempts to convince legislators of the desirability of introducing measures which would secure the compulsory incarceration and treatment of inebriates. For many years he was a member and chairman of the Inebriates Legislation Committee of the British Medical Association, and in 1876 he joined with a group of doctors and an interested lawyer, in founding the Society for Promoting Legislation for the Control and Cure of Habitual Drunkards (SPCLD), of which he was elected president. (MacCleod 1967, p.224) This organisation, along with the support of the British Medical Association, was instrumental in securing the passing of the Habitual Drunkards Act in 1878. In 1884 the name of the society was changed to that of the Society for the Study and Cure of Inebriety (SSCI).

Although Kerr's interest in the problem of narcotic addiction was entirely secondary to his dedication to the cause of temperance reform, and the diminution of the drink problem, his contribution to the debate on its etiology was important and lasting. It lay primarily in equating the two phenomena. He subsumed both under the term narcomania. In his Inebriety and Narcomania, he elaborated on the relationship between the two:

> let me define inebriety as a constitutional disease of the nervous system, characterised by a very strong morbid impulse to, or crave for intoxication. The morbid impulse and the crave of inebriety are not for inebriating agents for their own sake, but for the temporary relief of the inebriate nervine agony afforded by them ... I propose to call this abnormal state, especially in its marked

maniacal forms, by the comprehensive name - Narcomania. In other words, a mania for narcotism of any kind, an inexpressibly intense involuntary morbid crave for the temporary relief promised by every form of narcotic. (1894, p.42)

Although he accepted that inebriates could be classified with reference to the intoxicating agent, and that its nature could assume a variety of forms, varying with the 'disorder of which has been the exciting cause', and the differing 'circumstances of traumatism or disease which may have induced the affection', he took it as axiomatic that the factors implicated in all forms of narcomania were identical. (ibid, p.70) Despite the fact that he introduced the term narcomania in order to stress that the 'morbid crave' for alcohol was only one variant thereof, he constantly used the terms inebriety and narcomania as though they were interchangeable. His supporting evidence, moreover, was culled from examples of alcoholism, which he was not always careful to distinguish from drunkenness. Consequently, alcoholism was equated with other variants of addiction by definitional fiat.

This had certain advantages. It enabled physicians and reformers alike, to apply etiological theories evolved to explain a widespread and much discussed eighteenth and nineteenth century 'social problem', to phenomena which were not nearly as prevalent, and for which there were few elaborate explanations. Furthermore, since Kerr, along with many others, considered alcoholism to be a type of mental dysfunction, a variant of insanity, morphia addiction could be explained in accordance with the basic principles worked out by physicians specialising in the rapidly growing field of mental science. This had already occurred with respect to alcoholism, partly due to the indefatigable efforts of Kerr. By 1923, the view of Dr. Crichton Miller, Hon. Director of the Tavistock Clinic for Functional Nerve Cases, that the morphia addict was 'merely the psycho-neurotic who has lighted upon a chemical solution of his problem', was accepted as commonplace. (1923, p.164)

There were a number of factors which facilitated the simultaneous consideration of alcohol and morphine intoxication in the context of a common conceptual framework. For most of the nineteenth century alcoholism had been viewed as a vice rather than a disease. Kerr and those who joined with him in forming the SPCLD were convinced that it was a disease. They set out to enlighten the general public and the political establishment on this question. Their aim was to secure the passage of legislation which they considered necessary to ensure that treatment facilities would be provided for those afflicted with this malady. At the annual meeting of the British Medical Association in 1875, Lyon Playfair 'advised that no legislation was possible until Parliament and by implication the electorate was educated about the pathological character of alcoholism ... It was too easy to view alcoholism simply as immoral excess, its cure, simple moral restraint, and its expense, a personal responsibility'. (MacCleod 1967, p.223) Even by the mid-twenties, the educational process had by no means been completed, partly because the factors that campaigners singled out as being implicated in the causation of alcoholism made it extremely difficult for lay persons to decide whether it was a vice or disease. The Habitual Drunkards Act 1878, and the Habitual Drunkards (Amendment) Act 1888, which, amongst other things, altered the official designation of the 'habitual drunkard' to that of 'inebriate', in accordance with Kerr's views, were not particularly successful in securing either the cure of inebriety, or the widespread acceptance of the assertion that alcoholism could be classified as a physical infirmity, alongside more familiar maladies such as cholera and typhoid. Dr. Stanford Park, Medical Superintendant of the Bay Mount Sanatorium for Alcoholism, Drug Habit and Neurasthenia, still felt in 1923 that 'the fact that the public look upon inebriety as a vice and not a disease is one of the chief obstacles to the prevention and arrest of inebriety'. (p.159) The grouping of alcoholism with intoxications arising from lead, arsenic, ether, chloral, cocaine and opiates, can be interpreted as an attempt to justify the categorising of alcoholism as a disease by equating it with intoxications which were already regarded as such. Apparently, no-one suggested at the time that lead, arsenic or ether intoxications originated in morbid cravings for these substances. They apparently, were already viewed as medical rather than moral problems. The case of opiates is somewhat more difficult. When indulged in by denizens of the underworld, or persons of Chinese extraction, it was undoubtedly viewed as a vice. These categories of consumer, however, were considered to account for only a small proportion of those addicted to narcotics. The consensus of opinion was that most habituation to these substances arose out of the reckless prescribing activities of physicians, the laxity of the pharmacy laws, or, much later, the unscrupulous activities of dope pushers. As far as this latter group was concerned, their addiction was regarded as a medical problem. Even Billie Carleton was viewed in this light, despite the fact that it was clear that her consumption had been motivated by the desire for pleasurable self-indulgence.

Another factor that facilitated the equating of addiction to opiates with alcoholism was the close links which existed between participants in the anti-opium and temperance movements. Many members on the executive committees of the Christian Union and the Anglo-Oriental Society were also closely involved with promoting the cause of temperance. It was probably because of these close ties that the problem of addiction was brought to the attention of physicians who, like Kerr, were primarily interested in the problems of habitual drunkenness and alcoholism. Certainly, a large number of medical practitioners participated in the agitation against the Indo-China opium trade. In 1882, those attending the quarterly meeting of the British Medical Temperance Association, unanimously endorsed a resolution condemning the use of opium as 'most injurious to health and happiness'. (Knowledge 1882, Vol.2, p.249) Ten years later, more than 5,000 medical practitioners signed a declaration calling upon the government of India to prohibit the growth of the poppy, and the manufacture and sale of opium, except as required for medicinal purposes. (Friend of China 1892, Vol.XIII, p.11) The close ties between the participants in the two movements had significant repercussions on the ways in which physicians came to regard the problem of addiction to morphine and allied drugs. It also had a bearing on the content of theories advanced to explain the genesis of this phenomenon. This was so because it was mainly those members of the medical profession favouring temperance who evolved etiological theories of inebriety. These were subsequently held to account for narcotic addictions as well.

According to Harrison, the influence of the various temperance organisations in England, particularly that of the United Kingdom Alliance, was so great that there were few physicians who attempted to study the phenomenon from a scientific point of view:

The rich resources of the Alliance were spent on propagating ideal solutions, not on investigating existing reality ... The Alliance sponsored only the type of research which seemed likely to confirm its preconceptions, and which would produce statistics to shock politicians and the public into following its advice ... the temperance and prohibitionist movements had so advertised the <u>moral</u> dimensions of the problem that its scientific aspects could only be effectively studied on the continent. (1971, p.371. Emphasis in original.)

In consequence, no British physician developed a theory of alcoholism which systematically distinguished between variants of the disease on the basis of clinical symptoms. Such a step was essential if theories of addiction, to whatever substance, were to progress beyond the confused and haphazard stringing together of unsubstantiated assertions. Frequently these only amounted to the shielding of moral judgements behind a thinly veiled cloak of pseudo-scientific rhetoric.

The Swedish physician Magnus Huss, whose <u>Chronische Alkohols Krankeitoder Alcoholismus chronicus</u> first appeared in 1851, and which Bynum describes as probably the most important work on alcoholism until the twentieth century, gave the disease a strictly clinical definition based on symptoms referable to the nervous system. He separated the case-histories he reviewed into three large categories:

those in which somatic complaints predominate, those in which psychiatric complaints dominate, and those in which both are important ... He found six forms of alcoholism in which the chief complaints were somatic ... Psychiatric cases included mania, dementia, and hallucinations of sight, hearing, smell, taste and feeling. (Bynum 1968, p.182)

The precise details are not important in the present context. What is, is that no such systematic treatment of the subject can be found in the writings of those who in England were regarded as the leading experts on addiction. Many of these stood at or near the pinnacle of the medical establishment. Physicians of the calibre of Sir Humphrey Rolleston, Sir T.C. Allbutt, Sir William Collins and Dr. Norman Kerr. Pharmacologists of the stature of W.E. Dixon and Sir William Willcox.

Lammer, in drawing a distinction between <u>scientific conceptions</u> and <u>lay images</u>, notes that:

The more or less deliberate 'construction' and 'application' of ideas about any kind of reality with the aid of systematic 'methods of investigation' distinguish the scientific from the lay approach, and therefore constitute the main difference between views of reality among scientific and non-scientific groups. (1974, p.125)

The approach adopted by British experts to questions concerning the etiology of addiction was not scientific in the above sense. They established images of alcoholism widely held amongst temperance advocates and eugenicists, clothed them in the rhetoric of science, and disseminated them in texts which were primarily read by members of the medical profession. In this way, lay images were, for all practical purposes, converted into scientific conceptions simply by altering the context in which they were formulated and presented. Despite the fact that they rarely, if ever, employed systematic 'methods of investigation', their views were regarded as 'scientific' and incorporated in some of the more important texts of the time. They differed from Huss, not only in refraining from approaching the subject systematically, but also by employing a different theory of disease. Whereas Huss approached the study of chronic alcoholism by relying on a theory of disease which conceived of it as a distinct clinical entity, British experts considered chronic intoxicatins to be diseases in the sense that they constituted deviations from the normal.

Their adoption of this conceptual framework was dictated in large measure by the emphasis which they placed on the psychological components of addiction. The Departmental Committee Appointed to Inquire into the Question of the Law Relating to Inebriates and their Detention in Reformatories and Retreats, noted in its report that:

> There is no general consensus on the nature of inebriety. Some regard it as an exaggeration of ordinary self-indulgent drunkeness, and, therefore a vice, which should be dealt with by punishment alone. Others consider it a disease allied to insanity to be treated by medical measures, and not by punishment. The two views are irreconcilable. (British Parliamentary Papers 1908, Vol.XII, p.822)

Although many physicians did not actually advocate the control of inebriety by punitive measures, most of the leading experts regarded it as both a disease and vice. The committee was mistaken in implying that these conflicting approaches to the question were held by different groups of people. Kerr made it quite clear that drunkenness was 'at once a moral and a physical evil'. (1894, p.329) Whilst insisting that inebriety was as much a disease as typhoid or cholera, he continually stressed that it was essential to reassert the patient's moral control if a cure was to be effected:

> It is of the highest importance ... that firmness and perseverance in the paths of rectitude be sedulously cultivated ... In the invigoration of the control the resources of pharmacy play a secondary part ... Everything which can contribute to the improvement of the soul and the spirit, as well as the reparation of the tissue has its place in the medical armamentarium. (1894, p.374)

The conflict between the two approaches, although never really resolved, was bridged by physiological theories of mental functioning. Particularly important in this respect were the views of the influential psychiatrist Henry Maudsley, upon whose work Kerr relied heavily. Maudsley maintained that:

> The social development of distinctly human attributes like morality, virtue, and taste have a definite physical correlate in the structure of the brain: the longer, more numerous and complex cerebral convolutions which distinguish the brain of a civilised person from that of a savage correspond with the capacities for the exalted idea of justice, virtue, mercy, love, which the savage has not and cannot have ... Exposure to the correct moral environment for a long enough period of time produces the proper physical changes in the brain which makes it susceptible to the higher

virtues and become the innate endowment of the offspring.   (quoted
in Pruitt 1974, p.95; cf. Kerr 1894, p.228)

The view that variations in mental characteristics and moral virtues
were a function of anatomical and/or physiological differences in the
structure of the nervous system, was accepted as axiomatic by nearly all
British experts on addiction during the first quarter of the twentieth
century. Its appeal was partly related to the fact that it could easily
be fused with the widely held belief that chronic intoxications were a
product of cogenital defects. As Pruitt has noted, 'In the broader
context of contemporary biomedical theories, approaches to the problem
of alcoholism reflect nineteenth century notions of hereditary and
transmission of disease'. (p.93) This is evident in Sir Humphrey
Rolleston's discussion of alcoholism in the influential A System of
Medicine, jointly edited by himself and Sir T.C. Allbutt. Therein he
distinguished between disposing and exciting causes. The former:

> include the factors which are inherent in the individual himself,
> such as special idiosyncracy or susceptibility to alcohol due to
> hereditary causes, and also any acquired susceptibility such as may
> result from sun-stroke or injuries to the head. Hereditary taint
> may be traced in a very large proportion of alcoholic cases - it is
> said in nearly a moiety ... The influence of hereditary,
> therefore, consists in an unstable condition of the nervous system,
> which may be due either to drunkenness or to disorder of the nervous
> system in the parents. Thus drunkards beget 'neuropaths' or
> 'degenerates' and neuropaths again may have drunken offspring.
> (1910, Vol.2, pp.909-910)

T.D. Crothers identified similar processes at work in the case of
persons addicted to morphine. It was, he stated:

> a well-recognised fact that the transmission of the defects of the
> parents, in predispositions to the children, is a very active cause
> of nearly all functional and organic diseases of the nervous system.
> Eminent authorities agree that a large proportion of all cases of
> inebriety, border-land insanities, paranoiacs ... is due in large
> measure to heredity. Morphinism is one of these psychoses. (1902,
> p.66)

Although by 1923 the emphasis had shifted somewhat away from hereditary
defects towards congenital predispositions, these views were still held
widely. Dr. Campbell, in a paper published in the British Journal of
Inebriety, argued that the most likely subjects to become addicts were
those of the 'hereditary unstable neurotic type', a view concurred in by
Sir William Willcox, who took the view that 'even in those patients who
acquire the habit from the medical use of the drug' this factor was
evident. (Campbell 1923, p.149; Willcox, in Campbell 1923, p.163)

This approach was not without problems. Most physicians were aware
that in many cases of addiction, evidence for the presence of a family
history of alcoholism or morphinism was lacking. This difficulty was
resolved, as it was by Rolleston, by distinguishing exciting from
predisposing causes, and subsuming under both such a wide range of
different variables, of both an environmental and hereditary character,
so as to make any systematic etiological analysis virtually impossible.
In addition to congenital defects, Rolleston included amongst 'disposing

causes' the 'influences exerted on the patient by his surroundings, profession, occupation or trade ... The liquor traffic is naturally pre-eminent as a hot-bed of intemperance. Next, but long after, come trades necessitating exposure to severe weather, those of cabmen, drivers, nightwatchmen'. (op. cit., pp.109-110) Exciting causes were equally varied: mental distress, loss of relations, friends, money or reputation, the desire to forget, the desire to tide over a crisis, and overwork. Kerr included under this heading nerve shock - 'a weak brain is more susceptible to nerve shock than a strong one' - head and other injuries, sexual excess and idleness. (1894, p.200)

Equally questionable, was the categorising of every patient who was addicted to morpine or opium, or who occasionally drank to intoxication, as insane. As Levinstein pointed out:

> To describe the morbid craving for morphia as a mental disease it would be necessary, first of all, to show that the persons suffering therefrom are really impaired in their intellect and feelings. But this by no means is the case ... Authorities in military matters, artists, physicians, surgeons, bearing names of the highest reputation, are subject to this craving, without the least detriment to their capacities. (1878, p.9)

This was much too modern a view to be accepted widely in England at the time. It was taken as axiomatic that a person who periodically injected morphine, or who regularly consumed cocaine, must, by that very fact, be suffering from some form of mental instability. Nevertheless, it was clear to most physicians that many morphinomaniacs and habitual drunkards could not be grouped in the same category as those suffering from the more severe forms of mental illness. Sir Dyce Duckworth, in a lecture delivered at the London School of Clinical Medicine in 1908, noted that whilst clinical experience confirmed that certain cravings leading to immoderation in consumption were plain indications of an unstable brain and nervous system, it was necessary 'to recognise the opium habit especially in persons who cannot always be regarded as demoralised, or in a precarious state of bodily health'. (p.439)

The difficulty of classifying all addicts, particularly morphinists, as insane, arose partly because mental and medical science during the period under consideration was dominated by materialist theories of disease. This was clearly recognised by Sir William Collins, the only British expert on addictions who fully appreciated the moral and philosophical implications involved in attempting to ground explanations of the genesis of morbid cravings for intoxicants in theories which were based on the assumption that mental states were but a reflection of states of the nervous system. He held that the widespread acceptance of such theories was a product of the hold exerted by the positivist school of thought over the development of the modern medical curriculum, which:

> since it crystallised into form between 1850 and 1870, has been under the dominion of the materialist philosophy which led Prutz and Moleschott, Dubois Raymond and Littre, and their school, to incline to the view that without phosphorous there is no thought, and to define the soul as 'the ensemble of encephalic sensibility'[1] ... The notion that addiction to alcohol and drugs can be traced as effect to cause to some localised cerebral lesions belongs to the pathology that located the soul in the pineal gland ... that man is

what he eats, that the brain secretes thought as liver secretes bile, that morality is correlated with grey matter.$_2$ (1: 1916, p.138; 2: 1919, p.4)

Since no morphological lesions had been identified which could be traced to the repeated self-administration of either morphine or cocaine, and as many addicts manifested at best extremely mild forms of 'mental instability', it was difficult to classify them as insane in terms of this conceptual model.

Medical materialists had another string to their bow. This was the distinction drawn between organic and functional diseases. The view that confirmed morphine or cocaine addicts were insane was untenable if evidence of insanity was dependent upon identification of structural abnormalities of the nervous system, since addicts of long-standing displayed no such morphological defects. It was, however, possible to characterise insanity as a functional abnormality, a homeostatic imbalance of psychological equilibrium, unaccounted for by structural changes, and not associated with such alterations. Rather notes that:

There have been times in the past when medical thought was dominated by ideas of dynamism, polarity and ceaseless flux, times when morphological lesions of disease were looked on as no more than deposits left behind by the hurrying storm of pathological processes. There have been other times when more static forms of thought were dominant, when morphological lesions were regarded as the essence of disease, times when the attempt was made to deduce the whole picture of a disease from its associated lesions. The latter part of the eighteenth century qualifies by and large as a period of the dynamic in this respect, and the latter part of the nineteenth century as a period of the static. (1961, pp.502-503)

Medical theories of addiction in England evolved precisely at that time when there was a movement towards regarding certain types of mental abnormalities as functional rather than organic diseases. The main problems associated with identifying psychological abnormalities in terms of a functional model of disease, was the lack of precise criteria which would be used as evidence of the presence of pathological states. This is where a conception of disease as constituting a deviation from the normal came into its own. It is of course true, as Szasz has noted, that all illnesses, whether bodily or mental, involve deviation from some clearly defined norm. However, whereas physical illness is identifiable in anatomical and physiological terms, as are some diseases of the brain, mental illness, or diseases of the mind can only be stated in terms of 'psychological, ethical and legal concepts'. (Szasz 1974, p.15) Up until at least the mid-nineteen twenties, many psychiatrists and experts on addiction in Britain made no attempt to disguise their view that social, legal or ideological non-conformity were manifestations of mental abnormalities. Maudsley, for instance, defined insanity as 'such derangement of the leading functions of thought, feeling and will, together or separately as disable the person from thinking the thoughts, feeling the feelings, and doing the duties of the social body in, for, and by which he lives'. (Quoted by Savage, in Allbutt and Rolleston, 1910, Vol.8, p.823) Sir George Savage, one-time Physician Superintendant of the Bethlehem Royal Hospital, pointed out that as sanity and insanity were relative terms, the standards to be applied in their identification could not be of a general nature.

Sanity, he argued, 'must be gauged by conduct. Insanity had in most cases to be reckoned as a deviation from the ordinary line of conduct'. (ibid, p.824) Probably the clearest application of these criteria to morphine addicts was made by Crothers, who maintained that the mental symptoms attending the habitual consumption of morphine were pronounced and clearly defined:

One cannot use morphine long without suffering from weakened and obscure ideas of duty and right relations to others. Conceptions of truth and discriminations between truth and falsehood become more and more cloudy ... Religious manias, speculative manias, political and social changes of opinion, and endorsement of strange theories are the signs of mental change and the presence of morphine. (1902, pp.102-112)

The adoption of functional theories of mental illness enabled physicians to characterise addicts as sick or diseased despite the absence of morphological lesions, or physiological and biological imbalances associated with the syndrome. The flexibility of criteria based on non-conformity permitted a scaling down of the concept 'insanity' to include more benign forms of mental illness. Instead of regarding addiction as a manifestation of insanity, it came to be perceived as a psychoneurosis, a somewhat milder form of insanity, identifiable by deviations from accepted patterns of thought and conduct. According to Savage, the neurotic was a person:

whose nervous instability causes him to react unduly to stimuli, such reactions being called mental or nervous symptoms. Neurosis arises under certain conditions of general and nervous degeneracy ... Though restlessness, loss of control and undue tendency to react to stimuli are the most evident symptoms, those most dangerous socially are the moral effects and perversities; some neurotics have no sense of truth or honesty, and no altruism; they are cruel, destructive and sensual. (op. cit. pp.825-826)

By the nineteen twenties it was widely accepted that morphine and cocaine consumption indicated the presence of an underlying neurosis. (e.g., Dixon 1923-1924, p.111; Willcox 1926, p.5; Campbell 1923, p.149; Park 1923-1924, p.157)

The lack of any clearly specified and unambiguous criteria for identifying functional mental disorders, or for applying the term psychoneurosis, left the door wide open for distinguishing between different categories of addict in terms of their moral characteristics. Since psychoneuroses were only identifiable in terms of deviations from accepted standards of ideological, social and legal conduct, it should have been possible to relate the severity of the patient's mental instability to the extent of his deviation from established norms of conduct or thought. In practice, there was a tendency to regard the patient as more retractable the greater the social distance between him/her, and members of the medical profession. Crothers, for instance, drew a distinction between morphinists and morphinomaniacs which illustrates this point:

The term 'morphinism' describes a condition following the prolonged use of morphine either by the needle under the skin or by the mouth. Morphinomania is a term used to designate the condition of persons in whom the impulse to use morphine is of the nature of a mania, possessing the mind and dominating every thought, leaving but one supreme desire - to procure morphine and experience the pleasure it gives. (1902, p.42)

Although he maintained that it was not always easy to distinguish between the two, that they frequently merged into each other, and that the two types of addiction could be identified in persons of equivalent social status, he went on to argue that morphinism 'is often noted in the prosperous classes, while morphinomaniacs are seen lower down, among the tramps, criminals and degenerates'. (p.44) These social distinctions influenced recommendations for the type of treatment that should be applied to different categories of addict. Campbell, for example, was of the opinion that with regard to the 'degenerate class' it was useless to attempt to treat them, since those of the irresponsible criminal or borderland class ... need to be under custody'. (1923, p.153) Willcox, on the other hand, adopted what at first sight appears to be a more egalitarian approach to treatment, recommending that all confirmed habitues should be subject to compulsory restraint, 'under a proper system of certification, in order that adequate treatment under medical supervision may be carried out'. (In Campbell 1923, p.164)

Significantly, he was not party to the widespread belief that a large proportion of medical practitioners were victims of the morphine habit. (cf. Jennings 1909(a): vi) In his view, the morphine habit was rare amongst medical practitioners, nurses and pharmacists, 'and those whose occupation provides them with access to the drugs in question'. (ibid, p.163) Most other experts were of the contrary opinion. It was probably this consideration that accounts for their readiness to regard morphine addiction as a disease whilst drawing distinctions between different categories of addict. The drawing of fine moral distinctions was probably facilitated by the fact that most physicians who took to theorising about the causes of addiction probably had no first-hand experience of treating morphine habitues who belonged to the 'underworld', or to lower socio-economic groups. Dr. J.H. Morton, Medical Officer of Holloway Prison, noted in evidence before the Departmental Committee on Morphine and Heroin Addiction that 'the type of addict met with in prison was different from that met with in ordinary life. The majority of prison patients belonged to the underworld who were not leading normal lives and could scarcely be said to be normal mentally even before the acquirement of the drug habit'. (MH58/File 95006/3/5A) Dr Niall, a general practitioner who divided addicts into 'decent ordinary citizens who want to be decent, but must have a minimum daily dose of their dope to enable them to remain so', and 'loose livers who do not care a jot', stressed that the latter 'rarely came to a doctor ... they know perfectly well where to go'. (ibid)

In the final analysis, members of the medical profession trod a shaky course between regarding morphine and cocaine addiction alternatively as moral vice or disease. The scientific rhetoric in which their analyses of the latter were couched, barely concealed the predominant influence of the former. Thus, Allbutt and Dixon, after noting that opium smokers actually ingested only minute quantities of morphine, since most of its active ingredients were dissipated by combustion or collected about the pipe, concluded, nonetheless, that the practice was to be condemned, because of the 'degrading circumstances of its pursuit; in Eastern towns it is the recourse of the scum of the earth, and is associated with every kind of abomination'. (in <u>Allbutt and Rolleston</u> 1910, Vol.2, p.948) To add to the confusion, they went on to argue that the practice was not necessarily to be condemned in all cases with equal vociferousness: 'The opium-smoker is not rarely a man of active habits; and in moderation, like other uses of such drugs, the practice may enable the user to do a great deal of work on little food ... In depraved persons and imbeciles, who will abandon themselves to anything, it gradually produces the opium cachexia'. (<u>ibid</u>, p.949) In other words, that which was to be condemned was not the practice of opium smoking, or its supposed ill effects, since in this case there were none, but the character of the consumer.

Only Collins was aware that attempts to conceptualise addiction as a disease akin to physical illness, whilst simultaneously adopting a moral standpoint towards the non-medical consumption of drugs, was an endeavour riddled with inconsistencies. In his view, these theories betrayed some confusion of thought:

> The undoubtedly physical lesions which are the result of chronic alcoholism ... and which may affect, <u>inter alia</u>, the nervous as well as the digestive and eliminative organs, can only by a process of logical inversion, confounding consequents with antecedents, be cited as demonstrating the pathology of inebriety in terms of physical disease. (1919, p.3)

Practically alone amongst medical experts he persisted in regarding drug addiction as a vice. After his return from the First Hague Conference he noted in a lecture given at the Polyclinic, that there was a disposition in some quarters to regard the morphinist and cocainist as invalids who were to be pitied. His own view was that "no-one who had had the experience at first hand of these 'addicts' or who has read accounts of them ... can have failed to be impressed with the fact that many of them are social pests of the most dangerous kind. Bankrupt of moral sense and will-power, they are lying and deceitful, prodigal of time, plausible to a degree, backbiting and contentious, prone to vice and apt for crime". (1912, p.16) Collins was atypical. Despite the fact that his views on the morality of addiction were not markedly dissimilar from those held by many of his professional colleagues, albeit expressed more openly and forcefully, he was at least always consistent. His writings on the subject were free of the sophistry which cloaked moral condemnation in the garb of medical science. Although his achievements in the field of medicine were not as great as those of Allbutt, Rolleston, Willcox or Dixon, he was intellectually of a different calibre. Unlike them he had a thorough grounding in medical history and philosophy. To a large extent the differences in their approaches to these questions were rooted in their different epistemological allegiances. Collins, as is already probably apparent, was an exponent of voluntarism, whereas most other prominent experts can be described as determinists. On the central question of the role of the 'will' as a determinant of conduct, he adopted the position advanced by Bergson:

> The nervous system is the crown and <u>finis</u> of cellular differentiation, to the elaboration and sustenance of which all other cell activity if subordinate. It is the channel of choice, of indetermination. It is the role of life to insert some

indetermination into matter. The nervous system with its chains of neurones is a veritable reservoir of indetermination, to the construction of which the vital impulse has led up. (quoted in Collins 1916, p.141. Emphasis in original.)

In Collins' opinion, those who were committed to a physical causation theory of inebriety, and to a determinist philosophy, were bound to 'flounder in the quicksands of responsibility and irresponsibility, and will continue to search in vain for something out of a bottle, or, maybe, a hypodermic injection wherewith to redeem the sot and rehabilitate the will'. (ibid, p.143) None of the other leading experts on addiction shared these views.

During the period that the Departmental Committee on Morphine and Heroin Addiction conducted its enquiries, the consensus of opinion was that habituation to narcotics was a disease. If it was a disease of the will, which some reluctantly acknowledged that it partially was, this did not render the afflicted any less amenable to medical control. Those specialising in the field of psychological medicine, whose proficiency in the manipulation of the psyche was gaining wider recognition, could be relied upon to deal with this facet of the syndrome.

It is difficult to regard the views on the subject that have been reviewed as constituting an etiological theory of narcotic addiction. For the most part they represented an amalgam of ambiguous and unsubstantiated opinions evolved to explain drunkenness and alcoholism, put forward by physicians who were favourably disposed towards the goals of various organisations comprising the temperance movement. Later, in the 1880s and 1890s, they were applied uncritically to other types of chronic intoxication. The result was that by the nineteen twenties alcoholism and narcotic addiction were, for all practical purposes, regarded as identical phenomena. Physicians singled out the same variables as being implicated in their genesis. Methods of treatment were virtually interchangeable. Both were still accounted for in exactly the same terms that alcoholism had been explained in mid-Victorian England; by invoking 'Lamarckian Inheritance and beliefs about mind-body relationships in disease' which 'were incorporated in class attitudes which confused psychological problems, economic status, moral quality, and epidemiological factors'. (Pruitt 1974, p.94)

They were, however, accepted as valid statements of scientific fact by leading members of the medical profession. Three of those whose views referred to and quoted from above, were members of the Departmental Committee on Morphine and Heroin Addiction: Sir Humphrey Rolleston, Sir William Willcox, and Professor W.E. Dixon. All were acknowledged to be exceptionally gifted, and their contributions to medicine and pharmacology were widely acclaimed. The other members of the committee were Drs. J.W. Bone, R.W. Branthwaite, G.M. Cullen, J. Fawcett, A. Fulton and J. Smith-Whitaker. (For biographical details of cf. Stein 1978, pp.634-636) Since all members of the committee were physicians or pharmacologists by training, it was highly likely that these views, which reflected the contemporary consensus, would influence their findings.

10 The treatment of addiction

The Committee's deliberations and its examination of witnesses extended over a period of one year from October 1924. Most of the testimony it heard was from members of the medical and pharmaceutical professions. In addition, the Home Office and Ministry of Health submitted oral and written evidence.

The examination of witnesses was primarily directed at eliciting information in order to enable the committee to form conclusions respecting four questions:

(a) Whether there were any circumstances which made it necessary for those addicted to morphine or heroin to continue consumption of these drugs under medical supervision, in the absence of any expectation that patients would be permanently cured.

(b) If the answer to (a) was in the affirmative, whether certain conditions should be observed by physicians who were asked by addicts to undertake their treatment. For example:

(1) that it should be made a condition of the supply of the drug that the addict's consent should be obtained to the private notification of his case by the practitioner to the Regional Medical Officer; (2) that the addict should undertake to obtain his requisite supplies of the narcotic only from the practitioner who is undertaking his case. (MS58/File 95006/3/5A. Hereafter referred to as Evidence)

(c) Whether the right of a doctor to prescribe the drugs regulated under the Dangerous Drugs Act and the Regulations should be withdrawn if it appeared that his prescribing practices in relation

160

to these drugs violated their provisions, including the recommendations of the committee respecting (a), and by whom such rights should be withdrawn.

(d) Whether certain preparations containing morphine or heroin of a percentage less than that specified in the Dangerous Drugs Act and the Regulations, should be brought within their provisions.

The answers given to all of these questions, both by members of the commmittee and witnesses, hinged on their evaluation of:

(1) the extent of addiction;
(2) the factors implicated in its genesis;
(3) the demographic and psychological characteristics of addicts;
(4) the efficacy and availability of alternative methods of treatment.

The general view was that addiction to these drugs was not particularly prevalent. Sir Maurice Craig, physician and lecturer in psychological medicine at Guy's Hospital, was of the opinion that notification of names of addicts to Regional Medical Officers, and the securing of undertakings that they would not attempt to obtain supplies from more than one doctor, would:

> only be reasonable if it could be shown that the addiction problem in this country were of sufficient magnitude to justify their adoption. He did not himself think that the drug evil was so serious as to warrant these drastic measures which would probably defeat their own object. The patient's would not, as a rule, give their consent to notification, and measures in excess of the needs of the situation would only tend to drive the evil underground. (Evidence)

This was the line also taken by A.R. Melhuish, chairman of the Retail Pharmacists Union and Chemists Defence Association. In opposing the extension of the Regulations to yet more preparations containing morphine or heroin, he noted that 'so far as the experience of the pharmacist is concerned, the number of drug addicts is decreasing, and there are no signs of new addicts being created through pharmacists'. (ibid) The committee concluded that evidence collected from a variety of sources indicated that 'addiction to morphine or heroin is rare'. (Addition Report, p.10)

The considerations that probably influenced the committee's recommendations most, were those relating to the factors implicated in the causation of addiction and the demographic characteristics of addicts. In their report they noted that:

> Use of the drug in medical treatment was considered by witnesses, with but one exception, to have been the immediate cause of addiction in a considerable proportion of cases they had treated ... In many of these cases, it was considered that the drug had been administered injudiciously in various ways, either as regards the doses given, or the period for which the administration has been continued, or from the lack of care to diminish dosages and make the patient independent of the drug before treatment was concluded. (ibid, pp.12-13)

Only Craig took the view that few cases of addiction had arisen from therapeutic use of the drug. Sir James Purves-Stewart, Senior Physician to the Westminster Hospital, thought that it was 'evident that in the great majority of cases of the drug-habit, prescription of narcotic drugs by medical practitioners has been the starting point'. (Evidence)

There was also considerable agreement that physicians and others who had easy access to these drugs by virtue of their occupations, formed a large proportion of the addict population treated by medical practitioners. Purves-Stewart testified that of the 36 cases of male drug addiction that he had seen in private practice, 15 were doctors; of the female cases, 3 were the wives of physicians. F.S.D. Hogg, Resident Medical Superintendant of the Dalrymple House Retreat, noted that of the 195 cases that he had treated in twenty-five years, 44 had been medical practitioners, 7 students of medicine or chemistry, 3 chemists and 4 dentists.

The evidence attesting to the extensive culpability of physicians in creating addiction, and their own use of morphine and heroin for purposes of non-medical consumption, was bound to have some bearing on the recommendations made by the committee. It placed them in the position of devising proposals for regulating the negligence and deviance of members of their own and closely allied professions. Some witnesses went so far as to argue that special consideration be given to physician-addicts. Dr. Ivy Mackenzie, Consulting Physician to the Mental Observation Wards in Glasgow, 'did not hold it to be wise to allow a doctor-addict to treat himself, but he would not be in favour of any regulation to forbid this if the practitioner desired self-treatment'. (Evidence) G.M. Robertson, professor of psychiatry at the University of Edinburgh, 'said he would be inclined to deal very leniently with medical men who were the subjects of addiction and give them every chance'. (ibid) There were others, including Purves-Stewart, who were of the opinion that doctors who were addicts should not be permitted to treat themselves. This was also the attitude taken by a number of general practitioners. They were less inclined to be lenient toward such doctors than were more senior members of the profession. In their view they were dangerous and a menace to the community.

Involved here were questions of amour-propre, the underlying view being that the placing of restrictions on the prescribing habits of doctors would case an unnecessary slur on the profession as a whole. Considerations of this order were probably responsible for the acceptance by the committee of a recommendation put forward by the Director of Public Prosecutions. He suggested that if the Home Office had reason to think that a medical practitioner may be supplying, administering or prescribing any drugs covered by the Act or the Regulations, either to or for himself, or to or for other persons, otherwise than as required for purposes of medical treatment, the case should be referred to a medical tribunal. It would have powers to withdraw a practitioner's authorisation to be in possession of or prescribe the drugs in question. The Chemist and Druggist was quick to discern the extent to which this recommendation was based on professional self-interest, commenting in an editorial, that:

it is curious to note the difference of treatment between a medical man and a chemist. For the former a special tribunal is to be created ... to which certain breaches by medical men may be referred by the Secretary of State; the chemist, on the other hand, finds no relief from being dragged before a criminal court for a purely technical offence, and he has to submit to the indignity of inspection by policemen and other civil servants. (12 June 1926)

The part played by physicians in creating addiction and the evidence attesting to the large number of doctors who were themselves victims of the habit, probably accounts for the fact that in their report the committee minimised the role of mental abnormality in its etiology. This is particularly significant given the prevailing views on this question. The committee concluded that:

> The only immediate cause of addiction is the use of the drug for a sufficient time to produce the constitutional condition that is manifested in the overwhelming craving and the occurrence of withdrawal symptoms when use is discontinued. (Addiction Report, p.11)

The evidence given by witnesses on this question was frequently inconsistent. Robertson, although of the opinion that if a `normal person, mentally sound, and free from bodily disease were submitted to a course of morphine injections', he/she would become addicted, also held that `a psychopathic basis underlay the majority of cases of drug addiction'. At the same time, he held that `a considerable number of cases of drug addiction had their origin in the previous therapeutic use of the drug'. (Evidence) The only circumstance under which these various propositions could jointly hold true is if a `normal person, mentally sound', was also a `psychopath'. The evidence on this question submitted by Purves-Stewart and Dr. Farquhar Buzzard, Physician to St. Thomas' Hospital, were riddled with similar inconsistencies. In the face of this testimony, the committee concluded that:

> addiction may be acquired by injudicious use of the drug in a person who has not previously shown any manifestation of nervous or mental instability, and that, conversely, due care in administration may avert this consequence even in the unstable. (Addiction Report, p.13)

To a certain extent this conclusion, and the absence of any attempt to classify addicts on the basis of moral cum socio-economic characteristics, was dictated, not only by the evidence attesting to the large number of physician addicts, but also by the committee's selection of witnesses, most of whom were senior members of the profession. Dr. Robertson noted that the large number of medical men that consulted him was probably due to the fact that `addicts of this category were more likely to consult him than others, the laymen going to the general practitioner'. (Evidence) It is probably more realistic to conclude that laymen, particularly members of lower socio-economic classes, would not consult a physician at all.

Although no one disputed that addiction was a disease, there were considerable differences of opinion as to the most efficacious method of treatment. The major dividing line was between prison and other doctors. Dr. East, Medical Inspector of Prisons, and Drs. Sass, Watson and Morton, Medical Officers of Pentonville, Brixton and Holloway Prisons respectively, were all advocates of the immediate withdrawal method. They did note that the success that attended the application of this method in prisons 'was largely, if not entirely, due to the special circumstances of prison life'. (Dr. Morton, Evidence) In Dr. Watson's opinion:

> The circumstances and discipline of prison life were eminently favourable for the application of this plan of treatment. The patient realises that there are no means of procuring the drug and he makes up his mind to do without it. (ibid)

Mackenzie and Purves-Stewart also favoured this approach. The latter noted that those patients who had consulted him had already been treated unsuccessfully by the withdrawal technique. At the same time, all were agreed that immediate therapy should only be attempted in institutional settings, under medical supervision.

Hogg, Robertson, Craig and Niall preferred the gradual withdrawal method. Hogg noted that instant withdrawal was 'cruel and inhumane and carries a considerable degree of risk'. (Evidence) He considered that a successful cure by ambulatory treatment would be difficult to secure, but that if attempted the gradual withdrawal plan should be adopted. Robertson maintained that abrupt withdrawal 'was dangerous if the addict had been used to taking large doses. It was certainly a method which should not be attempted outside an institution'. (ibid) The committee concluded that, despite differences of opinion over which method was the most efficacious, it could be regarded as established that:

> abrupt or rapid withdrawal should not be carried out except in a well-appointed institution with the aid of skilled nursing and constant medical supervision. It is therefore, unavailable for the treatment of those who cannot or will not enter institutions. (Addiction Report, p.16)

This conclusion, when taken in conjunction with the view that addiction was a disease, that it was largely induced by physicians, that there was a dearth of adequate institutional facilities for treating addicts, a considerable proportion of whom were members of the medical and ancilliary medical professions, virtually dictated the position that the committee would have to adopt with respect to whether it was medically legitimate to prescribe narcotics to addicts in the absence of attempts to effect a cure. In a memorandum summarising the evidence, and views of members of the committee, it was noted that:

> The justification for the prolonged administration of morphine or heroin to addicts is, in the opinion of the Committee, largely dependent on the extent to which the 'sudden withdrawal' method of treatment is practicable in individual cases ... Even the warmest advocates, however, of 'sudden withdrawal' agreed, though in one or two cases with some reluctance, that it could not be carried out satisfactorily under the conditions of medical practice outside Institutions, owing to the want of effective control of the patient, and that, therefore, the method of gradual withdrawal is the only one available. It was further agreed, generally, that under these conditions complete withdrawal of the drug is difficult and cannot always be secured. It is therefore inevitable under present conditions that there should be in the community a class of persons from whom the drug cannot be completely withheld. Among these are

persons who, if regularly supplied with a small dose, can live an otherwise normal life, but become incapable of so carrying on their duties if that dose cannot be obtained. (MH58/File 95006/3/5B)

The committee therefore noted in their report that morphine or heroin could properly be administered to addicts by medical practitioners in the following circumstances:

(a) where patients are under treatment by the gradual withdrawal method with a view to cure, (b) where it has been demonstrated, after a prolonged attempt at cure, that the use of the drug cannot be safely discontinued entirely, on account of the severity of the withdrawal symptoms produced, (c) where it has been similarly demonstrated that the patient, while capable of leading a useful and relatively normal life when a certain minimum dose is regularly administered, becomes incapable of this when the drug is entirely discontinued. (Addiction Report, p.19)

It was also suggested that doctors should observe certain precautions when treating addiction cases. Where possible, patients should be persuaded to enter a suitable institution or nursing home. If, on the other hand, ambulatory treatment was attempted, patients should be kept under close observation and the amount of drug supplied should be kept to the 'limits of what is strictly necessary'. It was also advisable in such cases that the treating physician seek a second opinion. (Addiction Report, p.32)

These were the most important recommendations made by the committee. Their acceptance by the Home Office and the Ministry of Health required no amendment of the Dangerous Drugs Regulations. Regulation 7 of the Principle Regulations, that is those published in May 1921, was altered so as to make it clear that persons entitled to be in possession of dangerous drugs by virtue of their being under treatment for the cure of addiction were obliged, if already receiving prescriptions for these drugs from one practitioner, to disclose this to any other physician whom they might approach with a request for treatment. (HO45/Box 13351/File 423410)

The only other recommendations made by the committee were those concerning the appointment of a tribunal to consider the withdrawal of a doctor's authorisation to prescribe dangerous drugs, with which I have already dealt, and that relating to the extension of the Regulations to preparations containing opiates and cocaine in proportions less than those already covered by them. In this latter connection, it noted that:

There is little, if any, abuse or danger of addiction arising from any preparations at present excluded from the scope of the Dangerous Drugs Acts, with the possible exception of Chlorodyne ... The position as regards Chlorodyne would be met if it could be secured in some way that no preparation should be sold under the name of 'chlorodyne' which contained more than 0.1 per cent of morphine. (Addiction Report, p.35)

The views of Home Office officials on the recommendations, particularly those of Delevingne, are not known, since there are no documents which throw any light on the question. It is, of course, common knowledge that the proposals respecting the prescribing of narcotics to addicts were accepted and implemented. The response of the British Medical Journal and The Lancet was muted, their editorial staffs confining themselves to presenting factual resumes of the committee's report. Delevingne noted in July 1926 that 'no criticisms have come from any responsible representatives of the medical profession - at the recent meeting of the British Medical Association the recommendations of Sir H. Rolleston's Committee were attacked by one doctor, but they were defended by another and the subject was not pursued'. (HO45/Box 13351/File 423410)

Publication of the report was used by the Home Office as an opportunity for amending some of the Regulations. For the most part these conerned the keeping of records and the handling of poisons by pharmacists. For example, a new regulation stipulated that every person 'authorised in pursuance of Regulation 10 of the Principle Regulations to carry on the business of manufacturing, selling or distributing the drugs shall keep the same in a locked receptacle of which the key shall be kept by himself or a qualified assistant'. (HO45/Box 13351/File 423419/31) this, and other proposed changes, aroused the ire of pharmacists once again. The South-West London Chemist's Association informed the Home Office in June that:

> whilst it is the practice of pharmacists to keep under lock and key stocks of morphine, cocaine and their salts, and opium, it is not expedient for them to keep in a similar manner such preparations of them as are in frequent use in the pharmacy. In consequence a regulation such as the one proposed would prove irksome and ... quite unnecessary from the standpoint of carrying out, as pharmacists have endeavoured to do, the spirit as well as the letter of the Dangerous Drugs Acts. (ibid, 12 June 1926)

A.H. Anderson, one of the Home Office's inspectors under the Dangerous Drugs Acts, retorted that the statement that 'it is the practice ... to keep under lock and key stocks of morphine, cocaine', etc., 'is to all intents and purposes untrue'. (ibid)

The Chemist and Druggist also gave vent to its irritation at yet more bureaucratic interference, complaining that:

> The term 'addiction drug' has not yet lost its potency for inducing certain official minds to reel forth regulations. No sooner does a difference of opinion arise over the interpretation of a word than we get amendment piled on amendment of the principle regulations until it is impossible for any chemist to say exactly what he can or cannot do if he is to be sure of escaping the infamous penalties of the Dangerous Drugs Acts. (12 June 1926)

The Pharmaceutical Society sent the Home Office a lengthy letter in which, after complaining about lack of pre-publication consultations, they detailed their objections, which they later followed up with a deputation. These protests failed to dissuade the Home Office or the Ministry of Health from preceding as intended. Pharmacists, chemists and druggists did not carry as much political influence as doctors. Delevingne simply informed Smith-Whitaker that he did not 'attach a great deal of importance to the Pharmaceutical Society's criticisms'. (HO45/Box 13351/File 423410/6th July 1926) Their success in securing some minor alterations and clarifications of the original draft of the Principle Regulations in 1921, was due solely to the fact that they were supported in this endeavour by the representative organisations of the medical and other professions. The only suggestion of the Pharmaceutical Society that was accepted in 1926, was that the regulations should be consolidated. This was done in 1928.

CONCLUSION

Of all the Rolleston committee's recommendations, that which endorsed as legitimate medical practice the prescribing of dangerous drugs to addicts in the absence of an attempt to effect a cure, has been regarded as the most important in relation to its long-term repercussions on the development of narcotics control in Britain. It has been singled out for special attention, not because its implementation has had any significant impact, either at the time or subsequently, on the extent of addiction, the forms of drug use, or the attributes of the addict population in Britain, but because this policy has been viewed by American academics and reformers as a viable alternative to the system of narcotics control pursued since the nineteen-twenties in the United States. In order to avoid falling into the trap of concluding that the acceptance of this recommendation formed the basis of a 'system' of narcotics control that was radically different from the enforcement strategy then being implemented in the United States, it is essential to evaluate its significance in the context of the overall approach taken by the Home Office to issues of drug control, and the considerations that formed the basis of the committee's conclusions concerning this matter.

Neither the Home Office nor members of the committee considered that this proposal was particularly radical, primarily because, as the latter noted in their report, addiction to morphine or heroin was rare. In the opinion of most of the witnesses its extent was decreasing, partly because of the impact that enforcement of the provisions of the Dangerous Drugs Acts was having. The Committee on the Use of Cocaine in Dentistry had come to a similar conclusion regarding the extent of addiction to cocaine eight years earlier, noting in their report that:

> After careful examination of the evidence placed before us, we are unanimously of the opinion that there is no evidence of any kind to show that there is any serious or, perhaps, even noticeable prevalence of the cocaine habit amongst the civilian or military population of Great Britain ... apart from a small number of broken-down medical men, there is only slight evidence of its existence amongst the general population. (British Parliamentary Papers 1917-1918, Vol.8, p.4)

Given that there were only a handful of addicts relative to the size of the population, perhaps three or four hundred at most, the decision to permit them regular access to supplies of narcotics can hardly be said to have created a noticeable dent in the overall policy of narcotics control being pursued by the Home Office. This was directed at denying such access to the remaining 38 million members of the population. Certainly this does not constitute a very firm foundation for what Lindesmith (1965) and Schur (1962) have designated as a 'system' of narcotics control. The resources of the police, the Home Office

Inspectorate, the Board of Customs and Excise and the Ministry of Health, were all employed in the cause of preventing access to dangerous drugs. Few resources, on the other hand, were allocated to the treatment of addiction; nor does it appear that there was much concern over, or interest in, this facet of drug control. The Times, for example, considered that in the light of the Rolleston committee's other recommendations, this one did not even merit mention. (20 February 1926).

The scale of the addiction problem in the United States was of a different order. Estimates of the number of persons addicted to narcotics during the first quarter of the twentieth century vary considerably, and are, on the whole, unreliable. Duster estimates that prior to the passing of the Harrison Act in 1914, approximately 3 per cent of the population were addicted to narcotics. (Duster 1970, p.7) This, in the context of his definition of addiction, is probably far too high. Chein et.al. more realistically set the total number at somewhat less than 215,000 in 1915. (1964, p.329) Whatever estimate one accepts, one can reasonably conclude that in contrast to the situation in the United States, in Great Britain there was, for all practical purposes, no addiction problem.

It is reasonably certain that the small number of addicts was one of the main reasons for acceptance of the committee's recommendations concerning the sustaining of an addict's dependence upon narcotics. When, many decades later, it became apparent that their numbers were increasing, the authorities immediately took steps to bring them under closer surveillance. In 1965 the Brain Committee noted that there had been 'a disturbing rise in the incidence of addiction to heroin and cocaine'. (Second Report of the Interdepartmental Committee on Drug Addiction 1965, p.13) It made certain recommendations designed to meet the changed circumstances; notably, the setting up of addiction treatment centres, limiting the precribing of dangerous drugs of addicts to doctors working at these centres, and the notification of names of all addicts to a central authority. All of these proposals were eventually implemented, giving rise to a 'system' of drug control not radically dissimilar to the 'narcotic clinic' programme that existed in certain parts of the United States in the early part of the twenties. Significantly, the Brain Committee was also manned by members of the medical profession. This time, in contrast, the number of physician-addicts constituted a much smaller proportion of the known addict population, and committee members were not placed in the position of evolving policies designed to regulate the activities of their colleagues.

Although estimates of the number of addicts undoubtedly influenced the nature of the committee's recommendations, of equal, if not greater importance, was the information in their possession concerning the social context of drug use and the demographic characteristics of users. In their report they noted that cases of addiction 'appear to be proportionately more frequent in the great urban centres than elsewhere'. (Addiction Report, p.10) This was also characteristic of addiction in the United States. There was, however, one crucial difference. It was assumed that in Britain most persons addicted to narcotics did not consume these drugs as part and parcel of their association with other habitues. In other words, addiction for the most part had no sub-cultural basis. There were some obvious exceptions:

opium smoking amongst residents of Chinese extraction and Chinese seamen; morphine and cocaine consumption amongst members of the 'smart set'. Neither was presumed to be particularly prevalent. The former was concentrated in seaports, primarily London and Liverpool; the latter only in London. Even in the press it was never suggested that there was a drug-subculture outside of London. In the United States, on the other hand:

> The confessional writings of ex-addicts and information in medical journals and other sources clearly pointed to the existence of a subculture of addicts in almost every town ... every town had a rendesvous for addicts, whether in smoking dens or fashionable homes. (Morgan 1974, pp.8-10)

This was the case at least until after the passing of the Harrison Act. If one omits addiction arising out of the consumption of proprietary preparations containing narcotics, then even the British medical press, particularly the British Medical Journal and The Lancet, devoted far more attention to the problem of drug addiction in the United States, especially to the spread of cocaine addiction amongst Southern Negroes, than it did to the addiction problem at home during the first quarter of the century. In part this was due to the absence of a drug subculture, the only aspect of the addiction phenomenon that had the ingredients necessary to prompt the medical and lay press to take notice of it, albeit, if only for a few weeks or months at a time.

No less important than the absence of a subculture of drug-usage, was the evidence submitted concerning the demographic characteristics of addicts, and the circumstances under which most cases of addiction to narcotics arose. There was virtually no disagreement amongst witnesses on matters relating to both issues. Nearly all were agreed that a very significant proportion of addicts were either members of the medical and ancilliary medical professions, or belonged to upper socio-economic groups. Sir James Purves-Stewart, for example, reported that of the 26 women he had treated for addiction; '15 were ordinary "society women", 5 were demi-modaines, 3 were the wives of medical practitioners, 1 was a hospital nurse'. (Evidence) It is possible, even likely, that the information relating to the distribution of addicts on the basis of socio-economic criteria was an artefact of the committee's selection of witnesses disproportionately from more senior members of the profession. This is, however, besides the point, since this was the only information, other than that of their own experiences, that they could rely on in the course of making recommendations. The comparison with the American situation is once again instructive. Swatos, after surveying the information concerning this question contained in opiate-related articles that appeared in nine major American medical journals, covering the period from 1850 to 1910, notes that:

> The initial impression conveyed by these articles is that 'opium or morphia-takers are usually of the better classes', but there is by no means unanimous agreement that this is always the case. Others attest to addiction in the Chinese immigrants, the Southern Negro, urban prisoners, and the 'vicious classes' in general ... What tends to emerge at the level of simple status/class distinctions, then is a picture resembling much more the present day alcoholic population than 'drug addicts' in a modern sense. The much higher proportion of women, the prevalence of the phenomenon at all class

levels, the disregard of rural-urban and racial differences are all much more similar to the former problem as affecting more or less all social classes and status groups. (Swatow 1972, pp.741-743)

A closely related issue concerns the committee's evaluation of the addict's role-performance capabilities. The recommendation to sustain an addict's dependence on narcotics was premised on the assumption that some, perhaps many, were 'persons who, if regularly supplied with a small dose, can lead an otherwise normal life'. (MH58/File 95006/3/5B) Here again, this conclusion was probably drawn because the evidence submitted related to what was probably a non-representative addict population. This is important since 'street addicts' and 'physician addicts' differ in some important respects from each other, including the competence with which they carry out their occupational activities. Winick has noted in this connection that the 98 physician-addicts he interviewed:

> ranged from a few who were less successful than the average in their professional careers to some who were extraordinarily successful national figures. The typical physician interviewed was more successful than the average, in terms of income, honorific and institutional affiliations, and general professional activity. (Winick in Cressey and Ward 1969, pp.1076-1077)

The testimony given concerning the large number of physicians who were habituated to narcotics, and the iatrogenic origin of addiction, transformed the questions initially posed to members of the committee into issues of professional accountability. Since all its members were either practising physicians, medical administrators or pharmacologists, it is hardly surprising that they should prefer to regard their fellow professionals as 'sick' rather than as 'vicious criminals'. There were, of course, other considerations that justified proceeding this way. British physicians were for the most part agreed that narcotic addiction was a disease. There was also a consensus that if ambulatory treatment was attempted the method of gradual withdrawal should be used. Nevertheless, given that British experts on addiction, three of whom sat on the Rolleston committee, were also agreed that habituation to narcotics had an underlying psychoneurotic basis, that they alternated between considering it as a vice and a disease, depending primarily on the social status of the addict, the conclusion is inescapable that the committee would probably not have been as willing to advocate the sustenance of an addicts's dependence on narcotics if the evidence presented to it had indicated that addiction was concentrated primarily amongst members of lower socio-economic classes and denizens of the underworld.

It was not unduly difficult for Home Office officials to accept these proposals since the testimony given to the committee indicated that the problem was not particularly widespread. Furthermore, the prosecution of doctors in the criminal courts, for technical offenses, or offenses arising out of habituation to narcotics, was likely to prove counter-productive in the long-run. Due to the influence of the representative organisations of the medical profession, and a tradition of governmental decision-making based on mutual consultation between civil service departments and affected pressure groups, the co-operation of the medical profession was essential to the development of any system of narcotics control at the time. This was not likely to be achieved if physicians were to be prosecuted in the criminal courts. When, in the early sixties, evidence suggested that both the size and demographic profile of the addict population had changed significantly, the Rolleston Committee's recommendations were discarded as being no longer relevant to the new circumstances. The official response was to move away from a policy that endorsed the sustenance of an addict's dependence on narcotics, towards one directed at effecting a cure by the methods of drug-substitution and gradual withdrawal. This was precisely the policy that the Home Office had initially favoured in the early twenties, but which it had dropped in return for the future co-operation of the medical profession.

11 Conclusion: diplomats, administrators and pressure groups

THE CONVENTION

Since conclusions have already been drawn at the end of a number of chapters, and a summary of the main factors leading to the conclusion of the Hague Opium Convention has been presented in chapter 5, it remains only to briefly review some of the key issues linking the events surveyed in this study. In addition, an account will be offered of differing interpretations of parts of the Harrison and Dangerous Drugs Acts respecting the obligations of medical practitioners in prescribing narcotics.

The fact that the Hague Opium Convention was concluded, ratified and implemented, was a product of the intermeshing at particular points in time of a number of distinct sequences of events. These include: the state of Sino-American relations during the first decade of the twentieth century; certain domestic developments in the United States which facilitated the development of an imperialist ideology and encouraged overseas expansion; missionary opposition to the Indo-China opium traffic and the failure of their evangelising policies in China; the rise of Chinese nationalism; the Chinese anti-opium campaign; the attempts of British officials to curb exports of manufactured narcotics to the Far East during the First World War; the publicity given by the press to the presumed spread of addiction amongst soldiers and the 'smart set' during the years 1916-1919; the convening of an international conference to settle armistice terms with the enemy powers at the conclusion of the war; and the establishing of a League of Nations.

Insofar as a causal model is applicable to explaining the development of a concerted international approach to controlling the consumption and trafficking in dangerous drugs, priority must be given to those of the above factors which account for the origins of the Chinese anti-opium campaign and the decision of State Department officials to propose the convening of an international conference to discuss the Far Eastern traffic. Acceptance of the proposal by the British government was a product of two factors: the Chinese anti-opium campaign, and the hostility of a large proportion of backbenchers to the Indo-China traffic in opium. This hostility was fostered and promoted by the British anti-opium movements over a period of thirty years. Both of these factors made it virtually impossible for Foreign Office officials to reject the American invitation.

The significance of the Shanghai Commission was latent. In the context of subsequent developments its importance was twofold. First, it led to the appointment of Dr. Hamilton Wright as an American commissioner and an ad hoc employee of the Department of State. Secondly, the commission's recommendations were used as a diplomatic lever to justify further international negotiations on the issues with which it had been concerned. Wright played a crucial role in securing the convening of the Hague conference. His impact on the development of an international system of narcotics control was very considerable Given that senior State Department officials were initially opposed to convening a further international conference, and that British officials made their participation dependent upon acceptance of certain pre-conditions which other powers were reluctant to agree to, it is probable that if Wright had not taken the initiative in this matter and relentlessly applied pressure on the governments of the invited powers, the conference would never have been convened. For instance, in an attempt to accelerate the pace of pre-conference negotiations, he wrote to Mackenzie King suggesting that he use his influence to this end: 'My idea is this: that in your powerful position at Ottawa you could have a resolution introduced to the effect that the Chinese government has the sympathy of Canada in her war on opium, and perhaps hint ... an approval of the proposed conference'. (FO371/846/p.18302) Clementi Smith informed the Foreign Office that Wright 'has apparently captured the State Department ... over the opium business, and in working to his own ends, he continues to make statements which have no foundation in fact'. (ibid, p.447) Wright attempted to bring pressure on the Dutch authorities by warning their ambassador in Washington 'that if the Dutch authorities continued to procrastinate, the United States might convene the conference in Washington'. (Musto 1973, p.49) The British ambassador there informed Grey that Wright had 'the eagerness of the specialist who has been placed in charge'. (FO371/1075/361) In Becker's terms he was a 'moral entrepreneur', an enterprising individual whose declared aim was to restructure public notions of 'right' and 'wrong'. (1966) However, to describe individuals as 'moral entrepreneurs' merely provides a short-hand term for describing their activities. It does not account for their success. Wright's was largely a product of his status as an ad hoc employee of the State Department and amateur diplomat. He was not subject to the same constraints which circumscribed the activities of career diplomats. He could therefore appeal over the heads of his immediate superiors, use unorthodox methods, and advocate policies that more cautious and knowledgeable professional diplomats would hesitate to pursue. In its wider context, the role of the United States in the development of a system of international narcotics control was a product of its distinct organisational approach to the conduct of international negotiations.

In contrast to most European countries, the United States authorities frequently grant a superordinate role to non-career diplomats in the handling of international conference negotiations. (cf. <u>Jacobson and Stein</u> (1966) for a discussion of the negotiations preceding the signing of the 1963 Nuclear Test Ban Treaty)

Until the outbreak of the First World War, it was mainly issues relating to the consumption and traffic in opium in the Far East, which preoccupied officials and diplomats involved in regional and international negotiations on these matters. In Britain there were few restrictions on the consumption and commerce in the substances specified in the Hague Convention. The provisions of the Pharmacy and Poisons Acts placed few obstacles in the paths of those desiring to consume them. During the war this changed dramatically. In 1916 two developments occurred. One required the introduction of restrictions on the external commerce in opium and the proscription of opium smoking. The second justified the imposition of controls over domestic consumption of cocaine. The problems posed to shipping companies by the illegal exportation of opium led to a tightening of controls in relation to this substance. The prohibition on opium smoking, the manufacture of prepared opium, etc., was directly related to this. It was probably assumed that if such opium was not produced it was less likely to be illegally exported. Moreover, the view of British officials and politicians seems to have been that there was no conceivable justification for permitting individuals to indulge in this practice. (cf. FO371/1925/194) Publicity lent by the press to the spread of cocaine and morphine consumption amongst British and allied soldiers constituted the <u>raison d'etre</u> for introducing restrictions on the availability of cocaine. It may be assumed that the main reason for not introducing similar restrictions on the availability of morphine and proprietary preparations containing opiates, was the anticipated opposition from pharmacists, druggists, chemists, and their professional associations.

If the convention had not been put into force, it is reasonably certain that the domestic controls introduced to give continuing effect to war-time drug control policies would have been far less wide-ranging than those provided for in the Dangerous Drugs Act and the Regulations. That it was brought into force was a by-product of the conjunction at approximately the same period in time of four factors: the desire of Home Office officials to continue to give effect to war-time controls; the difficulties encountered by the Foreign Office, the Board of Trade and the War Trade Department in preventing the importation of morphia of British origin into China; the State Department proposal to implement the convention, if only by a number of powers; and Macleay's suggestion in response to this that the matter be raised at the Paris conference.

Reports from British diplomats in China on the spread of morphine addiction there, particularly in Manchuria, overlapped with those relating to the smuggling of opium by seamen employed aboard British ships. Foreign Office officials were initially extremely reluctant to do anything about this situation, on grounds that it would be 'quixotic' to prevent exports to Japan of products that could be obtained elsewhere, although it was never indicated where else they could be purchased in large quantities. The approach of Foreign Office and diplomatic personnel to the handling of this question was somewhat incongruous. At the same time that Jordan was raising this issue with the Japanese Minister to China, and Max Muller was stressing that it was essential to 'deal with morphia and cocaine simultaneously with opium if the suppression of the less harmful opium smoking was not to prove more of a curse than a blessing to China', Foreign Office policy was still directed at forcing the Chinese authorities to permit entry of the vast opium stocks that had been accumulated by speculators at Shanghai, or at least compensate them in return for its re-export to India. Their handling of this issue once again illustrates that they had no clear or consistent policy relating to the international traffic in these drugs. If left to the Foreign Office, it is unlikely that controls over exports of morphia and cocaine to Japan and other countries would have been introduced. It was only because the War Trade Department and the Board of Trade intimated that it would be feasible to do so, and that they did so at approximately the same moment in time that the Edinburgh Anti-Opium Committee and other organisations were lodging protests on this question, that Foreign Office officials embarked on a policy directed at introducing an import certificate system. It was probably negotiations on this issue which encouraged State Department officials to suggest in August 1918 that 'prompt measures' be taken to put into force the Hague Opium Convention. It was in response to this proposal, one which Foreign Office officials, along with those of the Colonial and India Offices, and the Board of Trade, objected to , that Ronald Macleay suggested that the matter be raised at the Peace Conference. Initially, this policy was not actively supported by the United States Commission in Paris. Although it is clear that some other delegations were interested in using the opportunity provided by the conference to resolve this question, particularly the Chinese, only those powers represented on the Supreme Allied Council were in a position to ensure that it was raised in the appropriate committees. Despite the fact that the British Commission actively pursued this policy, the entrusting of supervision over execution of the convention to the League of Nations, was dependent upon what role it was agreed it would play in international affairs. This was an issue which in no sense can be considered to have been determined in advance. Once this question had been resolved, it followed as a matter of course that it would be necessary to obtain the sanction of the conference for a resolution imposing upon signatories of the peace treaties the obligation to ratify the convention, and then bring it into force. There was no point in entrusting the League with a supervisory role if there was nothing to monitor.

There are two final points about the convention which should be reiterated. First, it was designed to regulate the <u>international traffic</u> in opiate-narcotic substances. <u>It was not directed</u> at controlling the non-medical consumption of these substances in European countries, for the simple reason that none of the European powers represented at the Shanghai or Hague conferences considered that they were faced with domestic narcotics problems of sufficient dimensions to require regulation by the means provided for in the convention. Even in respect of the Far Eastern problem, the convention was aimed primarily at curbing the traffic, not consumption. It was assumed that the convention would be self-regulating, in the sense that if the traffic was carefully controlled non-medical consumption would automatically be extinguished or diminished. This accounts for the fact that no attention was ever paid to the question of what policies should be pursued in relation to persons addicted to these substances. Whatever else the convention may be construed to have been, it was definitely not a repressive measure directed at curbing the activities of a 'deviant' segment of the population.

Secondly, none of the delegates to any of the international conferences, and none of the British officials involved in formulating policies on these issues, ever intended the convention to be interpreted in such a way as to imply that the drugs specified in Chapter III, that is, morphine, heroin, cocaine, their derivatives, etc., should be used for anything other than legitimate medical purposes. Without exception they considered that the non-medical consumption of these substances was harmful and should be prevented. They may have had few, if any, 'scientifically grounded' reasons for believing this, but that they considered their main use to be medicinal is beyond dispute. This was one of the reasons why there was no opposition to the inclusion of a resolution in the Shanghai Commission's recommendations urging the governments of the participating powers to introduce 'drastic measures' to control the manufacture, sale and distribution of these substances. The reluctance of the German authorities to ratify the convention stemmed, not from any disagreement with this generally held view, but from a desire to preserve the economic interests of their manufacturers in, as Max Muller succinctly put it, 'the legitimate business of poisoning Hindoos and Chinese'.

Taking a broad overview of the sequence of events which in 1919 culminated in ratification of the convention by the most important countries involved in the production of opium and the manufacture of narcotic substances, one thing is clear: there was nothing inevitable about the process. A large number of different factors were implicated, many evolving from independent sets of circumstances. Each link in the chain, itself frequently a product of the favourable conjuncture of disparate events, was a necessary pre-condition leading to the bringing into force of the convention. Conflict, inasmuch as it was a contributory factor, was not of the type usually attended to by sociologists of law. Their preoccupation is mainly with the intra-state variety. In the shaping of the convention, inter-state and inter-departmental conflicts were of much greater significance.

THE DANGEROUS DRUGS ACT AND ITS INTERPRETATION

As already noted in the conclusion to chapter 5, questions of inter-departmental responsibility and jurisdiction impinged significantly on shaping the content and emphasis of the Hague Convention. It was primarily because the Foreign Office was responsible for overseeing the Shanghai and Hague negotiations, whilst simultaneously its officials believed that no significant British interests were at stake, that they permitted those of the India and Colonial Offices, and colonial administrators, to dictate British terms for arriving at an acceptable international accord. Questions of inter-departmental responsibility were equally important in determining the policy adopted in Britain in relation to the management of addiction.

Soon after the convention was signed, the Treasury Commissioners approached the Foreign Office in connection with the legislation that it might be necessary to introduce to comply with its provisions. They suggested that the Board of Customs and Excise was 'the natural agency for giving effect to the policy decided upon', on the understanding that the Foreign Office would 'undertake the defence of the policy adopted and of any legislation required to give statutory effect to that policy'. (FO371/1330/467) Grey was not inclined to accept this solution. He argued that the 'Board of Trade, Colonial Office and India Office are the Departments most directly concerned. I will, of course, assist in defending it if desired and when I can'. (ibid, p.463) There then followed an extensive correspondence between the Home Office, the Privy Council Office, the Board of Trade, the Foreign, India and Colonial Offices on the question of which should assume responsibility for introducing and implementing such legislation. Each department involved in these exchanges was more than willing to shift the onus on to some other department. After the Colonial Office had suggested that it was the role of the Board of Trade to manage legislation of this sort, Stanley, a senior official, noted that he must 'demur to this altogether. The C.O. are too fond, it seems to me, of appearing to assume direction as to the business which the B.T. should undertake. Something ought to be done to put a stop to this'. (B.T. 11-14/C1000/19/C2091-1912) In reply he noted that the character of the convention was such that it did not fall within their usual functions, which 'have regard to matters relating to the maintenance and promotion of the Trade of the United Kingdom, whereas the measures contemplated by the convention are primarily designed to benefit the interests not of the United Kingdom, but the interests of H.M. Eastern Possessions and Colonies'. (ibid 23 March 1912) Eighteen months later he put forward the view that the Home Office was the department with primary responsibility for the matter, since the legislation would be restrictive in character, necessitate some form of supervision over factories, possibly some form of licensing, and the imposition of penalties for offences under any legislation which was passed. (FO371/1601/190) The Home Office, however, was no more interested in assuming responsibility for this matter than any of the others. It suggested that since the Privy Council Office was responsible for supervising the implementation of the Poisons and Pharmacy Acts, it should assume jurisdiction in relation to matters covered by the convention.

Although in retrospect demarcation disputes of this sort may appear trivial, their method of resolution is of importance. Departments vary in their functions, their methods of carrying these out, and also in the means they employ to ensure compliance on the part of regulated individuals and groups. Even within any one department, sub-divisions will frequently evolve distinct control strategies. Although control strategies are frequently dictated by legislative prescriptions, officials are usually left with a considerable degree of discretion for determining whether, and under what circumstances, the regulatory powers they possess will be invoked. Thus, to take but one of many examples that could be used to illustrate this point, legislation governing the safety, health and welfare of industrial employees in Britain, 'especially provides for its enforcement by means of criminal sanctions. Offenders can be tried summarily and may be fined ... in instances where the contravention was likely to cause death or bodily injury ... imprisonment for up to three months is permitted for offences such as personation, forgery of documents and making false declarations'. (Carson 1971, p.196) From a perusal of some of the Factory Inspectorate's files, Carson established that their preferred method of dealing with the 'substantial' amount of violations was by the use of formal administrative procedures, rather than by drawing on their powers to invoke the criminal law. They did not 'see themselves as members of an industrial police force primarily concerned with the apprehension and subsequent punishment of offenders. Rather, they perceived their major function to be that of securing compliance with the standards of safety, health and welfare required and thereby achieving the ends at which the legislation is directed'. (ibid, p.201)

Some legislative measures originate within regulatory agencies, as did the American Marihuana Tax Act 1937, for whose drafting and piloting through Congress officials of the Federal Bureau of Narcotics assumed primary responsibility. Others are a response to the demands of what Blumer designates as general social movements, 'movements such as the labor movement, the youth movement, the women's movement, and the peace movement. Their background is constituted by gradual and pervasive changes in the values of people – changes which can be called cultural drifts'. (1969, p.9) American anti-trust legislation introduced in the period 1890-1909, and the Pure Food Act 1906, were responses to changes of this order. On the other hand, legislation is frequently enacted to meet demands presented by specific social movements. Such a movement is one which 'has a well-defined objective or goal which it seeks to reach. In this effort it develops an organisation and structure, making it essentially a society'. (ibid, p.11) Examples of legislation that can be traced to the activities of such movements abound: the Anti-Corn Law League and repeal of the Corn Laws; the Women's Christian Temperance Union and the Eighteenth Amendment and the Volstead Act; the British Committee for the Abolition of the Slave Trade and the Abolition Act of 1807.

Neither the Hague Convention nor the Dangerous Drugs Act was primarily a result of the enterprising efforts of officials attached to regulatory agencies. Nor can they be traced directly to the endeavours of participants in identifiable social movements. As no special interest group in Britain was pressing for the introduction of legislation to control the availability of opiate-narcotics during the period 1912-19, and as the articles of the convention did not stipulate what methods should be instituted to ensure compliance with their terms, the particular department that would assume responsibility for such measures was of crucial importance in determining how the convention would be interpreted and enforced in the United Kingdom. In determining the content of legislation, and deciding upon a strategy of enforcement, officials were likely to be influenced by their acquaintance with control techniques they were currently applying, or had used in the past, in relation to other or allied matters over which they had administrative jurisdiction.

The areas of primary responsibility of a particular department delimits the types of organisations or individuals whose activities its officials are supposed to regulate or monitor. In order to carry out these supervisory functions, officials of regulatory agencies or departments establish direct links of a formal or informal character with their counterparts in such organisations. Edelman notes that 'the creation of an administrative agency in a policy area signals the emergence of a changed relationship between the groups labelled as adversaries. The agency, the regulated groups, and the ostensible beneficiaries become necessary instruments for each other while continuing to play the role of rivals and combatants'. (1964, p.57) The self interest of all parties lends itself to the development of some

form of _modus vivendi_. The policies of complex industrial societies
'demand technical knowledge which, frequently, the members of some
interest groups are best able to supply. In any case, they often
require the positive co-operation of interest groups if they are
effectively to be carried out'. (Eckstein 1960, p.23) Regulatory
bodies frequently rely on the assistance of the regulated in determining
the nature of the controls to be applied, and in their enforcement. The
pressure groups with which any one department develops particularly
close ties is likely to be dictated primarily by the nature of the tasks
it is entrusted with. As the policies being pursued by different
departments will frequently effect the interests of those represented by
one particular pressure group, the latter, in an attempt to influence
them, may establish close ties with more than one government department
or regulatory agency. Thus, for example, the Pharmaceutical Society of
Great Britain will liaise closely with the Home Office due to its
responsibility for enforcement of the Dangerous Drugs Acts, as well as
with the Department of Health and Social Security, since the latter
oversees the procuring policies of the National Health Service. More
usually, the main fuctions of a particular department are likely to
impinge on the interests represented by a specific pressure group to a
greater degree than those of other departments or agencies.
Consequently, it is on the development of close ties with these that
interest groups will concentrate. As Eckstein notes:

> The most important, and the most obvious, determinant of the
> selection of channels for pressure group activity, in any particular
> system, is the structure of the decision-making processes which
> pressure groups seek to influence. Interest groups (or any other
> groups) become pressure groups because they want to obtain
> favourable policy decisions or administrative dispositions; hence,
> obviously, they must adjust their activities to the processes by
> which decisions and dispositions are made. (ibid, p.16)

The consultative and administrative relations established between
interest groups and regulatory authorities, lead in some cases to a high
degree of mutual dependence. This is particularly likely to occur when
a department or regulatory agency has to rely on the co-operation of
some pressure group, or groups, in the course of carrying out a
multiplicity of different, though interrelated, functions. During the
period under consideration in the present study, the Board of Trade
relied heavily on the co-operation of employer and employee
associations, whilst the Ministry of Health established close links with
medical and ancillary medical interest groups.

Once a department has established a particular approach to ensuring
compliance with its policies, any measure that relies on alternative
methods which are radically at variance with these, carries the
potential for disrupting the interdependent relationships that it has
developed with associations representing the interests of those likely
to be effected by its implementation. Both the Board of Trade and the
Privy Council Office were reluctant to assume responsibility for
legislation required under the terms of the Hague Convention since they
concluded that its implementation would require the imposing of punitive
penalties for non-compliance with its provisions. Their view, it is
reasonable to assume, was that if such measures were necessary at all,
it was preferable that they should be introduced and enforced by a
department which did not have primary responsibility for monitoring the

activities of employers, or members of the pharmaceutical professions, so as not to disrupt the modus vivendi that they had arrived at with these groups in relation to their other departmental responsibilities. Since the imposition of criminal sanctions for violations meant that the enabling legislation would inevitably be a 'police measure', it seemed to them that the legislation would fall within the normal ambit of responsibility of the Home Office.

It is quite likely that if sole responsibility for drug control had been left in the hands of Home Office officials, the British approach to the control of drug addiction would not have been markedly dissimilar to that which has been pursued in the United States since the middle of the nineteen twenties. Sociologists, relying heavily on the work of Lindesmith in this field, have repeatedly drawn attention to differences in the methods of managing addiction that have been adopted by authorities in the two countries. Broadly speaking, the American system of narcotics control is punitively oriented, whereas persons recognised as being addicted to opiate-narcotics in Britain are enabled under certain conditions to obtain regular supplies of such substances. No reasons have been advanced to explain why British policy developed this medical cast.

Undoubtedly, one of the more important factors that accounts for this was the successful application of pressure by organisations representing the interests of medical practitioners and pharmacists on the Home Office, and the Ministry of Health, during that period when legislation relating to these matters was under consideration, as well as in the course of the early years of its implementation. Ministry of Health officials played a crucial role at both stages. The success of these pressure groups in achieving their objectives was due in large measure to the responsiveness of officials of that department to their demands.

One of the consequences of administrative specialisation and the development of relations of mutual-dependence between a particular department and pressure groups, is that officials attached to different departments vary in the extent to which they are willing to accommodate the demands of a specific interest group. Home Office officials, for instance, were extremely unresponsive to requests for policy changes emanating from medical and pharmaceutical pressure groups in connection with matters relating to the regulation of the sale and distribution of the drugs controlled under the provisions of the Dangerous Drugs Act. This contrasted with the attitude adopted by officials of the Ministry of Health, who were more inclined to accommodate their representations. They were probably inclined to do so for three reasons. First, those involved in formulating policy on these issues were themselves medical practitioners by training. They were therefore likely to share the views of their professional colleagues on the nature of addiction, and on the suitability of varying methods of 'treating' or controlling it. Secondly, they were heavily dependent upon the co-operation of these groups in carrying out many of their functions in the field of public health. Thirdly, since the Ministry of Health had only been established in 1919, its senior officials were probably concerned at this stage to ensure that other departments did not seek to appropriate jurisdiction over matters which could be interpreted as being directly related to issues of public health. It was only because the system of controls that it was necessary to introduce to implement the provisions of the Hague Convention enabled them to argue with some degree of plausibility that the legislation would necessarily be of a hybrid nature, that the 'British approach' to the management of drug addiction assumed a medical orientation.

In a memorandum dated 11 June 1919, Dr McCleary put the case for the Ministry of Health assuming responsibility for the control of dangerous drugs. His opinion was that there were two aspects to the Hague Convention: the control of exports, which fell within the jurisdiction of the Board of Trade, and the control of imports and internal consumption:

> In the question of controlling the importation of and the internal dealings in opium, morphia, etc. the public health aspects assume much greater importance. The object of the control which the convention would impose in this connection is the protection of the national health from the injurious effects of the illicit use of these drugs. This is obviously a public health matter. And it is most important that the suppression of the illicit usage should be effected without undue interference with the legitimate medical use of these drugs, which in medical practice are widely used, and are of essential importance. (M.H. 58(51)/File 95006/1/27)

He recommended that the Home Office be informed of the ministry's intention of obtaining official sanction for the taking over of responsibility for these matters.

At the Home Office, Delevingne had assumed personal responsibility for drafting the Dangerous Drugs Bill. In reply to McCleary's letter, he contended that:

> the control of opium, cocaine, and other dangerous drugs should remain with the Home Office ... The matter is very largely a police matter ... and on the police side as you know it has its international as well as its national aspects, especially in connection with the prevention of smuggling. Being so largely a police matter, the enforcement of the regulations has in the main been undertaken by the police, and there would be considerable objections to its being transferred to another department which is not in close relations with the police. The question stands on exactly the same footing as the control of poisons, with which it is closely allied, and it is clear that the control of poisons is a matter which should remain where it is, that is with the Privy Council Office and the Home Office. (HO45/Box 10969/File 399514)

It was eventually agreed between Delevingne and the Chief Medical Officer of the ministry, that there 'should be active and continuous co-operation' between the two departments on this issue. Delevingne, however, desired to ensure that the controlling voice in these matters should be his. On 1 September, the Second-Secretary at the ministry summed up his understanding of the arrangement between the two departments in a letter to him:

> It is agreed between our respective Departments that responsibility in connection with the matters under discussion ... is to be exercised concurrently, the Home Office looking after the police side with the Ministry of Health the public health side. (ibid)

Delevingne thought that this went too far. In reply he stresed that `concurrent responsibility' should not be taken to mean `anything more than the usual departmental consultation in matters of joint interest. Anything in the nature of a `condominium' would not be desirable'. (HO45/Box 10969/File 399514/5) At this point the Second-Secretary of the ministry concluded that it was unlikely that any further concessions could be extracted from Delevingne, and the question of departmental responsibility was left there.

Delevingne's interest in these matters dates from 1914. He then represented the Home Office at seven inter-departmental meetings held to determine the nature of the legislation it would be necessary to introduce in order to comply with the convention's provisions. The meetings were also attended by representatives of the India, Colonial, Foreign and Privy Council Offices, as well as those of the Boards of Customs and Excise and Trade. For the most part attention focused on devising solutions to administrative and technical problems, such as the procedures to be followed by the customs authorities in controlling exports and imports of the drugs in question; who should be licenced to receive them; the nature of the information regarding transactions which dealers should be obliged to enter in registers; the grounds for cancelling registrations or licenses, and so forth. Most of the solutions which were agreed were later incorporated in the Dangerous Drugs Bill.

One matter upon which there was clearly no disagreement was that consumption of these drugs should not be permitted for purposes of mere indulgence. When the articles of the convention relating to prepared opium were under discussion, F.D. Acland, Parliamentary Secretary to the Foreign Office, who chaired the meetings, interjected that he was not in favour of the gradual suppression of opium smoking, being of the opinion that its immediate suppression should be aimed at. (F0371/1925/194) This clearly went beyond what a literal interpretation of Article 6 required, as did the committee's proposals for regulating the availability of raw opium. Unlike the provisions concerning morphine, cocaine, etc., no article in Chapter I stipulated that the uses of raw opium should be confined only to `medical and legitimate' purposes. It was decided to consult Sir William Collins on the question of whether `people given to the drug habit could, presuming they were unable to obtain the prepared drug, satisfy their craving by taking raw opium, or themselves easily treat it in such a manner as to render it a substitute for the prepared drug'. (ibid, p.145) Collins was an inveterate opponent of any form of intemperance. In his view alcohol and drug addiction "are to be regarded as examples of the surrender of self-control in favour of self-indulgence, or the voluntary preference for the lower in the presence of the higher alternative of volition, exercised in obedience to appetite rather than to the `higher command' of conscience". (The Lancet 1915, p.848) In his reply he stressed that it certainly was the case that those addicted to opium smoking would substitute raw opium for the prepared product if supplies of the latter were not available. He concluded that it would be `necessary to control even the sale of small quantities to deal effectively with the drug habit'. (F0371/1925/193) In view of this, the committee decided that `it is essential that its distribution should be controlled in this country whether the strict letter of the Convention render it obligatory or not'. (ibid)

A similar approach was adopted in relation to the interpretation of the terms 'medical and legitimate uses only', in the context of the substances covered by the provisions of Chapter III of the convention. Acland stated that he considered that 'private consumers' should only be permitted to purchase these drugs on a doctor's prescription. It was agreed that these drugs should only be sold to (1) persons having a medical prescription, (2) registered doctors, dentists and veterinary surgeons, (3) persons licensed under the Cruelty to Animal Acts, and (4) other licensed persons. (ibid, p.345) This policy was fully in accord with the views of the Medical Secretary of the British Medical Association, who in response to enquiries from the committee, argued that he had 'no doubt whatever as to the desirability of limiting the sale to private consumers of the substances mentioned in article 14 of the convention to persons in possession of a doctor's prescription, and I think that the great majority of the medical profession would agree with the suggestion'. One of the advantages of such a limitation would be that 'any medical man who was found to be allowing his prescriptions to be used as a means of procuring these substances for the purposes of mere indulgence would be amenable to the discipline of the General Medical Council'. (F0371/1927/83, emphasis added.)

From the proposals that were agreed it is clear that no member of the inter-departmental committee had any intention of permitting consumers access to the drugs specified in the convention, solely for the purpose of satisfying their 'cravings' or, as the Secretary of the British Medical Association put it, for 'mere indulgence'. Delevingne strictly adhered to this approach in formulating the DORA regulations. These were conceived and implemented as if they were strictly police measures. The question of whether medical practitioners should be permitted to prescribe these drugs to persons addicted to their use was never discussed by the committee.

Home Office officials eventually conceded the right of medical practitioners to prescribe morphine and heroin to persons addicted to their use because of certain characteristics of the British administrative decision-making proces, and the power of the medical profession. Home Office officials, particularly Delevingne, were as hostile towards non-medical consumption of these substances as were many officials of the Narcotics Division of the American Treasury Department. There is no doubt that if questions concerning the treatment of addiction had been left to the Home Office to determine, then the policy adopted during the war in relation to prepared opium and cocaine would have been extended to the other substances specified in Chapter III of the convention. At the Home Office it was Delevingne who dictated decisions on all questions concerning the consumption and traffic in drugs covered by the convention. In his obituary in The Times he was described as 'something of an autocrat, preferring to keep matters in his own hands rather than to delegate them to others ... His mind perhaps lacked breadth in some directions, and he sometimes gave the impression ... of being too much of the bureaucrat who thought that to settle a matter you had only to tie it up in a bundle of regulations, preferably of his own drafting'. (1 December 1950) Although he could afford to alienate members of the medical and ancilliary medical professions with relative equanimity, Ministry of Health officials could not. Since they were also interested in influencing the way in which the Dangerous Drugs Act would be interpreted, the Home Office had to take their views into account. Members of the medical profession could bring more pressure to bear on ministry officials than they could on those of the Home Office because the former were dependent on their co-operation in carrying out a considerable proportion of their administrative responsibilities.

In the United States the situation was quite different. First, the number of persons consuming morphine and heroin for non-medical purposes was considerably greater. Secondly, the influence of the medical profession was strongest at the state level. Medical practice was regulated by state authorities, not by the federal government. Since the Constitution of the United States, as interpreted at the time, did not delegate powers for regulating public health to the federal government, there was no federal administrative entity with responsibility for matters handled in Great Britain by the Ministry of Health. Only in 1953 did Congress sanction the establishing of a Department of Health, Education and Welfare. Consequently, the relationships that evolved between American medical practitioners, their representative organisations, and officials of federal administrative agencies, were quite different from those that existed between their British counterparts. Brand noted in connection with the latter that:

The passage of Lloyd George's Insurance Act demonstrated, as never before, the radical change in public outlook which had taken place in England between 1870 and 1912. Central government compulsion for health and welfare had become acceptable to a degree considered intolerable in the eighteen-seventies. Simultaneously, the scope and direction of public health expanded from sanitary reform to the provision of curative medicine and personal health services. During the same years the physician's relationship to government evolved from the independent professional, loosely linked to community authority, to a status close to that of a state agent ... The notification acts, registration of birth and death requirements, and the extended participation in judicial processes-all brought the private practitioner within a larger framework of government health action. (1965, pp.232-235)

Ministry of Health officials, many of whom were physicians by training, were bound to be more sympathetic towards the protestations of practicing physicians concerning the conditions under which narcotics should be prescribed, than were officials of the Narcotics Division of the United States Treasury Department. Between the former two their had evolved close ties of mutual dependence. Neither ministry officials nor practicing physicians could carry out their respective responsibilities in the absence of mutual consultation and co-operation. Officials of the Narcotics Division had no special responsibilities respecting medical practitioners. Moreover, since the main medical pressure group in the United States, the American Medical Association, was much weaker than its British counterpart, and as there was no federal agency which necessitated its co-operation in carrying out policies relating to issues of public health, doctors had no means of bringing direct or indirect pressure to bear on federal officials with responsibility for enforcing the Harrison Act. Consequently, disputes between them relating to the rights of physicians to prescribe narcotics to those addicted to their use could only be resolved in the courts. It is differences of this order which largely explain why medical practitioners in the United States were prevented from prescribing narcotics to addicts, whilst in Britain they were enabled to do so.

This interpretation conflicts significantly with explanations advanced by Lindesmith, Duster and Schur. Lindesmith contends that:

> The present program of handling the drug problem in the United States is, from the legal viewpoint, a remarkable one in that it was not established by legislative enactment or by court interpretations of such enactments ... The basic antinarcotic statute in the United States is the Harrison Act of 1914. It was passed as a revenue measure and made absolutely no mention of addicts or addiction. Its ostensible purpose appeared to be simply to make the entire process of drug distribution within the country a matter of record ... There is no indication of a legislative intention to deny addicts access to legal drugs or to interfere in any way with medical practices in this area. (1965, pp.3-4)

Nothing could be further from the truth. The Harrison Act was introduced as a revenue measure for the simple reason that the United States Constitution did not delegate powers to the federal government to regulate medical practice. Consequently, some device had to be found to enforce the provisions of the Hague Opium Convention whilst 'appearing' not to violate its provisions. For similar reasons the Sherman and Mann acts were introduced under the interstate commerce clauses of the constitution. Dr. Hamilton Wright had been in charge of conducting negotiations with relevant pressure groups prior to its being discussed in the relevant congressional committees. He had returned from the Hague conference, as Musto notes, 'with two goals: increasing the number of signatories to the convention and dispelling any doubt that this nation would pass the necessary legislation ... (He) believed that the legislative goal should be elimination of narcotics except for medical purposes'. (1973, p.54) Since the federal government had no jurisdiction over the practice of medicine, it is extremely unlikely that the Harrison Act would have been passed by Congress at this time if the Senate had not already ratified the Hague Convention. Those who had been responsible for drafting that document had, as already noted, intended to confine the use of narcotics to legitimate medical purposes. This did not include their consumption by those addicted to their use. The reason why the act did not make any direct mention of 'addicts or addiction', was probably that those responsible for drafting it assumed, as had Home Office officials in Britain, that prescribing dangerous drugs to addicts merely to sustain their addiction did not fall within the ambit of legitimate medical practice. There is no justification for concluding that this omission meant that there was no 'legislative intention to deny addicts access to legal drugs'.

Lindesmith's contention that the policy of denying addicts legal access to narcotics conflicted with 'court interpretations', is based on his understanding of the Linder case:

> Unlike the doctors in the earlier cases ... Linder provided only four tablets of drugs for one addict ... Reiterating that the Harrison Law was a revenue measure, the Court added the following important statement: "It says nothing of 'addicts' and does not undertake to prescribe methods for their medical treatment. They are diseased and proper subjects for such treatment, and we cannot possibly conclude that a physician acted improperly or unwisely or for other than medical purposes solely because he has dispensed to one of them ... four small tablets <u>for relief of conditions incident to addiction</u>" (1965, p.9.

Emphasis added.)

The Court <u>did not</u> mean to imply that physicians were thereby entitled to prescribe narcotics to addicts in order to sustain their addiction, in the way that Britain physicians had been permitted to following acceptance of the Rolleton Committee's recommendations. It is only his distortion of the record by selective quoting that has given rise to the myth that agents of the Federal Bureau of Narcotics were enforcing the law in a manner which directly contravened 'court interpretations'. The opinion of the Court on this question is crystal clear. Referring to previous cases argued before it, the opinion reads:

> <u>Webb v. United States</u> ... came here on certified questions. Two were answered upon authority of Dormeus's case. The third inquired whether a regular physician's order for morphine issued to an addict, not in the course of professional treatment with design to cure the habit, but in order to provide enough of the drug to keep him comfortable by maintaining his customary use, is a 'physician's prescription'. The answer thus given must not be construed as forbidding every prescription for drugs, irrespective of quantity, <u>when designed temporarily to alleviate an addict's pains</u>, although it may have been issued in good faith and without design to defeat the revenues. (Linder v. U.S., 268, U.S. 5(1925), pp.18-21. Emphasis added.)

In other words, the Court ruled that the prescribing of narcotic drugs to an addict so as to 'keep him comfortable by maintaining his customary use', was illegal. The only conditions under which a doctor was legally entitled to prescribe narcotics to an addict patient was when the quantities involved were small, and they were prescribed or dispensed as a temporary means of alleviating conditions incident to addiction, a view that was reiterated in a number of separate places in the opinion. Lindesmith and others could reasonably argue that the opinion is riddled with ambiguity and inconsistencies, in that the only method of alleviating pains incident to addiction when no cure can be effected, is by maintaining the addict's 'customary use'. The Court's opinion in the Linder case is not exceptional in containing ambiguities and inconsistencies. Moreover, the views contained therein are identical with those held by officials of the Ministry of Health prior to referral of this question to the Departmental Committee on Morphine and Heroin Addiction.

The reasons for this and similar distortions and misinterpretations by Schur, Goode and Duster is that these analysts are all dedicated opponents of the American system of narcotics control. Theirs is not a quest for explanations but for solutions to a pressing social problem. As Slater and Nardin note:

> controversy about public afairs tends to be characterised by the search for pragmatic explanations aimed at identifying factors which can and should be manipulated to bring about change, rather than by a search for complete explanations which take account of factors which, while important, are beyond the reach of practical influence. Furthermore, such controversy often focuses on the identification of individuals or groups that seem to be responsible for the occurrence of or persistence of disapproved events, policies or situations, and against whom pressure can be mobilised to effect

186

reform. (1973, p.29)

By concentrating their ire on agents of the Federal Bureau of Narcotics, and neglecting wider institutional issues of the type discussed above, they fully justify Gouldner's criticism that 'insofar as this school of theory has a critical edge to it, this is directed at the caretaking institutions who do the mopping-up job, rather than at the master institutions that produce deviant suffering'. (1968, p.107) After all, since 1914 congressmen have had ample opportunity to amend these laws, and influence the mode of their implementation. Rather than doing so, they have consistently introduced more severe penalties for narcotics violations.

That the concerns of these theorists are primarily moral is easily demonstrated. Duster maintains, for instance, that a 'moral posture towards drugs should be assumed only after there is firm, adequate knowledge of the physical effects', thereby implying that there is some inexorable political necessity to enact legislation on the basis of scientific findings. (1970, p.236; cf. Goode 1972, p.183) Lindesmith argues that 'it may be contended that one of the most important long-range effects and advantages of the medical treatment of addicts is that it is the decent, just and humanitarian thing to do'. (1965, p.289) This argument, whatever its merits, is a politico-moral statement, not one that it is possible to deduce from a detailed analysis of the factors implicated in the enactment, enforcement, and interpretation of American narcotics legislation. On questions concerning the relationship between science and morality, one can safely leave the last word to Max Weber:

> To the person who cannot bear the fate of the times like a man, one must say: may he rather return silently, without the usual publicity build-up of renegades, but simply and plainly. The arms of the old churches spread widely and compassionately for him. After all, they do not make it hard for him. One way or another he has to bring his 'intellectual sacrifice' - that is inevitable. If he can really do it, we shall not rebuke him. For such an intellectual sacrifice in favor of an unconditional religious devotion is ethically quite a different matter than the evasion of plain duty of intellectual integrity, which sets in if one lacks the courage to clarify one's own ultimate standpoint and rather facilities this duty by feeble relative judgements. (1970, p.155)

Bibliography

BRITISH PUBLIC RECORDS

(a) Foreign Office (FO)

    371 (1906-1926)
    415
    228
    608

(b) Board of Trade (BT)

    11-14/C 1000/19
    11/24 CRT 1037/23

(c) Ministry of Health (MH)

    58 (51) File 95006

(d) Home Office (HO)

    45/Boxes: 10813, 10500, 13351, 10969, 11613, 11599,
              13231, 11240, 20037, 16176, 19978, 19980,
              19981, 11629, 11238, 19979, 12283, 11922,
              11028, 15597.

PRIVATE PAPERS

Anglo-Oriental Society for the Suppression of the Opium Trade. Minute
    Books, 1891-1895. London: Friend's House.

Davidson Papers. Special Box, Opium, 1907–1908. London: Lambeth
  Palace.
Grey (Sir E.) Papers. London: Public Records Office.
Hirtzel (F.A.) Papers. London: India Office.
Morley (J.M.) Papers. London: India Office.

OFFICIAL REPORTS (in chronological order)

Report of the Select Committee on Public Petitions.   Annual, 1875–1890:
  London.
Foreign Relations of the United States.   Annual, 1880–1920: Washington,
  D.C.
Hansard. 1880–1926: London.
Report of the Centenary Conference of the Protestant Missions of the
  World. 1882. London: James Nisbet and Co. 2 vols.
Royal Commission on Opium.   British Parliamentary Papers, 1894, vols.
  III, LX, LXI; 1895, vols. VI, XLII. London.
Report of the Committee Appointed by the Philippine Commission to
  Investigate the Use of Opium and the Traffic Therein.   1904.   Senate
  Document No.265, 59th Congress, 1st Sess. Washington D.C.
Report of the Hearings at the American State Department on Petitions to
  the President to Use his Good Offices for the Release of China from
  Treaty Compulsion to Tolerate the Opium Traffic, with Additional
  Papers. 1905. Senate Document No.135, 58th Congress, 3rd Sess.
  Washington D.C.
Report of the International Opium Commission.   1909.   Shanghai: North-
  China Daily News and Herald. 2 vols.
Report on the International Opium Commission and the Opium Problem as
  seen within the United States and its Possessions.   1910.   Senate
  Document 377, 61st Congress, 2nd Sess. Washington D.C.
Annual Statement's of the Trade of the United Kingdom.   Annual: 1911–
  1926. Published in British Parliamentary Papers, London.
Secret Remedies: What they Cost and What they Contain.   1909. London:
  British Medical Association.
More Secret Remedies, What they Cost and What they Contain.   1912.
  London: British Medical Association.
Report of the Committee on the Use of Cocaine in Dentistry.   1917–1918.
  London: Included in British Parliamentary Papers, Vol.8.
Report of the Committee Appointed by the Secretary of State for the Home
  Department to Consider Outstanding Objections to the Draft Regulations
  Issued Under the Dangerous Drugs Act, 1920.   London: British
  Parliamentary Papers, Vol.X, 1921.
Advisory Committee on Traffic in Opium.   Minutes, 1921–1927.   Geneva:
  League of Nations.
Report of the Departmental Committee on Morphine and Heroin Addiction.
  1926. London.
Report of the Departmental Committee on the Poisons and Pharmacy Acts.
  1930. London.
Estimated World Requirements of Dangerous Drugs in 1935. 1934. Geneva:
  League of Nations Supervisory Body.   Official No., C.462.   M.198.
  1934. XI.
Second Report of the Interdepartmental Committee on Drug Addiction.
  1965. London.

PERIODICALS

All Nations Missionary Magazine, 1902-1914. London.
British Journal of Inebriety, 1915-1926. London.
Chemist and Druggist. London.
China's Millions, 1875-1898.
Herald of Asia, Tokyo.
Illustrated Missionary News, 1894-1912. London.
Knowledge. London.
Medical Missions at Home and Abroad, 1889-1915. London.
Missionary Herald, 1891-1907. London.
Missionary Review of the World. New York.
National Righteousness, 1888-1915. London.
Pharmaceutical Journal, 1900-1926. London.
Regions Beyond, 1895-1910. London.
The British Medical Journal, 1900-1926. London.
The Chronicle of the London Missionary Society, 1879-1910. London.
The Church Missionary Intelligencer, 1888-1912. London.
The Friend of China, 1875-1916. London.
The Lancet, 1900-1926. London.

NEWSPAPERS

Daily Mail. London.
Daily Mirror. London.
Daily Telegraph. London.
Japan Weekly Chronicle. Tokyo.
News of the World. London.
North China Daily News. Peking.
North China Herald. Peking.
Pall Mall Gazette. London.
Peking Daily News. Peking.
The Sunday Post. Glasgow.
The Times, 1874-1926. London.

MISCELLANEOUS

Linder vs. U.S., 268 U.S. 5 (1925)
Roosevelt, T. Presidential Addresses and State Papers. (1904)   New
    York: The Review of Reviews Company.
Statutory Rules and Orders, 1914-1926. London: H.M.S.O.

BOOKS, MONOGRAPHS AND ARTICLES

Alexander, R. (1856) The Rise and Progress of British Opium Smuggling:
    Four Letters Addressed to the Right Honourable the Earl of
    Shaftesbury. London: Seeley, Jackson and Halliday.
Alexander, R. (1857) Contraband Opium Traffic: The Disturbing Element in
    All Our Policy and Diplomatic Intercourse with China. London:
    Seeley, Jackson and Halliday.
Allbutt, T.C. and Rolleston, H.D. (eds) (1910) A System of Medicine.
    London: Macmillan. 11 Vols.
Allbutt, T.C. and Dixon, W.E. (1910) 'Opium Poisoning and Other
    Intoxications', in Allbutt and Rolleston, 1910, Vol.2.

Asbury, H. (1968) The Barbary Coast. New York: Capricorn Books.

Barber, J. (1976) Who Makes British Foreign Policy? Milton Keynes: Open University Press.

Becker, H.S. (1966) Outsiders. New York: Free Press.

Beeching, J. (1975) The Chinese Opium Wars. London: Hutchinson.

Bergamini, D. (1972) Japan's Imperial Conspiracy. London: Panther Books.

Blake, C. (1960) Charles Elliot, R.N. 1801-1875. London: Cleaver-Hume Press.

Bloomfield, M.H. (1967) Alarms and Diversions: The American Mind Through American Magazines 1900-1914. The Hague: Mouton.

Blumer, H. (1969) 'Social Movements', in McLaughlin, B. (ed), Social Movements. New York: Free Press.

Bohr, P.R. (1972) Famine in China and the Missionary: Timothy Richard as Relief Administrator and Advocate of National Reform, 1877-1884. Boston: Harvard University Press.

Brand, J.L. (1965) Doctors and the State: The British Medical Profession and Government Action in Public Health, 1870-1912. Baltimore: John Hopkins Press.

Burton, D.H. (1968) Theodore Roosevelt: Confident Imperialist. Philadelphia: University of Pennsylvania Press.

Bynum, W.F. (1968) 'Chronic Alcoholism in the First Half of the 19th Century', Bulletin of the History of Medicine.

Campbell, H. (1923) 'The Pathology and Treatment of Morphia Addiction', The British Journal of Inebriety, April.

Carson, W.G. (1971) 'White-Collar Crime and the Enforcement of Factory Legislation', in Carson, W.G. and Wiles, P. (eds) Crime and Delinquency in Britain. London: Martin Robertson.

Chein, I., Gerard, D.L., Lee, R.S., and Rosenfeld, E. (1964) Narcotics, Delinquency and Social Policy. London: Tavistock.

Christlieb, T. (1879) The Indo-British Opium Trade and its Effects. London: James Nisbet.

Clark, F.E. (1900) 'The Empire of the Dead', North American Review, September.

Cohen, H. (1955) 'The Evolution of the Concept of Disease', in Proceedings of the Royal Society of Medicine.

Cohen, P.A. (1963) China and Christianity: The Missionary Movement and the Growth of Chinese Anti-Foreignism, 1860-1870. Boston: Harvard University Press.

Cohen, P.A. (1970) 'Ching-China: Confrontation with the West 1850-1900', in Crowley, J.B. (ed) Modern Asia: Essays in Interpretation. New York: Harcourt Brace and World.

Collins, W.J. (1916) 'The Ethics and Law of Drug and Alcohol Addiction', The British Journal of Inebriety, January.

Collins, W.J. (1919) 'Drinks and Drugs of Addiction', The British Journal of Inebriety, April.

Collins, W.J. (1919) 'The Aims and Future Work of the Society for the Study of Inebriety', The British Journal of Inebriety, July.

Conant, C.A. (1900) The United States in the Orient. New York: Houghton Mifflin.

Cook, S.J. (1969) 'Canadian Narcotics Legislation 1908-1923: A Conflict Model Interpretation', Canadian Review of Sociology and Anthropology, Vol.6, No.1.

Coolidge, M.R. (1909) Chinese Immigration. New York: Henry Holt.

Cressey, D.R., Ward, D.A. (eds) (1969) Delinquency, Crime and Social Process. New York: Harper and Row.

Crichton Miller, H. (1923) 'Communications on "The Pathology and

Treatment of Morphia Addiction"', in Campbell H.

Crowley, J. (1976) 'National Defence and the Consolidation of Empire, 1907-1913' in Livingston, J., Moore, J., Oldfather, F. (eds) The Japan Reader, Vol.1, Harmondsworth: Penguin books.

Crothers, T.D. (1902) Morphinism and Narcomanias From Other Drugs. London: W.B. Saunders.

Cunliffe, M. (1972) American Presidents and the Presidency. London: Fontana.

Das, M.N. (1964) India Under Morley and Minto. London: George Allen and Unwin.

Dennett, T. (1941) Americans in Eastern Asia. New York: Barnes and Noble.

Dixon, W.E. (1923-1924) 'Drug Addiction', The British Journal of Inebriety.

Dixon, W.E. (1925) 'Cocaine Addiction', The British Journal of Inebriety.

Duckworth, D. (1908) 'The Opium Habit and Morphinism', The Lancet, August 15.

Dukes, E.J. (1887) Along River and Road in Fuh-Kien, China. New York: American Tract Society.

Dulles, F.R. (1946) China and America: The Story of their Relations Since 1784. New Jersey: Princeton University Press.

Dunnell, M.B. (1901) 'The Settlement with China', The Forum, Vol.32.

Duster, T. (1970) The Legislation of Morality. New York: Free Press.

Eckstein, H. (1960) Pressure Group Politics: The Case of the British Medical Association. London: George Allen and Unwin.

Edelman, M. (1964) The Symbolic Uses of Politics. Urbana: University of Illinois Press.

Engels, F. (1969) The Condition of the Working Class in England. London: Panther Books.

Esthus, R. (1966) Theodore Roosevelt and Japan. Seattle: University of Washington Press.

Fairbank, J.K. (1953) Trade and Diplomacy on the China Coast. Mass.: Harvard University Press. 2 Vols.

Fairbank, J.K. (1971) The United States and China. Mass.: Harvard University Press.

Fay, P.W. (1975) The Opium War 1840-1842. University of North Carolina Press.

Field, M.H. (1957) 'The Chinese Boycott of 1905', Papers on China, No.11, December.

Forsythe, S.A. (1971) An American Missionary Community in china 1895-1905. Mass.: Harvard University Press.

Fry, E. (1878) England, China and Opium: Three Essays. London: Edward Bumpus.

Goode, E. (1972) Drugs in American Society. New York: Alfred A. Knopf.

Gosses, F. (1948) The Management of British Foreign Policy Before the First World War. Leiden.

Gouldner, A. (1968) 'Sociologist as Partisan: Sociology and the Welfare State', American Sociologist, Vol.3.

Greenberg, M. (1951) British Trade and the Opening of China 1800-1842. Cambridge University Press.

Harlow, V.T. (1964) The Founding of the Second British Empire 1763-1793. London: Longmans. 2 vols.

Harrison, B. (1971) Drink and the Victorians. London: Faber and Faber.

Hayter, A. (1971) Opium and the Romantic Imagination. London: Faber and Faber.

Healey, D. (1970) U.S. Expansionism: The Imperialist Urge in the 1890's.

University of Wisconsin Press.

Heclo, H. and Wildavsky, A. (1975) The Private Government of Public Money. London: Macmillan.

Henig, R.B. (1973) The League of Nations. Edinburgh: Oliver and Boyd.

Higham, J. (1955) Strangers in the Land: Patterns of American Nativism 1860-1925. New Jersey: Rutgers University Press.

Hofstadter, R. (1955) The Age of Reform. New York: Vintage Books.

Hsu, I.C. (1976) The Rise of Modern China. New York: Oxford University Press.

Ikle, F.C. (1964) How Nations Negotiate. New York: Harper and Row.

Isaac, R.J. (1976) Israel Divided: Ideological Politics in the Jewish State. Baltimore: John Hopkins University Press.

Israel, J. (1971) Progressivism and the Open Door: America and China 1905-1921. Pa.: University of Pittsburgh Press.

Jacobson, H.K., and Stein, E. (1966) Diplomats, Scientists and Politicians: The United States and the Nuclear Test Ban Negotiations. Michigan University Press.

Jervis, R. (1970) The Logic of Images in International Relations. New Jersey: Princeton University Press.

Jennings, O. (1901) On the Cure of the Morphia Habit Without Suffering. London: Balliere, Tindall and Cox.

Jennings, O. (1909-a) The Morphia Habit and its Voluntary Renunciation. London: Balliere, Tindall and Cox.

Jennings, O. (1909-b) The Re-Education of Self-Control in the Treatment of the Morphia Habit. London: Balliere, Tindall and Cox.

Kerr, N. (1894) Inebriety or Narcomania. London: H.K. Lewis.

Kerr, N. (1895) 'Alcoholism and Drug Habits', in Steadman, T.L. (ed) Twentieth Century Practice: An International Encyclopedia of Modern Medical Science. 20 vols. London: Simpson Low, Marston and Co. Vol.3.

Koss, S.E. (1969) John Morley at the India Office 1905-1910. New Haven: Yale University Press.

Lammers, C.J. (1974) 'Mono-and Poly-Paradigmatic Developments in Natural and Social Sciences', in Whitley, R. (ed) Social Processes of Scientific Development. London: Routledge and Kegan Paul.

Langer, W.L. (1935) The Diplomacy of Imperialism. New York: Alfred A. Knopf. 2 vols.

Leuchtenburg, W.E. (1952) 'Progressivism and Imperialism: The Progressives and American Foreign Policy, 1898-1916', Mississippi Valley Historical Review, Vol.XXXIX.

Levinstein, E. (1878) Morbid Craving for Morphia. London: Smith, Elder and Co.

Lim, M.J.B.C. (1969) Britain and the Termination of the Indo-China Opium Trade 1905-1913. Ph.D. Thesis. University of London.

Lindesmith, A.R. (1965) The Addict and the Law. New York: Vintage Books.

Linstead, H.N. (1936) Poisons Law. London: Pharmaceutical Press.

Lloyd George, D. (1938) War Memoirs. London: Odhams Press. 2 vols.

Lloyd George, D. (1938-a) The Truth About the Peace Treaties. London: Victor Gollancz. Vol.1.

Lomax, E. (1973) 'The Uses and Abuses of Opiates in Nineteenth Century England', Bulletin of the History of Medicine.

Lovett, H.V. (1932) 'The Home Government, 1858-1918', in The Cambridge History of India, Vol.VI. Cambridge.

Lowes, P.D. (1966) The Genesis of International Narcotics Control. Geneva: Librairie Droz.

Macleod, R.M. (1967) 'The Edge of Hope: Social Policy and Chronic

Alcoholism 1870-1900', Journal of the History of Medicine.

Mahan, A.T. (1898) The Problem of Asia.

Maki, J.M. (1961) Conflict and Tension in the Far East. Key Documents 1894-1960. Seattle: University of Washington Press.

Malloy, W.M. (1910) Treaties, Conventions, International Acts, Protocols and Agreements Between the U.S.A. and other Powers 1776-1909.

Merrill, F.T. (1942) Japan and the Opium Menace. New York: Secretariat, Institute of Pacific Relations.

Miller, D.H. (1921) 'The Making of the League of Nations', in House, E.M. and Seymour, C. (eds) What Really Happened at Paris: The Story of the Peace Conference. London: Hodder and Stoughton.

Miller, D.H. (1928) The Drafting of the Covenant. New York: G.P. Putnam. 2 vols.

Miller, S.C. (1969) The Unwelcome Immigrant: The American Image of the Chinese 1785-1882. University of California Press.

Moore, W.J. (1882) The Other Side of the Opium Question. London: J. and A. Churchill.

Morgan, H.W. (ed) (1974) Yesterday's Addicts: American Society and Drug Abuse 1865-1920. University of Oklahoma Press.

Morse, H.B. (1918) The International Relations of the Chinese Empire. London: Longmans, Green and Co. 3 vols.

Morse, H.B. and MacNair, H.F. (1931) Far Eastern International Relations. Boston: Houghton Mifflin.

Mowry, G.E. (1958) The Era of Theodore Roosevelt, 1900-1912. London: Hamish Hamilton.

Musto, D.F. (1973) The American Disease. New Haven: Yale University Press.

Neu, C.E. (1967) An Uncertain Friendship: Theodore Roosevelt and Japan 1906-1909. Mass.: Harvard University Press.

Noble, G.B. (1968) Policies and Opinions at Paris 1919: Wilsonian Diplomacy, the Versailles Peace and French Public Opinion. New York: Howard Fertig.

Owen, D.E. (1934) British Opium Policy in India and China. New Haven: Yale University Press.

Park, S. (1923-1924) 'Inebriety: Disease or Vice? The Need for Public Education on the Subject', The British Journal of Inebriety.

Park, S. (1925-1926) 'The Institutional Treatment of Inebriety', in The British Journal of Inebriety.

Pelcovits, N.A. (1948) Old China Hands and the Foreign Office. New York: American Institute of Pacific Relations.

Peterson, T. (1956) Magazines in the Twentieth Century. Urbana: University of Illinois Press.

Phipps, J. (1835) China and the Eastern Trade. Calcutta: Thacker and Co.

Platt, A.M. (1969) The Child Savers. Chicago: University of Chicago Press.

Pruitt, A.A. (1974) 'Approaches to Alcoholism in Mid-Victorian England', Clio Medica.

Purcell, V. (1963) The Boxer Uprising. Cambridge: Cambridge University Press.

Rather, L.J. (1961) 'An Early Nineteenth Century View of Functional vs. Organic Disease', Archives of Internal Medicine.

Rowland, P. (1968) The Last Liberal Governments: The Promised Land, 1905-1910. London: The Cresset Press.

Savage, G.H. (1910) 'Mental Diseases', Allbutt and Rolleston (eds) 1910.

Schelling, T.G. (1960) The Strategy of Conflict. Mass.: Harvard University Press.

Schofield, M. (1971) The Strange Case of Pot. Harmondsworth: Penguin Books.

Schrecker, J.E. (1971) Imperialism and Chinese Nationalism: Germany in Shantung. Mass.: Harvard University Press.

Schur, E.M. (1962) Narcotic Addiction in Britain and America. London: Tavistock.

Scull, A. (1972) 'Social Control and the Amplification of Deviance', in Scott, R.A. and Douglas, J.D. (eds) Theoretical Perspectives on Deviance. New York: Basic Books.

Shotwell, J.T. (1937) At the Paris Peace Conference. New York: Macmillan.

Slater, J., Nardin, T. (1973) 'The Concept of a Military Industrial Complex', in Rosen, S. (ed) Testing the Theory of the Military Industrial Complex. Mass.: D.C. Heath.

Steadman, T.L. (ed) (1895) Twentieth Century Practice: An International Encyclopaedia of Modern Medical Science. 20 vols. London: Simpson, Low and Marston.

Steiger, G.N. (1927) China and the Occident: The Origins and Development of the Boxer Movement. New Haven: Yale University Press.

Stein, S.D. (1978) The Origins of the Hague Opium Convention 1912, and its Implementation in England and Wales 1919-1925. Ph.D. Thesis, University of London.

Stein, S.D. (1980) The Sociology of Law, British Journal of Criminology, Volume 20, No 2.

Steiner, Z.S. (1969) The Foreign Office and Foreign Policy, 1898-1914. London: Cambridge University Press.

Storry, R. (1967) A History of Modern Japan. London: Penguin Books.

Strachey, J. (1903) India: Its Administration and Progress. London: Macmillan.

Swatos, W.H. Jr. (1972) 'Opiate Addiction in the Late Nineteenth Century: A Study of the Social Problem, Using Medical Journals of the Period', International Journal of the Addictions.

Szasz, T. (1974) Ideology and Insanity. London: Penguin Books.

Taylor, A.H. (1969) American Diplomacy and the Narcotics Traffic 1900-1939. Duke University Press.

Temperley, H.W.V. (ed) (1920) A History of the Peace Conference of Paris. London: Henry Froude and Hodder and Stoughton. 4 vols.

Terry, C.E. and Pellens, M. (1928) The Opium Problem. New York.

The Opium Revenue of India. Unsigned Pamphlet (1857) London: Wm. H. Allen. British Museum Catalogue No. 8022.d.69.

Tong, T.K. (1964) United States Diplomacy in China 1840-1860. Seattle: University of Washington Press.

Varg, P.A. (1952) Open Door Diplomat: The Life of W.W. Rockhill. Urbana: University of Illinois Press.

Varg, P.A. (1968) The Making of a Myth: The United States and China 1897-1912. Michigan University Press.

Vevier, C. (1955) The United States and China 1906-1913: A Study of Finance and Diplomacy. New Jersey: Rutgers University Press.

Wallace, W. (1975) The Foreign Policy Process in Britain. London: Royal Institute of International Affairs.

Weber, M. (1970) 'Science as a Vocation', H.H. Gerth, C.W. Hills (eds) from Max Weber: Essays in Sociology. London: Routledge and Kegan Paul.

Wehrle, E.S. (1966) Britain, China and the Antimissionary riots 1891-1900. Minneapolis: University of Minnesota Press.

Willcox, W. (1926) 'The Prevention and Arrest of Drug Addiction', The British Journal of Inebriety.

Willoughby, W.W. (1925) Opium as an International Problem: The Geneva Conferences. Baltimore: John Hopkins Press.

Winick, C. (1969) 'Physician Narcotic Addicts', Cressey, D.R. and Ward, D.A. (eds) (1969) Delinquency, Crime and Social Processes. New York: Harper and Row.

Winskill, P.T. (1892) The Temperance Movement and its Workers. Edinburgh: Blackie and Sons. 4 vols.

Wolpert, S.A. (1967) Morley and India 1906-1910. Berkley: University of California Press.

Wright, J.W. (1901) 'Protestant Dominion Over Weak Communities', The American Catholic Quarterly Review.

Young, E.P. (1970) 'Nationalism, Reform and Republican Revolution: China in the Early Twentieth Century', Crowley, J.B. (ed) Modern Asia: Essays in Interpretation. New York: Harcourt Brace and World.

Young, M.B. (1968) The Rhetoric of Empire. Mass.: Harvard University Press.

Author Index

Dulles, F. R. 32, 38, 39
Dunnell, M. B. 37
Duster, T. 168, 186
Eckstein, H. 178
Edelman, M. 44, 177
Engels, F. 130, 131
Esthus, R. 35, 46
Fairbank, J. K. 7, 42
Field, M. H. 41
Forsythe, S. A. 11
Fry, E. 9
Goode, E. 186
Gosses, F. 83
Gouldner, A. 186
Harlow, V. T. 6
Harrison, B. 150
Hayter, A. 131
Healey, D. 31, 33
Heclo, H., Wildavsky, A. 85, 86
Henig, R. B. 118
Higham, J. 44
Hofstadter, R. 30
Hsu, I. C. 7
Ilke, F. C. 58, 60
Isaac, R. J. 16
Israel, J. 43
Jacobson, H. K., Stein, E. 173
Jennings, O. (a) 146, 147, 157
Jervis, R. 36
Kerr, N. 148, 149, 152, 154
Koss, S. E. 21
Lammers, C. J. 151
Langer, W. L. 29, 30
Leuchtenburg, W. E. 30, 33
Levinstein, E. 145, 147, 154
Lim, M. J. B. C. 48
Lindesmith, A. R. 167, 184, 186
Linstead, H. N. 90
Lloyd George, D. 122
Lomax, E. 129
Lovett, H. V. 82
Lowes, P. D. 81
Macleod, R. M. 148-9
Mahan, A. T. 33
Maki, J. M. 29, 34
Malloy, W. M. 34, 39, 40
Merill, F. T. 109
Miller, D. H. 117, 119, 120
Miller, S. C. 12, 39
Moore, W. J. 14
Morgan, H. W. 169
Morse, H. B. 11
Morse, H. B., Macnair, H. F. 8
Mowry, G. E. 30, 33
Musto, D. F. 53, 61, 172, 184
Neu, C. E. 35, 46
Noble, G. B. 117

Subject Index

Campbell, Sir F. 87
Carleton, Billie, see Stewart, Florence L.
Cecil, Lord R. 118
Chefoo Convention, additional article to 23
China, acquiescence in Ten Year Agreement by 23; acquiescence with
    demand for territorial concessions by 29-30; Anti-opium campaign in
    17; Boxer uprising in 35; boycott and 41-42; effects of opium on 7;
    emigration problem and 40; First Opium War 7; foreign policy
    objectives of 28; impact of missionaries on 11; legalisation of opium
    trade 7-8; position of missionaries in 10-11; reform movement in 18-
    19; restriction on British opium imports to 22; spread of morphine
    addiction in 106
China Reform Association 41
Chinese immigration 37-42
Christian Union for the Severance of the Connection of the British
    Empire wth the Opium Trade (CM), founding of 9; objectives and tactics
    of 10; links with the temperance movement of 150
Christianity, attitude of Chinese towards 10
Christlieb, T. 13
Clemenceau, G. 117
Cleveland, S.G. 40
Cocaine, consumption by allied soldiers of 14-4; Hague Convention
    articles on 72-6; proposals of 1910 interdepartmental conference on
    64; restriction of exports to Japan of 111; spread of consumption in
    India and Burma of 65
Cocaine, Straits Settlements governor suggests control of 25
Collins, Sir W. 69, 106, 110, 158, 181
Colonial Office, views on post-Shanghai conference of 63
Conant, C. 31-2
Conferences, First International Missionary 9
Crafts, W. F. 47
Curzon, Lord G. 116
Dangerous Drugs Bill 1920, enactment of 126; lack of parliamentary
    interest in 126-27; pharmacists opposition to 125; provisions of 124-
    26
Dangerous Drugs Regulations 1921, Committee on the Draft Regulations,
    136-37; objections of pharmacists, doctors and others to 128, 133-37;
    provisions of 127-28
Delevigne, Sir M. 95, 127, 143 166, 180-82
Departmental Committee on Morphine and Heroin Addiction, circumstances
    leading to appointment of 140-43; evidence to 161-64; membership of
    159; tecommendations of 165; terms of reference of 143-44
De Veulle, R. 102-04
Dixon, W. E. 151
Dope parties 99-101, 103
Dora 40B, see Regulation 40B, etc.
Drug Addiction, ambulatory treatment of 141-42; institutional facilities
    in Great Britain for 142; origins of medical views on 144-59
East India Company, assumption of control of opium by 6; policy on opium
    of 6-7
Edinburgh Anti-Opium Committee 16; suggests restriction on morphine exports
    110
Ellis, J. E. 21
Finger, H. J. 69
Foreign Office, mediating role of 79, 81, 84-85; opposition to post-
    Shanghai conference by 62; reply to United States proposals for post-
    Shanghai conference by 66

Frazer, Sir E. 107
Geary Law (1892) 40
George, L. 83, 117
Germany, interests in trade in cocaine and morphine of 65, 72; policy at
    Hague conference of 73-77; manufacture and distribution of morphine in
    China by nationals of 108
Giddings, F. H.
Gladstone, W. E., opposition to opium policy 9
Godley, Sir A. 51
Government of India, opposition to post-Shanghai conference of 63
Great Britain, foreign policy goals regarding China of 28; see opium
    policy - Great Britain
Grey, Sir Edward 22, 23, 50, 63, 67, 86
Hague Conference, adhesion difficulties at 77-78, 81; British delegation
    to 68-69; powers represented at 69; United States delegation to 69;
    see Hague convention
Hague convention, articles relating to adhesion in 77-78, 81; articles
    relating to China in 71-72; articles relating to morphine and cocaine
    in 72-76; articles relating to prepared opium in 70-71; articles
    relating to raw opium in 69-70; deficiencies of 113; outline structure
    of 69; ratification difficulties of 88; reference to Paris Peace
    Conference of 115
Harmsworth, C. 121
Hartington, Marquess of
Hay, J. 34-35, 36
Hayes, R. B. 39
Hirtzel, F. A. 51
Home Office, advocate bringing into force of Hague convention 115
Hosie, Sir A. 53
Hurst, C. 119
Import certificate system, Board of Trade proposes 110; defects of 112-
    13; enforcement respecting Japan of 111; extension of 111-13
India, organisation of opium production in 8; poppy cultivation acreage
    in 9; see Government of India
India Office, delaying tactics of 50; support for government of India by
    51
Indo-China opium traffic, agitation against; American missionary
    petition against 46; arguments in defense of 14-15, 21; arguments of
    campaigners against 13-14; China seeks gradual cessation of 22; Great
    Britain and 15-16; immorality of 13-14; legalisation of 7-8; Ten Year
    Agreement on 22-23
International opium commission 50-60; British delegates to 53; Chinese
    resolutions at 54, 58-9; India Office objections to United States
    terms of reference for 52; participating countries in 50, 54;
    resolutions of 56-8
International Reform Bureau, 47
James, W. 33
Japan, Imports of Morphine to 108
Japanese Nationals, Trade in Morphine in China by 107, 110-11
Jones, Sir W. G. 125
Jordan, Sir John, 20, 22, 23, 68, 85-86, 89, 106-07, 112, 114, 173
Kerr, Dr N. 151, Biographical Details 148
Kerr, P. 121
King, W. L. M. 53, 172
Knox, P. C. 61
Laidlaw, R. 53
Langley, W. 77, 87

Lansing, R. 120-21
League of Nations, supervisory role relating to traffic in narcotics of 20
Lodge, H. C. 31-32
Lyon, T. H. 110
Macleay, R. 115-16, 121, 174
Mahan, A. T. 31-32
Maxwell, J. 9
McKinley, W. 32
Mayer, Sir W. 68, 70
Miller, D. H. 119-20
Missionaries, attitudes to Chinese and 42; attitudes, to opium consumption of 10; British opium policy and 12-13, 46; Chinese conversions and 11; hostility of Chinese towards 10-12
Moore, W. J. 14
Morley, J. 21, 22, 51, 83
Morphine, spread of consumption in India and Burma of 65, spread of consumption in Straits Settlements of 65; Army Order in Council (1916) relating to 94; consumption by allied soldiers of 93-4; desirability of controlling consumption of 65; Hague convention articles on 172-76; Hong Kong governor suggests control of 25; international opium commission resolution on 57; manufacture in Great Britain of 108-09, 113; proposals for control of manufacture of 113; proposals of 1910 interdepartmental conference on 3-4; spread of addiction to in China of 106; spread of consumption in China 25; Straits Settlements governor suggests control of 25
Most Favoured Nation Clause 28-29, United States and 43
Muller, M. 20, 68, 72, 108-09, 113, 116, 173
Narcomania 149
Olney, R. 31
Open Door Policy 33-37, 45
Opium, American missionary petition against 46, 49; cultivation in India of 6; distribution in Far East of 6, 8; excise, definition of 6; exports from India of 7; parliamentary debates on 16; imperial edict against 17; Malwa, definition of 6; medical effects of 54; prepared, definition of 6; Royal Commission on 13, 15-16
Opium Policy - Great Britain, agree participation in investigatory commission 50; reaction to United States agenda for post-Shanghai conference 64
Opium Policy - United States, investigatory commission proposed 50; official justification for 28; proposals for post-Shanghai conference, 61-62, 65; source of 1906 initiative 27, 46-48; State Department hearing on (1904) 47, 49
Opium preparations, consumption of in Great Britain 129-33
Opium Smoking, International Opium Commission resolution on 56
Opium trade, revenues from 8
Parliament, composition of 20; Dangerous Drugs Bill and 126; Dangerous Drugs Regulations and 134; opium debates in 16, 20-21
Pease, E. 9
Pharmaceutical Society of Great Britain, opposition to Dangerous Drugs Regulations by 134; supervisory role regarding poisons of 91
Pharmacists, see Pharmaceutical Society of Great Britain; Dangerous Drugs Bill; Dangerous Drugs Regulations
Pharmacy Acts 1868, 89-90; 1908, 89, 91
Philippine Opium Commission 47
Phillips, W. 37
Platt, O. H. 32